FIRESCAPING YOUR HOME

Page 4: Mammoth Lakes, California, in fall.

Cover photographs by (clockwise from top): Erin Donalson/Dreamstime; Patrick Alexander/Flickr; Daniel Ripplinger/Dreamstime; Kobernus, Patrick/Wikimedia; Salvador Ceja/Dreamstime; W. Bulach/Wikimedia; Eric in SF/Wikimedia.
All other photography and illustration credits appear on page 249.

Published in 2023 by Timber Press, Inc., a subsidiary of Workman Publishing Co., Inc., a subsidiary of Hachette Book Group, Inc.
1290 Avenue of the Americas
New York, New York 10104
timberpress.com

Printed in China on responsibly sourced paper
Text design by Kelley Galbreath
Cover illustration by Jennifer Luxton

The publisher is not responsible for websites (or their content) that are not owned by the publisher.

The Hachette Speakers Bureau provides a wide range of authors for speaking events. To find out more, go to hachettespeakersbureau.com or email HachetteSpeakers@hbgusa.com.

ISBN 978-1-64326-135-5

Catalog records for this book are available from the Library of Congress and the British Library.

FIRESCAPING YOUR HOME

A MANUAL *for* READINESS *in* WILDFIRE COUNTRY

ADRIENNE EDWARDS
and **RACHEL SCHLEIGER**

Timber Press
Portland, Oregon

Contents

Preface   6

11   Introduction: Becoming Fire Resilient
     While Supporting Habitat

21   Habitat: Your Biotic Community
     and Ecoregion

39   The Nature and Behavior of Fire

63   Hardening Your Home Against Fire

79   Creating Defensible Space

99   What to Plant, Where, and When

121 A Native Plant Palette for Fire-Safe
     Gardens

195 Maintaining Plants for Fire Resilience

211 Recovery: Helping Land Heal After Fire

225 Our Fire Future

Resources and Further Reading   236
Source Notes   239
Acknowledgments   248
Photography and Illustration Credits   249
Index   251

Preface

Fire restores.

KJERKIUS GENNIUS, 36 BC

MY EARLIEST CHILDHOOD MEMORY is of a house burning around me. That day was an odd juxtaposition of personal and historical events. On my mother's birthday, November 21, 1963, President John F. Kennedy visited San Antonio, Texas. Joyce Winkler, who took care of the kids while my parents were at work, took my older sister, who was in kindergarten, to see him. The next day, Kennedy was assassinated in Dallas, and my little brother started a fire in our house. He and I were playing in the garage with toy vehicles, and the most coveted was a green policeman riding a motorcycle. My brother set it down and I grabbed it. When I wouldn't give it back, he decided to climb up on our dad's real motorcycle. I, sassafras that I was, told him to get down or I would tell. As he was climbing down, the motorcycle fell over, spilling gasoline out of the tank and onto his clothes. Joyce came out and took him inside to change him. I continued playing until the gasoline on the garage floor made it to the hot water heater.

The gas water heater exploded into flames. I shot up, then froze, afraid to move as the flames reached the ceiling. It was so very hot. There was a stack of cardboard boxes near the garage door, and I stiffly inched behind them to get away from the heat. But my three-year-old self thought, "Boxes can burn," so I moved back out from behind them.

I didn't remember how I got out of the burning garage. I knew I was not strong enough to open the garage door myself and assumed that firemen broke down the door and rescued me.

More than fifty years later I tracked down Joyce and asked her about that day. She had raced around the outside of the house, handed my brother to the neighbor next door, then run into the back of the garage where the water heater was, through the flames, to save me. I would not have survived long enough for the firemen to arrive. My sister told me later that I had blisters on my face, legs, and hands. It took months before I would go to sleep without begging for the lights to be left on so I could "see" my way out in case there was a fire.

As an adult living in fire country, I still have a visceral reaction (goose bumps, nausea) to fires that burn houses. Yet I have a healthy respect for the good that fire does in the environment. As a volunteer with the Forest Service I have strung fire with a drip torch for prescribed burns, and I rejoice in the riot of wildflowers and wildlife that follows fire. We all can learn to appreciate the good that wildland fire does, and support the native plants and animals that surround us while we live in fire landscapes with our homes and communities intact.

—Adrienne

I GREW UP IN THE MONTANE FORESTS of the Sierra Nevada, my town surrounded by national parks and national forests. Throughout my child-hood I would visit the local fire stations and listen through the spiel I think every kid remembers . . . fires are dangerous and destructive, don't play with fire, and stop-drop-and-roll. That was the extent of my education on fire until in 2013 my fiancé (now husband) started a job contracting with CAL FIRE and the Forest Service doing rapid assessment fire mapping. He started going to fire camps to map fires, and I began noticing how many fires there were every year in California, since it was a big part of our daily conversa-tions. As time went on, it seemed like he was gone longer, and the fires he was working at were getting a lot more news coverage than ever before. Every year seemed worse than the last.

FIRESCAPING YOUR HOME

My curiosity was sparked (pun intended) and I began asking a lot of questions. Have these types of fire events been going on the whole time I've lived in California and I've never noticed? Or are fire events worse now than they ever have been? Why was I never educated more about this as a kid or adult? Why is nobody creating a fire curriculum to educate the masses? This was also the time I started reading books to get an understanding of fire science, fire ecology, and the history of fire and fire policy. I learned that not all fires are dangerous and destructive—in fact, many of the species, habitats, and ecosystems that are present where fire is common benefit from fire. Some species even require fire as a part of their life cycle!

This paradigm shift I had about fire really got me thinking about all the people affected by fires and how no formal curriculum exists to educate the public (at any age). It just so happened around this time (2018) that I got the opportunity to update a biology course at Butte College called Current Issues in Biology and have it be fire focused. A few months later, fire affected my family. On November 8, 2018, the day the Camp Fire started, my family evacuated our home in Magalia, just north of Paradise. We were very lucky that our home didn't burn down although the fire fully encircled it and was inches from it in a few spots, but half of our neighbors weren't so lucky. My family members, like so many, were just thankful to still have each other and mourned for those who lost everything. We didn't return to our home for three months. After this, I was more motivated than ever before to get my fire-focused course ready for the following school year to empower and educate college students and help mend their fire paradigms. A few years later the opportunity to write this book came along, and it became my next passion project.

—Rachel

Introduction

Becoming Fire Resilient While Supporting Habitat

You can decrease your fire risk while also providing habitat for the wild creatures you share your landscape with. Cleveland sage (*Salvia clevelandii*) is fire resilient and friendly to pollinators.

THIS GUIDE IS INTENDED FOR ANYONE living in the wildfire-prone areas of California, Oregon, and Washington. Fire season is getting longer, wildfires are becoming larger in many parts of our region, and extreme fire events are becoming more frequent due to warming and drying conditions. At the same time, more people are choosing to live adjacent to fire-prone wildlands. The result is not only that more structures are burning in human-built communities but also that the integrity of natural communities is at risk from our activities.

We can coexist with fire by learning more about the wildlands where we live and how to support fire-resilient landscapes. Fires do not have to be viewed as tragedies. Larger wildfires are not, per se, bad for landscapes when structures are not in harm's way (although excessive smoke is clearly a public health concern). When we understand that fire is an inevitable process, like rain, we can move away from describing all wildfires as "devastating" and work together to manage them.

Living in fire-prone landscapes should not mean that you must scrape away all vegetation within hundreds of feet of structures. Landscaping in fire country, or firescaping, is more nuanced than that. The right firescaping strategies for your home will depend on your habitat—the kind of biotic community you live in. This book provides detailed suggestions for habitat-supportive firescaping specific to the varied landscapes of West Coast states, which encompass some of the most diverse and extreme habitats in North America.

Our sincerest hope is that this book will empower you to ameliorate not only your own fire risk but also the impact of fire risk management on surrounding wildlands.

Wildfire Realities

Here in the West, we have altered landscapes in the past few hundred years in ways that have made habitats drier and less resilient to drought. For example, the Central and San Joaquin Valleys of California once contained vast wetlands that probably extinguished most fires there. Today, water is channeled to municipalities and into one of the most productive agricultural regions in the world; less than 5 percent of the original wetland area remains. Extensive clear-cutting and soil degradation in temperate rainforests of the Pacific Northwest have reduced rainfall and fog. Smaller second-growth trees are more abundant and less resistant to drought and fire. Great Basin and desert grasslands/shrublands, once with plenty of bare soil between groups of plants, are now stitched together by nonnative annual grasses that are highly ignitable and speed the depletion of winter rainwater from soils. These and other alterations have made landscapes more likely to burn.

Human-caused climate change is also setting us up for increased wildfire risk. Projections for climate change impacts in our western states include more rain and less snowpack, more frequent and extreme drought and flood events, and higher overall temperatures. With increased drying influenced by overall climate change, as well as the Pacific Decadal Oscillation (a shifting pattern of cold and warm water masses in the Pacific Ocean that affects the jet stream and thus weather across North America), fire season has become progressively longer and more costly in the West. Fires burn hotter when high temperatures combine with extremely low humidity.

In some regions, such as the North Coast, Sierra Nevada, and Klamath regions, fires have increased in size in the past few decades driven by increased climate variability. Hotter, dryer weather conditions reduce moisture available in both live and dead plant materials, while wetter years significantly increase ignitable fuels in grasslands and savannas.

Since 2000, an average of 7 million acres have burned each year across the

BELOW Interface WUI areas are where structures are built adjacent to wildland vegetation, like this neighborhood in Pacific Palisades, California.

BOTTOM Intermix WUI areas are where structures are dotted inside wildland vegetation, like this development in Waldo Canyon, Colorado.

12

United States, more than double the average acreage that burned annually in the 1990s. In 2020, wildfires burned 10.3 million acres in the US, and roughly 60 percent of those acres were in California (more than 4 million acres), Oregon (more than 1 million acres), and Washington (more than 700,000 acres). According to the California Department of Forestry and Fire Protection (CAL FIRE), more than half of the twenty largest wildfires in California history occurred in 2020 and 2021.

In parallel with the changing nature and frequency of wildfire, the years between 1970 and 2014 saw a 60-percent increase in the number of houses in wildland areas of the western United States. This trend was widespread. Throughout the continental United States, roughly one out of three houses and one out of ten hectares (24.7 acres) are now in the wildland-urban interface (WUI), as it is known. More than half of all US homes and other buildings are situated in designated disaster zones for wildfires, earthquakes, floods, hurricanes, and tornadoes, yet development is growing faster in these areas than elsewhere, and for wildfires this is largely through expansion into undeveloped areas in the WUI.

Increased development into the WUI increases wildfire risk, for two main reasons. First, almost 85 percent of wildfires in the United States are started by people, so more people living in an area equals more wildfire starts. Second, houses are very effective at igniting other houses, so houses grouped together facilitate wildfire spread. Houses are, for the most part, made out of dead wood. Add to those facts the reality that climate change is increasing the frequency of extreme weather events— including heat waves, severe drought, and high winds—that make landscapes more flammable, and you have the tinderbox conditions that can make wildfires more pervasive and destructive.

Two types of WUI areas, where development meets or intermingles with undeveloped wildlands, are most frequently associated with destructive wildfires. *Interface* WUI areas are where housing is concentrated adjacent to wildlands. *Intermix* WUI areas are where houses and wildland vegetation commingle. These two main types of WUI community are associated with

13

TOP This rural house in the Laguna Mountains of eastern San Diego County, California, is situated on very dry, forested land.

ABOVE Many quickly growing urban centers are being developed directly next to wildlands, like El Cerrito in the Bay Area. Any structure can burn if it's within the range of flying embers or firebrands, even if miles away from a wildfire front.

The Plight *of* Insects and Birds

Available long-term data show major species and population declines in insects, including essential pollinators, in the past fifty years. Total insect biomass has trended significantly downward in multiple long-term studies, and the number of insect species now considered endangered has climbed dramatically. Globally, threats to insect biodiversity include climate-change-driven massive wildfires, increased storm intensities, more severe droughts, deforestation, insecticides, large-scale industrialized agriculture, introduced species, urbanization, pollution, nitrification, and disruption of species interactions by all these factors.

Birds depend on insects for food. Accompanying the decline of insects has been a shocking decline in bird abundance in the past fifty years. Both rare and common species—even species that thrive in human-disturbed environments—have suffered population losses. Bird numbers in the United States have declined across all habitats except wetlands by 29 percent, by roughly three billion birds, since 1970. Only a few types of birds have increased in number over that time, including waterfowl

and raptors, due to increases in wetland migratory habitats and banning of the pesticide DDT.

Besides feeding birds, insects and spiders provide a range of goods and services, among them honey, silk, wax, dyes, food, waste processing, pollination, and pest control services. Insects and spiders also bring beauty and motion to the great outdoors. If you'd rather not think about spiders, imagine butterflies as dancing colors winking across the landscapes around you. Now try to wrap your head around the fact that butterfly numbers in the West, and not just monarch butterflies, have declined by roughly 1.6 percent per year over the past four decades.

How can we save insects from global declines? Experts urge us to convert lawns into diverse natural habitats, grow native plants, reduce or eliminate the use of pesticides and herbicides, limit the use of exterior nighttime lighting, and minimize runoff of soaps, de-icing salts, coal-tar driveway sealants, and other polycyclic aromatic hydrocarbons (PAHs). Even frequent low mowing and leaf blowers kill insects, so minimizing or eliminating these practices also helps.

different risk factors. These risk factors need to be taken into account when you are developing a firescaping plan for your home.

In California alone between 1985 and 2013, half of all buildings destroyed by wildfire were in interface WUI areas, and 32 percent of the total were in intermix WUI areas. So more than 80 percent of structures lost to wildfire were in the WUI, and structures in interface WUI areas were at higher risk despite having less wildland fuel than intermix WUI areas. Structures nearer to established Firewise communities (those that participate in the Firewise USA program, a public education project of the National Fire Protection Association) were destroyed at significantly lower rates than structures farther away from Firewise communities.

Development that isn't considered to be in the WUI is either urban or rural. Urban built environments have no wildland areas nearby, and rural areas are defined as those with fewer than one house per 40+ acres. Even homes in urban and rural communities are not necessarily safe from wildfire risk.

Our Beloved Western Habitats and Species in Peril

People move into homes in the WUI to be near wildlands and what they offer. Ironically, to reduce fire risks to housing, we make Swiss cheese of the wild landscapes we love. Residents are directed by fire management agencies, regulators, and insurance companies to clear all vegetation away from struc-tures. Common recommendations include substantial clearing out to at least 100 feet from any structure.

"Defensible space" has been the battle cry for preventing property losses from wildfires. However, excessive clearing of vegetation around buildings can:

- **reduce wildlife habitat** and native biodiversity;
- **increase erosion** and energy use;
- **increase regional temperatures,** deplete soil moisture, and eliminate natural windbreaks;
- **reduce aesthetic value,** privacy, and property values; and
- **make structures more susceptible to ignition** from blowing embers, called firebrands.

Designed landscapes that ignore the needs of wildlife degrade WUI habitats.

We need to make our homes and our WUI communities more resistant and resilient to fire. But how do we do that without causing the deterioration of what made us want to move near wildlands in the first place? That's the question central to this book. Answering it begins with understanding that we live in an era of declining biodiversity, and that the major culprits are habitat loss and degradation, invasive species, and climate change.

Habitat fragmentation, like what happens in the WUI, is the leading threat. When we break up native plant habitats and communities, the remaining fragments tend to be degraded in quality.

Key Terms

A **wildfire** is a landscape fire started naturally or by humans, subject to suppression. **Firescaping** refers to landscaping in wildfire country.

Resilience is the ability to recover from or adjust easily to misfortune or change. This refers both to the ease with which nature can rebound from fire (which is simply an ecological disturbance) and to fostering fire-resistant community practices in the built environment.

The **built environment** consists of human-made surroundings that provide the setting for human activity, ranging in scale from buildings and parks or green spaces to neighborhoods and cities. The built environment can include supporting infrastructure, such as water supply or energy networks.

A **wildland-urban interface** (WUI) is an area where structures and other human development meet undeveloped wildlands and their fuels. An **interface** WUI is where developed areas have sparse or no wildland vegetation but are within close proximity of a large patch of wild land. An **intermix** WUI is where houses and wildland vegetation directly intermingle.

Defensible space is an area where flammable material has been cleared, reduced, or replaced with less-flammable material as a barrier to approaching wildfires.

Biodiversity refers to the number of different species present in an area and the relative abundance of each of those species.

Traditional ecological knowledge (TEK) is evolving knowledge acquired by indigenous and local peoples over hundreds or thousands of years through direct contact with the environment.

16

The second biggest threat to native biodiversity is invasive species. Yet not all nonnative species are necessarily bad, and some native species can go rogue in altered landscapes. We'll contrast plants that are good (noninvasive plants that provide pollinator food and shelter as well as wildlife habitat) with plants that are poor (nonnatives that provide little to no wildlife value), bad (invasive species that spread easily by seeds or other propagules), noxious (aggressive invasive species that spread on their own and change plant community composition), and fire enablers (species that increase fire risk).

Climate change is a third threat to biodiversity. It is driving changes in phenology (the timing of life cycle patterns) and in animal migrations, and will likely drive some extinctions unless we can help threatened species migrate to suitable habitats.

Documented declines in the abundance and diversity of life should inform us that we can no longer install landscapes without considering our outdoor neighbors or sense of place. Designed landscapes in the WUI that ignore the needs of insects, birds, and other wildlife further degrade the habitats that we fragment with our developments. Many groomed yards with lush lawns and exotic shrubbery lack pollen, nectar, nesting, and sheltering resources for native wildlife, including insects. Pesticide use simply adds insult to injury. Our home landscapes should be more than just artful arrangements of exclusively nonnative plants that appeal to our exterior decorating sensibilities. By the same token, making our landscapes fire safe should include considering the impact of our choices on our native ecosystems.

The WUI is modified by our built environment, but the gardening choices we make can produce very different habitat qualities. It is our ethical responsibility to do the least amount of ecological harm and ideally to create an oasis of support for pollinators, birds, and other wildlife around our homes. Fortunately, scientists continue to compile evidence that habitat restoration, pesticide reduction, expanding food and shelter for native biodiversity, and being able to predict where species might do better or worse with climate change could counteract our negative impacts in the WUI.

Putting Goals for Fire Readiness and Habitat Health Together

This book gathers resources not just on fire safety but also on the nuances of landscaping and gardening that can help you reside lightly with specific regard for wildland communities. Caring for our western landscapes should acknowledge a sense of place through respecting the native species that occur where we live. We can mitigate the negative impacts of development in the WUI by manipulating defensible space to create habitats that are fire resistant while also providing oases for native biodiversity.

The incongruity of clearing all vegetation to create defensible space around structures and destroying wildland habitat in the process has led some agencies and groups to add criteria for "sustainable" practices in creating defensible spaces. One example is the SAFE (Sustainable and Fire Safe) Landscapes blog hosted by the University of California Agriculture and Natural Resources website (ucanr.edu/blogs/Safelandscapes/). However, what is considered sustainable is simply summarized as using plants that are drought tolerant and that support habitat for birds, butterflies, and other wildlife. Is that enough, or should sustainability in the WUI include more?

We believe that sustainability in the WUI requires a two-pronged approach. One focus for living in fire landscapes should be to minimize the potential for wildfires to ignite structures. Ideally, that means understanding fire behavior, knowing about wind patterns and fire regimes, building structures that are fire resistant and positioned effectively in the landscape, and maintaining defensible spaces. Hand in glove with that focus on structures should be a focus on creating gardens that are wildlife oases rather than dead zones that wildlife cannot use. The sure bet for supporting native wildlife is to plant species they evolved with—that is, native plants.

There are no one-size-fits-all guidelines for living in fire landscapes. However, the landscape you create around your home should satisfy three basic conditions:

- It must be fire resilient.
- It should minimize the negative impacts of habitat fragmentation.
- It should minimize the introduction of invasive species.

Robin Wall Kimmerer, plant ecologist, member of the Potawatomi Nation, and proponent of traditional ecological knowledge (TEK), wrote in her book *Braiding Sweetgrass*, "It was through her actions of reciprocity, the give and take with the land, that the original immigrant became indigenous. For all of us, becoming indigenous to a place means living as if your children's future mattered, to take care of the land as if our lives, both material and spiritual, depended on it." Kimmerer and others have given voice to the idea that all beings and lakes and mountains and rocks and soil are not just resources but also kin—kin who support us and each other. The utility of recognizing nature as kin—who give us gifts of beauty, of food, of shelter, of medicine, of music, of breath—is that we can reciprocate those gifts by taking care of where we live, by making room for the residents who evolved in that place. We can do this in

Succulent gardens can be fire resistant as well as drought tolerant. A focus on native plants will further support native insects and other wildlife.

each plan, planting, and maintenance action we take. This is how our presence in and near wildlands can bring more benefit than harm to our kin and maintain a sense of place.

This book reframes some of the widely available fire safety recommendations with an awareness of reciprocity. We begin by examining how habitats have become degraded by human presence and suggesting that an essential part of decreasing your vulnerability to wildfire is knowing and respecting your wildland biotic community. We then discuss how fire behaves and the importance of understanding how fire can move across landscapes, and we guide you in evaluating the prevailing conditions where you live. The next three chapters provide practical advice on home and landscape hardening. Beyond offering general guidelines, we incorporate the latest research to further inform decision making about fire resistance and wildland integrity. We then provide a directory of native landscaping plants to consider growing where you live in place of nonnative invaders. The final two chapters focus on what to do in the aftermath of a fire and look toward a future when our WUI communities are as fire resilient as our wildlands.

We can reside in or near wildlands without destroying them. We can support the integrity of wild places while gardening. We can create gardens that bring us joy but also reduce the risks of damaging wildfires. May this book help show the way.

Habitat

Your Biotic Community and Ecoregion

Learning more about your local wild tapestry can help you make choices that increase your home's fire resilience while reducing the impact of habitat fragmentation and invasive species.

AH, THE TAPESTRY OF NATURE. We love it so much that we want to live in it—that is, in the wildland-urban interface (WUI). Roughly a third of homes in the continental United States are now in the WUI, imposing heavy costs on native species and their habitats. Living in the WUI, by definition, fragments habitat. When we punch holes in our beloved native wildland habitats for housing, we impact not just the species that live there but also the web of interactions between species. Jane Goodall said it like this: "Every time a little species vanishes, it may not seem important. But the thread is pulled from that tapestry and the picture gets weaker as more threads are pulled, until that tapestry, once so beautiful, is hanging in tatters."

We also impact wildlands in the WUI through the introduction of invasive or "weedy" species. This is especially critical to consider given that roughly half of the area stretching from southwestern Oregon to northern Baja California is considered one of only thirty-six biodiversity hot spots around the world. These are defined as places that have lost at least 70 percent of their original native vegetation but still contain at least 1,500 species of vascular plants that are native nowhere else. Biodiversity hotspots cover only 2.5 percent of Earth's land surfaces but support nearly 60 percent of the world's plant, bird, mammal, reptile, and amphibian species.

Human-caused habitat fragmentation tears holes in tapestries of wild land; invasive species stain and shred those tapestries. Together, our fragmentation of wildland habitats and the invasive species we introduce affect habitat quality, as well as fire susceptibility and resilience. As you think about how best to protect your home from wildfire, learning more about the wild tapestry around you will help you make choices that will reduce the impacts of both fragmentation and invasive species in the WUI. Further, you will have a greater understanding of the fire regime(s) that maintain the biotic communities in your area, and what to expect when they burn.

Habitat Degradation in the WUI

Habitats are simply places where organisms live. Habitats around the WUI are being increasingly degraded by human activities.

Habitat fragmentation creates islands of habitat within a background matrix that may hinder organisms from living and/or moving across a landscape. Habitat fragmentation also affects the quality of habitat remaining, in two important ways.

Habitat fragmentation has two powerful effects: populations become smaller and "edgier," and populations become more isolated.

22

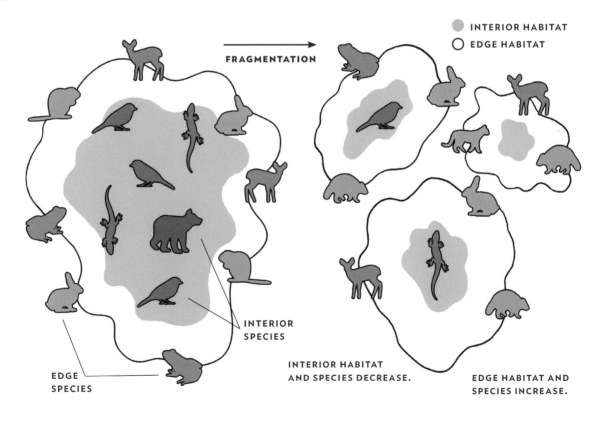

FRAGMENTATION

INTERIOR HABITAT
EDGE HABITAT

INTERIOR SPECIES

EDGE SPECIES

INTERIOR HABITAT AND SPECIES DECREASE.

EDGE HABITAT AND SPECIES INCREASE.

First, as habitat patches become smaller, they become "edgier," with more area adjacent to habitat edges. Think of it this way: a string long enough to go around several small patches is longer than a string encircling a single habitat of the same area. As habitat patches become smaller, they tend not to support viable populations of species that require habitat away from edges—that is, interior habitat.

Second, the greater the distances between remaining habitat patches, the more difficult it is for organisms to move between them (especially if the background matrix is inhospitable, like concrete), and the more isolated populations become. Small patches may even allow some interior species to live temporarily but have insufficient habitat quality for successful reproduction. These "population sinks" continually receive migrant individuals who may reproduce, but the habitat patch is too small or degraded to provide sufficient resources for them to persist there.

Research indicates that human-caused habitat fragmentation not only reduces biodiversity but also impairs ecosystem functions, by decreasing biomass (and carbon storage) and altering nutrient cycles, particularly nitrogen retention, among other things. Habitat fragmentation is likely to worsen impacts due to climate change, invasive species, and pollution from the lighting we use, the noises we make, and the chemicals we release into the environment. Layered on top of that, fragmented habitats with reduced biodiversity have fewer sources of plants and animals for habitat recovery after wildfires.

Invasive species

Essentially, habitat fragmentation—when habitat patches decrease in size, are composed of more edges, and are increasingly isolated—can drive turnover to different species assemblages, including invasive species. All else being equal, some species are highly sensitive to habitat fragmentation and others less so. Most invasive species have an easier time gaining a foothold in fragmented landscapes than in intact wild landscapes. Invaders may already be naturalized in the surrounding wildlands, or brought into the WUI by the people who settle there. Sadly, very few invasive species are restricted in commerce, and invasive species are still commonly sold in nurseries and online.

Although we can make good estimates, no one really knows how much native vegetation should be retained to maintain healthy support for any given wild ecosystem. We don't even really know how much native habitat exists in developed WUI areas on average, although that could be easier to figure out in a specific ecoregion or biotic community. Identifying the threshold at which invasive species cause significant harm to an area is also poorly understood. No research can establish at what point human-modified landscapes no longer support viable communities of native flora and fauna, because viability varies with species. And climate change shifts all the variables into moving targets.

What we do know is that invasive species should be avoided and aggressively removed, even if fire resistant. Invasive nonnative plants can spread into wildland ecosystems and displace native species, hybridize with native species, alter biological communities, and/or alter ecosystem processes (including fire regimes). Not only do invasive species negatively affect habitats (including backyard habitats), but many weedy species, particularly nonnative annual grasses, mustards, and thistles, also happen to be fire enablers. They can grow in difficult conditions, increase fuel loads (both live and dead), and make fuels more continuous.

Many invasive plant species are flashy (they catch fire easily), and invasive species fill in gaps between plants horizontally and vertically (they are ladder fuels). Illustrious invaders in this regard include nonnative annual grasses like cheatgrass (*Bromus tectorum*), broom shrubs (*Cytisus multiflorus, Cytisus scoparius,* and *Spartium junceum*), and in riparian systems, giant reed (*Arundo donax*) and tamarisk (*Tamarix* species). Invasive species such as yellow starthistle (*Centaurea solstitialis*) can also deplete soil moisture early in the growing season, leaving more dead and stressed fuels.

BELOW LEFT English ivy, an invasive species, is commonly sold in nurseries.

BELOW RIGHT Scotch broom (*Cytisus scoparius*) has invaded much of the West and is among the most flammable plants in our landscapes. It forms dense stands up to 6 feet tall or more that burn dead or alive and can transfer fire into the tree canopy.

24

How to
Recognize Invasive Species in Your Area

California, Oregon, and Washington all have councils that provide extensive information on invasive species. Consult these resources for the latest information about invasive species and how to avoid/control them:

- **In California,** the California Invasive Plant Council (Cal-IPC) is the most comprehensive source and provides a downloadable list of plants to avoid in landscaping, at www.cal-ipc.org.

- **The Oregon Invasive Species Council** (OISC) maintains its Invasive Species Digital Information Hub at www.oregoninvasivespeciescouncil.org/infohub, where you can click on a button to find out about species of all kinds, not just plants, to look out for in Oregon.

- **The Washington Invasive Species Council** (WISC) maintains separate lists of noxious animals, insects, weeds, and diseases at invasivespecies.wa.gov/. The Washington State Noxious Weed Control Board provides downloadable noxious weed lists at www.nwcb.wa.gov/printable-noxious-weed-list.

   Not all invasive plants are well documented; monitor any species that you observe spreading too quickly for comfort. If you see a plant you can't identify, try taking a photo and uploading it to the free iNaturalist app (iNaturalist.org) for identification.

25

Habitat quality and wildfire risk

Habitat fragmentation affects habitat quality. Habitat quality in turn affects how fires can move through landscapes. For example, many invasive annual grasses have been found to increase fire occurrence and frequency relative to similar areas without those invaders.

Historical accounts of pre-European settlement are scarce, but forests, woodlands, shrublands, grasslands, and deserts of our area have changed drastically over the past 450 years. Multiple lines of evidence give us a rough idea of precolonial vegetation. Native Americans managed different habitats to varying degrees for food, tools, medicines, and shelter. The earliest written descriptions were mostly recorded after the decimation of Indigenous peoples due to introduced diseases and ethnically motivated violence. Transitions to colonial farming and ranching techniques had impacts that extend to today, such as overgrazing in landscapes prone to periodic drought. Mining also deeply scarred many mountain and riparian habitats. Even mill ponds changed the hydrology and vegetation of riparian habitats during European settlement.

A trained botanist or naturalist can read landscape quality and interpret some of its history simply by looking for telltale signs of past disturbances. Common indicators used in such an assessment are overgrazing, soil compaction, mining, surface erosion, groundwater depletion, excessive nutrient inputs, soil salinization due to irrigation, development, extent of invasive species, wildlife habitat, vegetation structure, biodiversity, and fire scars.

A wildfire fueled by nonnative annual grasses burns a California hillside.

Here are some common ways in which disturbances to water, land, and vegetation can affect both habitat quality and wildfire risk:

- **Draining or ditching land** changes the available soil moisture and the water storage capacity of the land. For example, wetland meadows that have been drained or ditched lose both wetland species and soil organic matter. The result is that the land is drier and more vulnerable to wildfires.

- **Impounding water** behind dams or weirs changes soil moisture and sedimentation patterns. Onstream reservoirs result in the land being wetter immediately surrounding the reservoir but drier downstream.

- **Deep ripping or plowing of land,** along with laser leveling, results in the loss of isolated wetlands, vernal pools, and perched water tables (stores of water trapped above an impermeable layer of soil). As a consequence, the land is drier and more vulnerable to wildfires.

- **Significant and prolonged groundwater depletion** in the root zone of plants, including trees, increases drought-related mortality and stresses the plants, as is happening in the Sierra Nevada and Cascade foothills. The result is drier fuels that are more vulnerable to wildfire.

- **Erosion and compaction of the soil surface** changes the properties of soil and results in biodiversity losses. This effect can be seen in foothill and mountain areas that have been subjected to mining in the past. In these areas, plants are slower to take up nutrients and water, so they become weaker. The amount of dead biomass on the ground increases, making more fuel available to wildfires.

- **Changes to the vegetation structure,** sometimes as a result of fire suppression in forests, leads to a loss of native biodiversity and an increase in live and dead biomass and ladder fuels.

27

Key Terms

Habitat fragmentation is the breaking apart of continuous habitat into distinct pieces.

Habitat degradation refers to the results of a set of processes—natural (for example, drought, heat, cold, climate change) and human (such as forestry, agriculture, and urbanization)—that reduce habitat quality.

Edge effect refers to changes in population or community structure that occur at the boundary of two or more habitats; areas with small habitat fragments exhibit especially pronounced edge effects that may extend throughout the range. Interior species richness tends to decline in small patches because of the larger amount of edge habitat, leading to higher probabilities of local extinction.

Species richness is the number of different species in an ecological community, landscape, or region; simply a count of species, not considering the abundance of each species. **Species evenness** refers to the relative abundance of all species within a community, landscape, or region.

Interior habitat is living space beyond the influence of both microclimatic and biotic edge effects, which therefore manages to sustain the viability of the plant and animal communities that depend on its generally stable environmental conditions.

- **Invasion by nonnative species** such as cheatgrass leads to a loss of native biodiversity and an increase in live and dead biomass and fuels that are more easily ignited.

- **Removal of native species,** as in chaparral habitats that are burned too frequently, leads to a loss of native biodiversity and an increase in nonnative annual grasses and fuels that are more easily ignited.

When we understand the harm human development is doing to the WUI, we can find ways to support habitat health while also increasing wildfire resistance. For example, one way to reduce the impacts of fragmentation in the WUI is to provide corridors of native habitat, and more native plants in the intervening spaces. In other words, we can reduce our negative impacts on the wild environment by making our homesteads more like the wild biotic communities where we live. That gives us good reason to find out as much as we can about our habitat.

Habitats, Biomes, Ecoregions, and Biotic Communities

The broadest class of habitat is the biome. The western United States encompasses these distinct biome types:

- **Forest biomes** have lots of trees and are found in the mountains and along the northwestern coast.

- **Woodlands** have fewer trees, with grasses and herbs underneath, and are common in the foothills of California.

- **Grasslands, shrublands, and savannas** (sparsely treed woodlands) are common in the great valleys of California and in eastern Oregon and Washington.

- **Deserts and very dry shrublands** extend from inland southern California through large areas of eastern Oregon and Washington.

Yet, if you have ever driven through different regions of the West, you know that each of these broad biome classifications has a lot of variation. Temperature and precipitation patterns—as well as elevation, topography, and soils—dictate the kinds of habitats possible in a particular place.

Even within the same biome, vegetation can show a lot of variation. Mammoth Lakes, California, is in a forest biome that also supports sagebrush.

29

Before European settlement, native plants evolved in the absence of non-native species and some disturbances that are common today. Plants formed recognizable communities. Each species might be widespread in several habitats, or narrowly restricted to very specific ones.

Today communities of plants can be distinguished both by their adaptations to their environment (abiotic, nonliving factors that define habitats) and by other species in the environment (biotic entities). Ecologists have long debated the merits of categorizing different communities mostly in terms of abiotic factors and generalized plant communities ("ecoregions") versus the primary plant species ("biotic communities") of an area. It turns out that both visions can be extremely useful.

Ecoregions

Ecoregions are areas where ecosystems are generally similar, defined by geography and the amount of solar radiation and moisture they receive. Ecoregions defined primarily by climate, physical geography, water, soils, air, and potential natural communities have been identified by the US Environmental Protection Agency (EPA) across the United States, as a framework for researching, managing, and monitoring ecosystems and their components. The EPA has identified ecoregions at several different levels, ranging from general to more detailed. Level III mapping subdivides the United States into 104 ecoregions, including 19 within the West Coast states. Level IV mapping further subdivides Level III ecoregions. Level IV mapping is still under way in many states but has been completed in California, Oregon, and Washington.

The EPA's description of your ecoregion can give you a good idea of the terrain, climate, soils, dominant vegetation historically, and common land uses today where you live. What you don't get is information about specific plant communities or their specific fire regimes.

Biotic communities

Biotic communities are groups of living organisms, including plants and animals, that inhabit the same region and are interdependent. Biotic communities can change over time, and they can pop up in different places. The convenience of recognizing biotic communities generally is

---

How to
Identify Your Ecoregion

You can find the EPA's Level III and Level IV ecoregion maps for your state at www.epa.gov/eco-research/level-iii-and-iv-ecoregions-state.

The Jepson Flora Project has identified ten different ecoregions in California that you can view at ucjeps.berkeley.edu/eflora/geography.html.

How to
Learn About the Plant Communities Where You Live

These helpful resources can tell you more about the plant communities where you live:

- **The California Native Plant Society** maintains the electronic version of *A Manual of California Vegetation* at vegetation.cnps. org/, where you can search by common or scientific name of species that are the most abundant. The electronic edition is updated regularly as more data are collected and analyzed.

- **In Oregon, the Classification of Native Vegetation** is maintained online by the Oregon Biodiversity Information Center of the Institute for Natural Resources at Oregon State University (see inr.oregonstate.edu/ biblio/classification-native-vegetation-oregon-2019 to download the pdf). Rather than alliances, the Oregon manual lists each association, then identifies in which of eight primary ecoregions (Coast Range, Willamette Valley, Klamath Mountains, West Cascades, East Cascades, Columbia Basin, Blue Mountains, and Northern Basin and Range) each association occurs.

- **In Washington, the Washington Natural Heritage Program (WNHP)** also distinguishes between coarse-scale vegetation classification (ecological systems) and fine-scale classification (associations). The Natural Heritage Program published the Ecological Systems of Washington State, available at www.dnr.wa.gov/publications/ amp_nh_ecosystems_guide.pdf.

Consult these resources to find out about rare species:

- **The California Native Plant Society** maintains an Inventory of Rare and Endangered Plants of California, downloadable at rareplants.cnps.org.

- **The Oregon Biodiversity Information Center** maintains lists of rare, threatened, and endangered organisms in Oregon, available online at inr. oregonstate.edu/orbic/rare-species/ rare-species-oregon-publications.

- **The Washington State Department of Natural Resources** maintains lists of rare, threatened, and endangered species online as well, at www.dnr.wa.gov/NHPlists.

The Joshua tree, a characteristic plant of the Mojave Desert, gives its name to Joshua Tree National Park in California and to just one of the plant alliances found there.

Key Terms

An **ecoregion** is a major eco-system defined by distinctive geography and receiving uniform solar radiation and moisture.

A **biotic community** is a group of living organisms, including plants and animals, that inhabit the same region and are interdependent.

A **plant community** is an assemblage of plants that co-exist in a similar environment.

The **US National Vegetation Classification** is a hierarchical system designed to classify existing vegetation on the basis of both outward appearance and geographic occurrence.

A **plant alliance** is a group of plants that reflects regional climate, soils, water sources, nutrients, and disturbance regimes. A **plant association** is a subgroup of a plant alliance.

Dominant species are the most common in terms of biomass, density, height, and/or coverage. **Characteristic species** are distinctive representatives of vegetation in a locale or region.

that, like families, you can predict certain behaviors of those communities. Discrete plant communities can be recognized based on dominant members and their common associates. That is the foundational logic behind the US National Vegetation Classification, a system of classification that provides a common language for managing and conserving plant communities.

In this classification system, plant communities are grouped into alliances based on typical species; associations, additional species commonly found in the company of particular alliances, are also detailed. Alliances are named for typical species that are either dominant, co-dominant, or characteristic. Dominant species are the most abundant, covering greater than 50 percent of the area, and co-dominant plants cover roughly 30 percent to 60 percent. Characteristic plants may not reach 50 percent cover but are distinctive to an area, such as the iconic Joshua trees (*Yucca brevifolia*) of the Mojave Desert.

Classifying plant communities in this way allows scientists to

- **recognize and preserve** rare communities,
- **better predict** where to find rare or troublesome species,
- **intuit some environmental parameters,**
- **identify localized biodiversity** hot spots,
- **monitor the effects** of disturbances on community dynamics, and
- **associate fire regimes** with particular biotic communities.

Each West Coast state maintains online resources detailing how biotic communities are categorized and how you can find what type(s) you live with. Classification consistent with the National Vegetation Classification can tell you about topography, elevation, soils, how common or rare your community is, where else it occurs, and fire characteristics.

As we develop the WUI, we need to be particularly aware of rare species to preserve overall biodiversity where we live. If you happen to be living in a rare biotic community, you may want to take greater care to not disturb any more than you have to for fire safety.

Understanding Your Wildfire Risk

Here are some aids to assessing the risk of wildfire where you live:

- **The Understand Risk web page** on the Wildfire Risk to Communities website (wildfirerisk.org/understand-risk/) has an interactive data viewer to help you understand your community's wildfire likelihood.

- **The Wildfire web page** on FEMA's National Risk Index website (hazards.fema.gov/nri/wildfire) maps wildfire risk and rates communities on relative risk of wildfire losses.

- **Risk Factor** is a tool provided by the nonprofit First Street Foundation to help homeowners determine their flood and wildfire risk. Just go to riskfactor.com and enter your address.

34

Key Terms

A **fire regime** is the characteristic pattern of fires that naturally occur in a particular ecosystem. This pattern includes seasonality, fire-return interval, size, spatial complexity, intensity, and severity.

The **fire return interval** is the average length of time between fires in a particular area.

Fire suppression is extinguishing, controlling, or in some cases entirely preventing fires from spreading or occurring.

Prescribed fire or a **prescribed burn** is fire ignited under predetermined conditions to meet management objectives.

Chaparral is a shrubland plant community found mostly in California and southern Oregon composed of plants that tolerate hot, dry summers. With a fire return interval of between thirty and more than a hundred years, chaparral habitats can become dense, tangled thickets of woody shrubs.

A **stand-replacement fire** is a high-severity fire that kills most of the aboveground portions of shrubs and trees, so that the stand must be replaced by plants that can resprout from roots or establish from seeds.

Your Region's Fire Regime

A fire regime is the general pattern of fires that naturally occur in a particular ecosystem. A fire regime is characterized by an average return time (fire return interval). Vegetation type, climate, and weather patterns are the strongest determinants of a fire regime. Specifically, the fire regime of an area depends on plant composition and structure, stage of succession after previous fires or disturbances, past management, topography, and landscape patterns. These components of fire history, along with climate and weather, will determine fire size, spatial complexity, intensity, and duration. Obviously, fire regimes are complex.

Forest fire suppression was a national policy in the United States for roughly 120 years, interfering with natural fire regimes and fire return intervals in most habitats. Ironically, the legacy of fire suppression has been a buildup of fuels, leading to more devastating wildfires today. In the wake of recent massive wildfires, abundant media attention has been focused on the need for more prescribed fires to reduce wildfire fuels. However, fires that recur more often than the capacity of a community to recover can be much

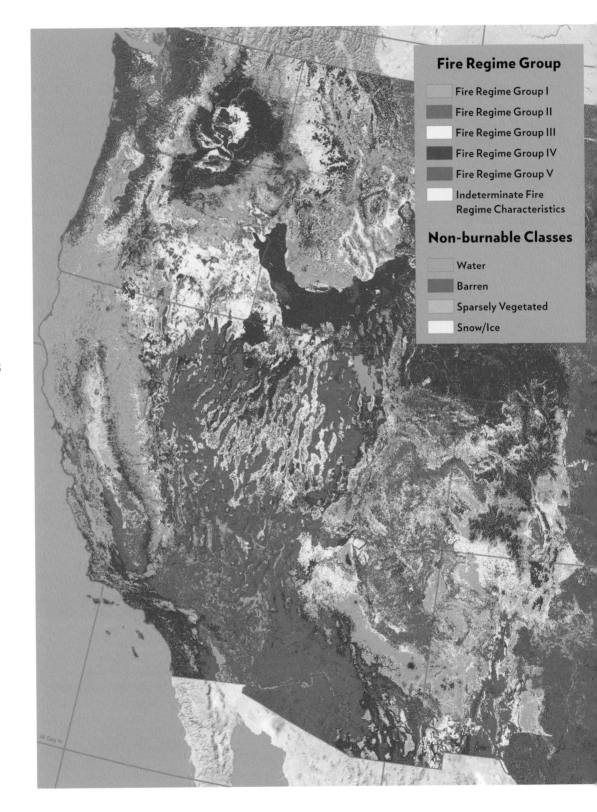

Fire Regime Group

- Fire Regime Group I
- Fire Regime Group II
- Fire Regime Group III
- Fire Regime Group IV
- Fire Regime Group V
- Indeterminate Fire Regime Characteristics

Non-burnable Classes

- Water
- Barren
- Sparsely Vegetated
- Snow/Ice

more devastating than fire suppression. For example, a particular forest type may have a fire return interval of every three to ten years, but chaparral may be destroyed by a fire return interval that frequent.

Fire return intervals across the western states range from every few years to greater than 150 years for some types of chaparral adapted to infrequent, high-intensity fire. Some high-elevation desert areas have fire return intervals that span hundreds of years. This knowledge should enter into our thinking about how best to protect our homes while respecting our western habitats and the needs of other creatures.

Learning the fire regime of the region where you live can help you understand plant community adaptations to fire, and how likely a fire is to occur in your area. The LANDFIRE fire regime map of the continental United States (available for viewing at landfire.gov/frg.php) indicates fire regimes in five groups:

- Group I, frequent (0–35 years) low-severity burns
- Group II, frequent (0–35 years) fires of stand replacement severity
- Group III, fires of mixed severity every 35–100+ years
- Group IV, fires of stand replacement severity every 35–100+
- Group V, fires of stand replacement severity every 200+ years

Analyses of wildfire risk tend to sort homes into three or four categories of wildfire risk: very high (in the WUI with high-risk fuels where high-intensity wildfires tend to recur), high (in or near fuels and terrain conducive to catastrophic fires and vulnerable to ember ignition), moderate (farther away from high-risk areas but still vulnerable to ember ignition), and low (but not zero). However, even urban areas not considered vulnerable to wildfire can experience conditions that allow fires to spread from house to house. Wherever you live, it is a good idea to be wildfire risk aware.

OPPOSITE This map of fire regime groups of the western United States is provided by LANDFIRE, a program of the US Forest Service and the US Department of the Interior.

37

The Nature and Behavior of Fire

Fire is a force of nature driven by fuel, heat, and oxygen. Understanding how fire spreads can help you plan how to defend your property.

FIRE IS A FORCE OF NATURE. Like water, like wind, like sunshine and darkness, it shapes us.

Fires transform matter, and they are mesmerizing to watch. Staring into the dancing flames of a safe fire can lower blood pressure and make us feel more relaxed. We delight in the warmth and colors of the flames.

But a wildfire is a different matter entirely. When you are up against the possibility of a wildfire threatening your home, you need to have a clear understanding of how fires start and spread. This knowledge is not just for firefighters. It can help you plan how to harden your yard and home to defend against fire.

This chapter exposes the complexity of fire behavior and the variables that make every property unique. Recognizing that complexity and taking inventory of those variables can empower you to refine your landscaping plans for safety and beauty, and to support healthy habitat. The goal is to become a knowledgeable caretaker of the land where you live.

What Is Fire?

Fire is a chemical reaction (combustion) that releases energy. During combustion, oxygen combines with fuel (such as the hydrocarbons in wood) to produce carbon dioxide, water, and energy in the form of heat and light. Basically, fires release carbon that was stored in living organisms to the atmosphere. Because incomplete combustion is common during wildfires, such fires produce smoke, ash, and embers, and often leave unburnt fuels behind.

For a fire to continue to burn, combustion must be self-sustaining. A self-sustaining fire is a chemical chain reaction, in which the products of a chemical reaction contribute reactants to another reaction. Besides oxygen and fuel, a self-sustaining fire requires heat. Heat ignites fuel in the presence of oxygen. All three of these components affect fire ignition probability and behavior. Remove any one of those and combustion will cease.

Once a fuel ignites, its combustion produces heat, and heat helps sustain a fire. Heat removes moisture from and preheats fuel, and warms the surrounding air. Any substance that reduces the amount of heat available to a fire can slow or stop the fire. Water, for instance, combines with heat to produce steam and thereby reduces the heat available to drive combustion.

Each color in a flame indicates a temperature range. In rainbow order of light wavelengths, red is the coolest fire color; orange, yellow, green, blue, and

The fire triangle portrays fire as a chemical reaction among fuel, heat, and oxygen. Remove any one of those to put the fire out.

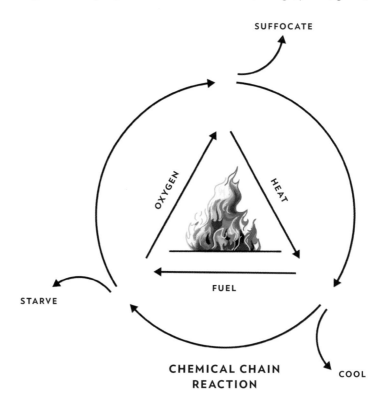

SUFFOCATE

OXYGEN

HEAT

FUEL

STARVE

CHEMICAL CHAIN REACTION

COOL

How Do Wildfires Start?

According to the US National Park Service, nearly 85 percent of wildland fires are caused by humans. Natural sources of ignition are limited to lightning, volcanic eruptions, and spontaneous combustion; lightning-ignited fires are more common in the eastern portions of our geographic region. The most common ignition sources are arson and accidental ignition, powerline arcs, mechanized equipment and vehicles throwing sparks, debris burning, cigarettes, and campfires.

Accidental ignition often occurs from behaviors that only become dangerous under drier conditions. Mowing and using power equipment without spark arresters, campfires not extinguished properly, fireworks, parking vehicles in dry vegetation, driving vehicles with dragging chains or other sources of sparks, and target shooting with metal targets are just a few of the everyday behaviors that can become dangerous during high fire risk conditions. The nearly 23,000-acre El Dorado Fire in southern California in 2020 was started by a smoke-generating pyrotechnic device at a baby gender reveal party in a public park. The fire destroyed or damaged nine homes and killed a veteran firefighter, Charlie Morton.

violet are each associated with increasingly hotter temperatures. A grass fire or surface fire on a forest floor might range in temperature from 212°F to 1472°F. Forest fires typically range from 1500°F to 2192°F, with flame heights extending to more than 165 feet. Of course, the color can vary with the type of material burning as well. Burning of various chemical compounds can create colored flames (copper chloride can create a green flame, for example). Oranges and yellows are generally what we see in wildfires, along with smoke.

It is important to note that combustion can occur in the absence of flames, in which case it is called thermal pyrolysis or smoldering combustion. Pyrolysis of wood typically starts at around 482°F. Such nonflaming combustion releases heat on a solid surface and can convert wood to blackened biochar. Charcoal is an example of biochar. Biochar is rich in carbon and can be used both as a soil amendment and as a method of storing carbon in soil for thousands of years.

BRANCHES PREHEATED BY CONVECTION AND RADIATION

TREE TRUNK PREHEATED BY RADIATION

BRUSH PREHEATED BY RADIATION

LOG PREHEATED BY CONDUCTION AND RADIATION

LITTER OR DUFF PREHEATED BY CONDUCTION AND RADIATION

Fuels in the forest are preheated by radiation, convection, and conduction during a wildfire.

Wildfires and the Transfer of Heat

Until recently, we believed that fires with sufficient oxygen and fuel spread by just three mechanisms of heat transfer: radiation, convection, and conduction. Radiation and convection are considered the most important drivers of heat transfer in wildfires. They drive the ignition of ladder fuels, fuels that connect and can carry fire from the ground into the crown of a forest or shrubland.

- **Radiant heat** is the emission of energy in waves, such as the heat you feel when sitting by a roaring woodstove or fireplace. Radiation from a fire in the forest can preheat litter or duff, fallen logs, brush, tree trunks, and branches.

- **Convective heat** spreads as a result of differences in temperature-driven air densities. As air is warmed by fire it becomes less dense and rises. Cooler, denser air falls in to replace the warmed air. Cooler air feeds more oxygen to the flames, then heats as the oxygen is consumed by the flames, becoming less dense and rising. This sets up a convective column of cycling air patterns around a flame. Tree branches rising high above the ground can be preheated by convection during a wildfire.

- **Conduction** is the transfer of heat directly from one material to another. When you touch a hot stove, heat is conducted directly to your skin. Wood is a poor conductor of heat, so conduction is not generally very important in wildfires unless there are human-built structures present. Conduction does affect fallen logs and litter or duff on the forest floor during a wildfire.

Recent research has identified a fourth mechanism of heat transfer, called flame or fire buoyancy. We all know from watching fires that flames are naturally inconstant and unstable. Flames develop peaks and troughs that create vortices, and these vortices can spiral flames forward through the troughs to heat and ignite fuels. Imagine corkscrews drilling forward in flame troughs to drive bursts of flame forward, igniting fuels more quickly. Understanding this fourth heating mechanism increases our ability to predict wildfire dynamics.

Wildfires burning as never before have turned our attention to learning more about how heat transfer mechanisms correlate with fuel, topography, and weather conditions. These are the three main variables that determine wildfire behavior. Each of these variables, in turn, has several aspects, which we'll be exploring in the sections that follow.

Key Terms

Fire behavior is the manner in which fuel ignites, flame develops, and fire spreads as determined by the interaction of fuels, weather, and topography.

Combustion is another name for fire, a rapid oxidation process that chemically combines hydrocarbons with oxygen to produce carbon dioxide, water, and energy (as heat and light).

Pyrolysis is smoldering combustion. **Smoldering** is a slow, low-temperature, flameless combustion that can transition back into flames.

Biochar is charcoal that is produced by pyrolysis of biomass in low oxygen.

Radiation is energy (heat or light) sent as rays through the air.

Convection is movement of heat through the air due to temperature differences. These differences drive the flow of warmer, less-dense materials upward relative to cooler, more-dense materials.

Conduction is transfer of heat from molecule to molecule.

Flame or fire buoyancy is the tendency of flames to develop peaks and troughs that create vortices that in turn can spiral flames forward through the troughs to heat and ignite fuels.

Wildfire Behavior and Fuels

Fuel is anything that can burn. In the WUI, fuel is living and dead organisms plus everything we bring with us to live there. In this chapter we focus on the behavior of wildfire in the absence of the stuff we bring with us. We go into detail about the built environment and fire in the next chapter.

RIGHT Flame buoyancy creates vortices that alternately push flames up into peaks and down into troughs. Flames intermittently burst forward through the troughs to heat and ignite fuels.

BELOW RIGHT Every wildfire is different. The three main variables that affect wildfire behavior are fuel, weather, and topography.

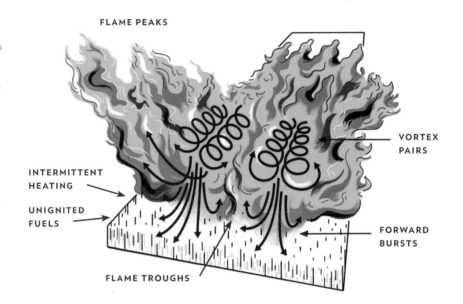

FLAME PEAKS

VORTEX PAIRS

INTERMITTENT HEATING

UNIGNITED FUELS

FORWARD BURSTS

FLAME TROUGHS

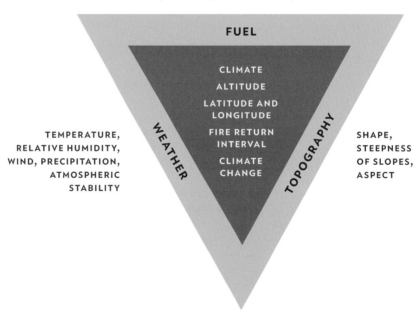

FUEL AVAILABILITY, CONTINUITY, ARRANGEMENT, SIZE, DRYNESS, TEMPERATURE, CONDITION

FUEL

CLIMATE
ALTITUDE
LATITUDE AND LONGITUDE
FIRE RETURN INTERVAL
CLIMATE CHANGE

WEATHER

TOPOGRAPHY

TEMPERATURE, RELATIVE HUMIDITY, WIND, PRECIPITATION, ATMOSPHERIC STABILITY

SHAPE, STEEPNESS OF SLOPES, ASPECT

Factors That Can Create Dangerous Fire Behavior

How many of these factors are present around your home on any given day? The more there are, the greater is the risk of dangerous fire behavior.

Fuel
- dry or unusually dry fuels
- large quantities of fine fuels
- fuels exposed to direct sunlight
- fuels dried by prolonged drought
- ladder fuels
- high concentration of dead buildup of branches/duff/litter

Weather
- strong wind
- sudden changes in direction/velocity of wind
- thunderstorms
- high or unusually high temperatures

Topography
- ridges
- steep slopes
- chutes, saddles, box canyons
- narrow canyons

All fuels have different flash points, or temperatures at which they ignite. Wood ignites at flash points around 482°F to 689°F, depending on the species, size and shape of the wood, and associated resins. Once a fire starts, it will dry and heat adjacent fuels that will ignite once they reach their flash point. The flash point of each fuel varies over time with moisture content, loading, and arrangement.

Fuel moisture

Fuel moisture is the single most important determinant of whether a fuel will ignite, and it can change from day to day. Fuel moisture is simply how much water a fuel contains. The more water contained in a fuel, the more energy is required to ignite the fuel because energy goes into evaporating the water first so the fuel will be dry enough to burn. (Similarly, the more water you have in a pot, the more energy it takes to boil the water.)

For monitoring fire potential, fuel moisture is expressed as a percentage of the dry weight of the fuel. Downed trees that are completely dry, for

How to
Monitor Fuel-Related Wildfire Risk

Check online and step outside to monitor your community's fuel-related wildfire risk in general and specific risks to your property on any given day.

- To monitor fuel moisture: You can use the National Fuel Moisture Database (NFMD) maintained by the US Forest Service within the Wildland Fire Assessment System to monitor fuel moisture in your region throughout the year. The NFMD is based on live and dead fuel moisture monitored on the ground. Just search for "National Fuel Moisture Database" in your browser.

- To determine your fuel load and arrangement: Take a close look at the surface material on your property. What kinds of materials are present (duff, litter, fine woody debris, coarse woody debris)? How are they arranged horizontally and vertically? How compact is the arrangement? Where and how can you create breaks in those fuels?

example, have a fuel moisture level of 0 percent. Precipitation and humidity are the main drivers of fuel moisture, but temperatures, sunlight, wind, precipitation type, and the size and shape of fuels all affect the amount of water in fuels at any given time.

Living and dead plant fuels are always exchanging moisture with the environment. Live plants adjust that exchange through photosynthesis and respiration. Fuel moisture in live plant material decreases as fire season progresses in Mediterranean (summer-dry) climates. Dead plant materials, on the other hand, act more like sponges; their moisture is constantly responding to changes in weather conditions.

Dead fuel moisture is an important way to assess fire potential and is one indicator used by the US Forest Service to determine when to conduct prescribed burns. The National Fire Danger Rating System used by the Forest Service classifies dead fuel moisture based on fuel size and lag time. Lag time, loosely defined as the time it takes for a piece of dead fuel to change moisture content to nearly match the atmospheric moisture in its local environment, is proportional to a fuel's diameter. Smaller fuels respond more quickly to changes in atmospheric moisture, ignite more easily, and burn more quickly than larger fuels.

The National Fire Danger Rating System classifies dead fuels in this way:

- **one-hour fuels,** less than ¼ inch in diameter: needles, leaves, and grasses
- **ten-hour fuels,** ¼ to 1 inch in diameter: finger-diameter twigs and branches
- **hundred-hour fuels,** 1 to 3 inches in diameter: arm-diameter branches or logs
- **thousand-hour fuels,** 3 to 8 inches in diameter: leg-diameter or larger branches or logs

The key takeaway here is that on any given day, dead fuel moisture can increase or decrease in response to weather conditions. Heavy precipitation in a short time period will not raise fuel moistures as much as lighter precipitation over a longer period. Frozen precipitation causes moisture to linger on fuel surfaces. Extremely saturated or extremely dry soils can increase water runoff, leaving fuels drier. Low humidity takes moisture from fuels; fuels, in turn, take moisture from the air when the humidity is high. Regardless of moisture levels, all dead fuels should be removed (or stored and processed) away from structures.

For living fuels, fine, light fuels hydrate more quickly than heavy fuels. Around your home, irrigating plants periodically can increase their moisture content and reduce their ignitability. Be aware of what drought-stressed plants look like (drooping or dehydrated leaves). The optimal way to irrigate during dry conditions or in dry habitats is to water only when the sun is not shining and to water infrequently but deeply to encourage deep roots. For chaparral and desert plants, a very early morning spray down with a hose on a weekly or monthly basis during dry spells is often all that is needed to keep those plants sufficiently hydrated.

Fuel loading

Fuel loading, also referred to as fuel volume, is a measure of the surface material available to burn. This includes the duff (broken-down organic matter), litter (like dead leaves), fine woody debris (twigs), and coarse woody debris (logs) in an area. Fuel loading is reported in tons of fuel per acre. The higher the overall fuel loading, the more heat will be produced during a fire.

Some fire readiness manuals refer to fuel types, distinguishing herbaceous from woody vegetation, but fuel loading is a more comprehensive term. Woody plants contain more carbon fuel (that is, wood) than herbs and grasses, and therefore contain more fuel that can burn.

Key Terms

Fuel is any combustible material, including vegetation (such as grass, leaves, ground litter, shrubs, and trees), and any man-made materials/structures/vehicles that feed the fire.

The **flash point** or **ignition point** is the temperature at which a fuel ignites.

Fuel moisture is the quantity of water in a fuel, expressed as a percentage of the total dry weight.

Lag time is how long a piece of fuel takes to change most of its moisture content to match its environment.

Fine fuels are fuels such as grass and pine needles that ignite readily and are consumed rapidly when dry.

Duff is the layer of soil with partially decomposed and extensively decayed organic matter, immediately above the mineral soil layer. **Litter** is the top layer of intact, and recognizable, plant debris on a forest floor.

Fuel loading or **fuel volume** is a measure of the duff (broken-down organic matter), litter (like dead leaves), fine woody debris (twigs), and coarse woody debris (logs) in an area.

Fuel compactness is how tightly fuels are packed in the horizontal and vertical planes.

Ladder fuels are fuels that connect and can carry fire from the ground into the crown of a forest or shrubland.

A **surface fire** is a fire that travels through dead and downed woody materials, grasses, and shrubs. A **canopy/aerial/crown fire** is a fire burning in the canopies of trees and/or shrubs.

Fuel loading models are used by fire managers and analysts to predict fire effects from fuels in a given area. These provide a simple and consistent way for managers to describe fuel loading conditions on the ground for input into fire behavior and effects software. Such software can predict a given wildfire's rate of spread and flame length based on detailed information about the fuel load.

You may live in a region where fuel loads are higher than expected historically due to fire suppression and/or timber harvesting practices. Although fire behavior where you live depends on the condition and amount of fuels, topography, and winds, some fires are driven more by excess fuels and some fires are more likely to be driven by extreme winds. In either case, decreased fuel moisture during drought increases fire hazard.

Fuel arrangement

Fuel arrangement refers to how fuel is assembled across a landscape. Anyone who has laid out kindling and wood for a campfire knows that the arrangement can make or break your ability to start the fire. Assessing the arrangement of fuels in both horizontal and vertical planes improves our ability to understand the potential movement of fire across a landscape. Besides the overall arrangement of fuels relative to each other, how compact or dense the arrangement is affects how air moves between the fuels, how they dry, and how oxygen circulates in a fire.

Horizontal fuel arrangement is how continuous the fuel is across a surface. Fuels uniformly distributed across a landscape provide a constant source of fuel for fire along the ground. This is the case in, for example, a grassland, where plants are all of similar height and are touching each other. By contrast, a patchy distribution of fuels would be expected in an old-growth forest with canopy gaps and occasional dead trunks on the ground. This type of arrangement can provide natural firebreaks. So can bare ground, rocks, wetlands, or irrigated vegetation with higher moisture content that break up a continuous layer of vegetation.

Vertical fuel arrangement is the distribution of vegetation from the ground up. Vertical arrangement affects the height at which fire damage can occur. For example, contrast the vertical fuel arrangement of a grassland and a very dense forest. The vertical plane can be divided into four layers: ground, surface, ladder, and aerial (canopy).

- **Ground fuels** are combustible materials lying at or beneath the soil surface, including deep organic litter/duff, peat, tree roots, and buried logs and trunks.

- **Surface fuels** are combustible materials lying on or immediately above the ground, including leaf and twig litter, grasses and herbs, small dead wood, downed logs, stumps, large limbs, and low shrubs.

- **Ladder fuels** connect surface fuels to the canopy layer of trees.

BELOW Grasslands are characterized by an even distribution of fuels in the horizontal plane, providing a way for fire to travel along the ground.

BOTTOM This Ponderosa pine forest has a patchy distribution of fuels in the horizontal plane. In the vertical plane, smaller trees can act as ladders to conduct fire upward.

- **Aerial or canopy fuels** are green and dead materials located in the upper canopy, including tree branches and crowns, snags (dead standing trees), epiphytes (mosses, lichens, and other plants growing in the canopy of trees), and very tall shrubs.

Surface fuels are the easiest for firefighters to extinguish, and aerial/canopy fires are almost impossible to stop. Eliminating ladder fuels adjacent to trees that are near structures is one of the most effective ways to reduce fire severity and impacts near those structures.

Wildfire Behavior, Climate, and Weather

Wildfire ignition and spread depend on both long- and short-term atmospheric conditions. Long-term patterns, averaged over many years, represent climate. The two biggest factors in an area's climate are precipitation and temperature. Climate defines major plant communities and their potential relationship with fire.

OPPOSITE Surface fires can spread into a canopy when there are abundant ladder fuels.

BELOW The vertical plane in a forest contains fuels in four different layers.

50

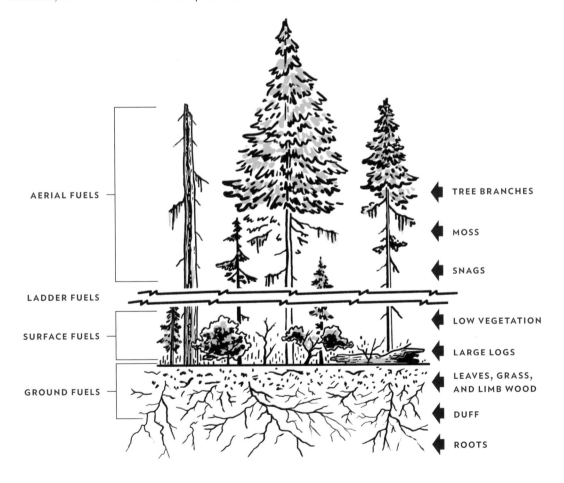

AERIAL FUELS

TREE BRANCHES

MOSS

SNAGS

LADDER FUELS

SURFACE FUELS

LOW VEGETATION

LARGE LOGS

GROUND FUELS

LEAVES, GRASS, AND LIMB WOOD

DUFF

ROOTS

THE NATURE AND BEHAVIOR OF FIRE

How to
Monitor Weather-Related Wildfire Risk

Find appropriate sources of current weather information and keep a journal of how weather changes on your property over time. You can monitor the status of red flag warnings through numerous online portals, including these:

- **National Weather Service** fire weather maps (www.weather.gov/fire/)

- **California Department of Forestry and Fire Protection** (CAL FIRE) Red Flag Warning and Fire Weather Watches web page (www.fire.ca.gov/programs/communications/red-flag-warnings-fire-weather-watches/)

- **Oregon Department of Forestry Fire Information and Statistics** web page (www.oregon.gov/odf/fire/pages/firestats.aspx)

- **Washington Department of Natural Resources Information on Wildfires** web page (www.dnr.wa.gov/Wildfires)

You can also access local weather information on apps like Weather Underground and on local news stations. You can even set weather apps to send you alerts when weather hazards are present in your area.

52

The West Coast of the United States experiences the greatest extremes of climate of any area in North America. Climate zones in California range from the hottest desert in North America to cool high-altitude alpine tundra. Mediterranean (wet-winter and dry-summer) climates prevail along the coast, in the valleys, and in the foothills. Western Oregon is Mediterranean, and parts of eastern Oregon and Washington are semi-arid high desert. Western Washington contains North America's only temperate rainforest.

Short-term patterns of precipitation, temperature, and winds represent weather. Weather influences the fire danger on any given day. Warmer temperatures increase ground and fuel temperatures to make ignition more likely, and winds spread fires. Researchers with the US Forest Service developed the Hot-Dry-Windy Index in 2018 to help fire managers identify days when the weather can contribute to especially dangerous wildfire behavior. As the name of the index suggests, days that are hot, dry, and windy are the most problematic.

On these days, the National Weather Service issues red flag warnings to indicate a high risk of wildfire ignition and spread due to a combination of low relative humidity, strong winds, dry fuels, and the possibility of dry lightning strikes. During periods when there are red flag warnings, extra firefighters are put on duty in fire-prone areas, more fire engines are staffed, and more equipment is readied to respond to new fire events.

Zeke Lunder, who publishes wildfire commentary on his site The Lookout, points out that wildfires that go on for weeks or months burn through an enormous range of weather conditions. "We often get low- and moderate-severity fire when an area burns at night, under heavy smoke, after rain, or late in the season when temperatures drop, humidities rise, and days get shorter. Conversely, we often get the majority of our high-severity fire in the few hours of late afternoon when smoke clears out and winds blow up the drainages," he writes.

Wind and wildfire behavior

Wind fans the flames of fires. With respect to the fire triangle, wind drives more oxygen to a fire. Wind direction dictates the direction of fire spread. Wind carries firebrands and embers ahead of a fire front, leading to spot fires (the most common source of building ignitions). Wind moves air heated by convection forward to dry fuels faster, allowing them to ignite more easily. High winds can whip a wildfire into burning even sparse fuels.

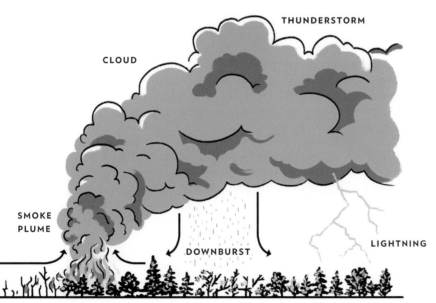

Pyrocumulonimbus clouds, driven by severe wildfires, can cause tornado-like fire whirls, erratic downbursts of wind, and lightning strikes that can ignite fires far from the fire front.

Wind is a function of climate and weather but also of topography. Wind turbulence can cause erratic fire behavior, and wind turbulence is greatest over rough surfaces (rough topography or "bumpy" vegetation) and surfaces that can heat up significantly (think bare fields and asphalt) on hot summer afternoons. Wind can be funneled and can eddy like water through canyons and low mountain saddles. Wind turbulence can also occur in vertical air layers of changing wind speed and direction, driving atmospheric inversions, wind shear (apparent when clouds or columns of smoke are abruptly "sheared" off), and low-level jet winds (common in the Great Plains) that tend to occur when thermal eddies are less important—say, at night.

Severe wildfires can propagate their own wind systems due to convection currents generated by heat. These convection currents create strong updrafts. Hot air, smoke, and ash rise and mix with water vapor to create a pyrocloud, which can be either of two types. Pyrocumulus are smoky cumulus clouds that generally don't cause additional problems. Pyrocumulonimbus clouds are thunderstorm clouds that can cause lightning and erratic downbursts of air (that can also contain embers). The downbursts slam heavy air to the ground beneath the fire, like a giant sledgehammer. These downbursts can reach velocities of 100 mph or more. The opposing updrafts can lead to fire whirls, essentially flaming dust devils, that might be as much as 100 feet in diameter and last a few minutes.

A far more dangerous form of fire-generated turbulence is a fire tornado or firenado, which can be more than a thousand feet wide with winds greater than 65 mph. A stunning example of this effect was recorded and circulated online during the 2018 Carr Fire in Redding, California.

Prevailing winds

Prevailing winds in California, Oregon, and Washington tend to blow at various angles in from the ocean, but wind patterns are more complicated than that. Weather patterns and topography modify prevailing winds throughout the year. Winds are strongly affected by topographic shapes and by local heating and cooling. Daytime breezes may flow onshore or upslope, but with nighttime cooling, winds reverse direction to produce offshore and downslope winds, usually of lesser magnitude.

Temperature and pressure differences on windward and leeward sides of mountain ranges generate large-scale seasonal winds, reversing usual wind patterns in most of our area. These winds, called foehns or föhns, drive warm, dry air downslope on the leeward side of mountains and are a significant contributor to high-fire-risk conditions. As touched on earlier, wildfires can be separated into fuel-dominated wildfires, where fire intensity is dictated by fuel characteristics, and wind-dominated wildfires, where fires are associated

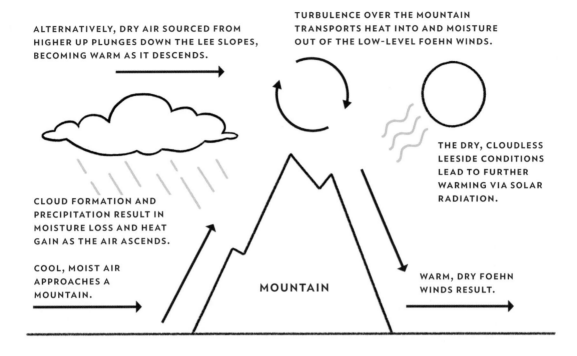

ALTERNATIVELY, DRY AIR SOURCED FROM HIGHER UP PLUNGES DOWN THE LEE SLOPES, BECOMING WARM AS IT DESCENDS.

TURBULENCE OVER THE MOUNTAIN TRANSPORTS HEAT INTO AND MOISTURE OUT OF THE LOW-LEVEL FOEHN WINDS.

THE DRY, CLOUDLESS LEESIDE CONDITIONS LEAD TO FURTHER WARMING VIA SOLAR RADIATION.

CLOUD FORMATION AND PRECIPITATION RESULT IN MOISTURE LOSS AND HEAT GAIN AS THE AIR ASCENDS.

COOL, MOIST AIR APPROACHES A MOUNTAIN.

MOUNTAIN

WARM, DRY FOEHN WINDS RESULT.

with foehn winds and human ignition sources. Primarily wind-driven fires appear to occur west of the high-elevation Sierra Nevada from Butte County in northern California south to San Diego County, as well as in western Oregon and Washington.

Major foehns in West Coast states have familiar names, including the Chinook winds in the Northwest (and Rockies), the Sundowner winds of the southern California transverse ranges, and the Santa Ana winds in California. Chinooks are wet winds that blow in from the coast—also referred to as the Pineapple Express—and drop moisture on windward mountain slopes before descending as warm, dry winds on eastern mountain slopes. Chinooks are most common in winter and therefore not generally associated with fires. Other major foehns blow toward the coast. Sundowner winds are associated with the east-west Santa Ynez Mountains and often precede or follow Santa Ana winds.

Santa Ana winds are associated with the Sierra Nevada and usually occur late summer through early winter, during fire season. Santa Ana winds are strong, dry downslope winds that develop from high pressure systems to the east, in the Great Basin and Mojave Desert, and flow toward the Coast Range. Two forms have been identified: "cold" Santa Ana winds are accompanied by high pressure off the Northwest coast, and "hot" Santa Ana winds are accompanied by high pressure off the California coast.

Foehn (föhn) winds increase fire potential on the leeward side of mountains.

Major foehn winds in our region can be associated with increased drying and warming, and increased fire risk.

Since 1950, 90 percent of large wildfires (100 acres or more) in California, as well as 95 percent of the burned area, have been associated with "hot" Santa Ana winds. This includes some of the largest and deadliest fires, such as the Santiago Canyon Fire in September 1989 (southern California) and the Camp Fire in November 2018 (northern California). "Diablo wind" was coined more recently to refer to Santa Ana winds that blow over the central Sierra Nevada and Coast Range near the Bay Area; they have also driven catastrophic fires, including the Oakland firestorm of 1991.

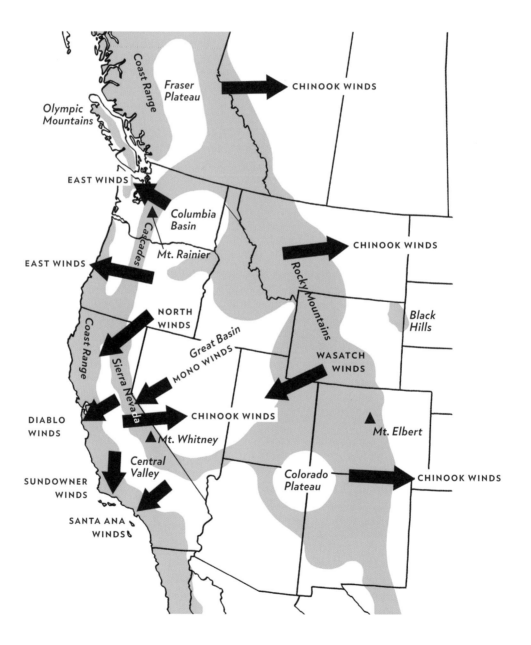

How to
Determine the Prevailing Wind Patterns Where You Live

Note the general wind direction and speed at different times of the year (especially fire season) at different locations around your home, at different times of day (in many foothill communities surrounding the Central Valley of California, for example, wind flows uphill during the day and downhill at night), and over time (make it a multiple-year study). Notice where leaves and debris collect around vegetation and structures, as these are places where the wind eddies. Conversely, where does wind scour the ground?

Here are a few options you may consider to study your wind patterns:

- **Purchase inexpensive equipment** (such as a handheld anemometer) to measure wind speed and direction.

- **Set up weather vanes or wind socks,** and record compass directions with a map of your property or phone app.

- **Use wind websites** like WindFinder. com (or phone apps) to incorporate your understanding of the small-scale patterns into the larger-scale wind movements around your community. These are also great resources to help you understand your potential vulnerability during a nearby fire event. (Rachel used Wind-Finder a lot during the North Complex Fire of 2020 and the Dixie Fire of 2021 to see if winds would be pushing those fires, and embers, in her direction.)

- **Go to WeatherUnderground.com** for current wind maps that can be selected by state. Although they are at a larger scale, they do reveal wind patterns relative to major topographic features by region.

You can then create a wind map of your property, a sketch of places that are fairly sheltered versus places where wind is more prominent. This information will be useful for designing your landscape to moderate the localized movement of wind, and fire.

Other foehn winds in the western United States are the Mono/north winds in northern and central California and the east winds in western Washington and Oregon. Some of the strongest foehns channel through mountain passes at speeds of 60 mph or more, with recorded wind gusts of more than 90 mph. Better predictions of these large-scale wind events can buy time to prepare your homestead for fire weather.

Key Terms

The **Hot-Dry-Windy Index** is a measure of atmospheric heat, moisture, and wind designed to help fire managers predict the effects of any given day's weather on fire behavior.

A **red flag warning** is a forecast warning issued by the National Weather Service in the United States to inform the public, firefighters, and land management agencies that conditions are ideal for wildland fire combustion and rapid spread.

Spot fires are blazes ignited beyond the perimeter of the main fire by flying sparks or embers.

Relative humidity is the ratio of moisture in the air to the maximum amount of moisture the air would hold if saturated, for a given temperature.

A **pyrocumulus cloud** is a dense cumuliform cloud associated with fire or volcanic eruptions. A **pyrocumulonimbus cloud** is a type of cumulonimbus cloud that forms above a source of heat, such as a wildfire or volcanic eruption, and may sometimes even extinguish the fire that formed it.

Foehns or **föhns** are warm, dry winds on the leeward side of mountains. **Leeward** means situated on or toward the side sheltered from the wind; downwind. **Windward** means situated on or toward the side facing the direction from which the wind is coming.

Fuel-dominated fires are fires where fuel is overabundant relative to natural forests, largely due to fire suppression or some timber logging practices.

Wind-dominated wildfires are those associated with foehn winds and human ignition sources.

Wildfire Behavior and Topography

Topography, basically the lay of the land, can affect fire behavior in myriad ways. Topographic aspect, slope, landform shape, and elevation determine the amount of solar radiation and moisture, and the local wind patterns in a given place. These features directly influence fuels. Furthermore, any time winds align with the orientation of canyon topography, there is potential for a strong wind-driven fire. Conversely, in areas with flat topography, wind direction can change in a flash, making fire burn direction unpredictable.

Aspect is the compass direction a slope faces, also known as exposure. The compass orientation of a slope is reported in degrees of a circle, with due north at 0 or 360 degrees, due east at 45 degrees, due south at 180 degrees, and due west at 225 degrees. The aspect of a place regulates solar radiation, temperatures, and moisture. These factors affect the amount, condition, and plant community types (fuels) present. South- and southwest-facing slopes are more directly exposed to sunlight and generally have higher temperatures, lower humidity, lower fuel moisture, and sparser, lighter fuels. Southwest-facing slopes are the most vulnerable to fire spread because they are typically the driest areas of a landscape, although with fewer fuels to burn. North aspects have more shade, lower temperatures, higher humidity, higher fuel moisture, and more abundant and heavier fuels.

Slope is how the ground inclines, either upward or downward. Slope can be expressed as either a percentage or an angle (in degrees). As a percentage, it represents the amount of rise (vertical distance) divided by the run (horizontal distance). As an angle, it represents the amount of deviation from a flat surface, where flat ground has 0 degrees of slope and a vertical cliff has 90 degrees of slope. Fire burns more rapidly uphill than downhill, and the steeper the slope, the faster a fire burns. This is because fuels above the fire are in closer contact with upward-moving flames. Generally speaking, for every 10 percent increase in slope, flame lengths double. Burning material can also roll downhill and ignite new fires. With more rapid fire spread uphill and the potential for burning fuels to roll, defensible space zones on sloping terrain need to be bigger than on flat terrain.

These ridges in southern California chaparral habitat clearly show the differences in vegetation between mountain slopes with various aspects. Slopes facing north (with a northern exposure, facing the left-hand side of the photo) are amply clothed in vegetation (especially woody), while those with a southern exposure are more sparsely vegetated.

59

The flame length is the distance from the middle of the flaming zone at the base of a fire to the tip of the flame. This illustration shows a flame driven by wind on a flat surface. For every 10 percent increase in slope, the flame length doubles, which results in fires burning more rapidly uphill than on the level.

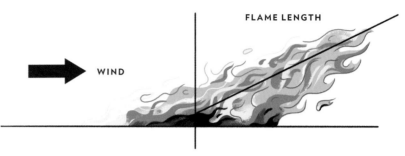

FLAME LENGTH

WIND

MIDDLE OF THE FLAMING ZONE

Landform shape—landscape features like canyons, ridges, and saddles—can dramatically impact fire behavior. The lay of the land can shift wind direction and speed, rate of spread, and fire intensity. For example, in contrast to fires in flat landscapes, fires that are racing uphill can send embers over ridges, and a fire's rate of spread can speed up as air is sucked uphill ahead of a fire front. The shape and position of landscape features also influence which plant communities live there.

Elevation is the height of terrain above mean sea level. Elevation affects the amount and timing of precipitation, exposure to winds, and the moisture status of fuels. At high elevations, fuels remain wet later in the season but are also exposed to more lightning strikes that could ignite fires.

Barriers, anything that hinders the spread of fire, are another aspect of topography related to wildfire risk. Barriers are among the greatest tools for fighting fires where fires are not wanted. Natural barriers include rivers, lakes, rock outcrops, or even high-moisture fuels. Human-made barriers include roads, highways, reservoirs, and firelines (breaks in fuel made by cutting, scraping, or digging down to mineral soil). Very recently burned areas act as barriers to wildfire simply due to a lack of fuel. Smaller-scale barriers around structures can also reduce fire hazards.

Managing All the Variables

Fire behavior is the sum of all the variables discussed in this chapter—fuel, weather, and topography—combined with their variable interactions. This complexity makes wildfires hard to predict. Layered over all of this are the predicted effects of climate change, with prolonged warmer and drier

Key Terms

A terrain's **aspect** is the compass direction its surface faces.

A property's **slope** is a measure of its steepness relative to the horizontal plane.

Flame length is the average maximum length along the axis of a flame. It directly relates to fire intensity.

60

How to
Assess Your Topography

Apps and online tools can help you assess your topography.

- **To determine your aspect:** Google Earth or a compass app on your phone can help you identify the aspect(s) of your property and/or home.

- **To determine your slope percentage and angle:** To calculate percentage and angle of slope you can use a clinometer, or a clinometer app on your phone. You can also calculate by hand the percentage of slope for a given area by dividing the amount of elevation change by the amount of horizontal distance covered (rise over run), then multiplying the result by 100. For example, if a given property gains 1,000 feet in altitude (the rise) and the horizontal distance as measured on a map is 2,000 feet (the run), 1000/2000 = 0.5 x 100 = 50 percent slope.

- **To determine your elevation:** You can easily determine the elevation where you live by using Google Earth or a compass app on your phone.

- **Also observe and note** the landform shapes and barriers present on your property.

conditions becoming more frequent, even as some areas receive more rain. This is why there is such a push for property owners and communities to control the variables they can, to the greatest extent possible. This decreases the risks associated with wildfires and makes fire behavior more predictable, and thus more survivable.

Some variables are easier to control than others. Topography and climate are relatively constant. (Although climate is not as constant a variable as topography, especially with current climate change estimations, the rate of change is still substantially less compared to weather variables.) Weather is constantly changing, and there's not much we can do about it. What is most alterable is fuel, along with the wind flow and moisture around structures.

The bottom line is that you can note constant variables such as your property's slope and prevailing wind patterns and use this knowledge to help make decisions about how to manage alterable variables. Monitor wind flow and fuel moisture fairly constantly, especially during fire season. Most important, manage the sources of fuel around your home. This is the topic of the chapters that follow.

Hardening Your Home Against Fire

Roofs are perhaps the most vulnerable parts of structures in a wildfire event. Tile, kept clear of debris and in good repair, is a smart choice in wildfire country.

IT'S ESSENTIAL TO THINK OF OUR HOMES AS FUEL—dead, standing fuel. Remember, our homes are typically constructed of dead trees, whereas the live ones in our yards are filled with water. That's one key reason why structures need additional protection. The main objectives of being wildfire ready are to keep your loved ones safe and decrease the chances of structures burning down. Being wildfire ready requires two actions: (1) hardening structures, the focus of this chapter, and (2) creating conscientiously planned landscapes around them, the focus of the next three chapters.

This chapter discusses annual care—tasks that a homeowner can complete at little or no cost each year before wildfire season to harden structures—and how to modify or replace the parts of your home and other structures that are most susceptible in a wildfire event. As you read through it, remember that your home is only as fire resistant as its weakest link (often wooden decks, siding, shingles, and wood fences). Your weakest link should be your priority when planning how best to harden your home against wildfire. Unfortunately, these weakest links also tend to be costly to address. This chapter will suggest some ways to think about how to balance potential fire hazards and costs.

WIND

EMBERS

RADIANT
HEAT

DIRECT FLAME CONTACT

The three main sources of ignition driving structure loss during wildfires are embers, radiant heat, and direct flame contact.

In many cases, you should consult with a local professional who understands structure-hardening objectives in order to plan and execute your strategy. Engaging a professional can help keep you safe (from falling off ladders or roofs, for example) and help you make your home as fire resistant as feasible.

Annual Assessment and Care of Structures

Meticulous inspection and maintenance of structures cost relatively little to do but make a big difference in wildfire readiness. Once a year before wildfire season, do a general assessment of your home and other structures. Clean up any combustible debris and remove spiderwebs at the same time. Realize that anything you have in your yard with sufficient surface area (living or dead vegetation, furniture, art—anything) can catch dead plant debris (leaves, needles, and such), accumulate spiderwebs (that can catch dead plant debris), and also catch embers. Thus, even noncombustible or ignition-resistant materials can be a danger if not maintained properly.

During the structure assessment, check for disrepair or integrity issues such as these:

- **dry rot or decaying wood,** which has a low combustion point and provides places where embers can lodge

- **gaps, nooks, and crannies,** which provide places where debris and embers can settle

- **cracks in roofing material** or its underlayment where embers can lodge

- **lint buildup** in dryer vents and hoses, which is highly ignitable

The Three Types *of* Ignition Sources

Structure loss during wildfires occurs as a result of exposure to three types of ignition sources:

1 **Embers or firebrands.** Fast-moving, hot wildfires can loft embers far in advance of a fire front (miles, under extreme conditions), and embers inevitably fall from the sky to accumulate like hail on roofs, in gutters, and in other trouble-some areas. An astounding 60 to 90 percent of all structure ignitions during wildfires—whether you are in a rural, WUI interface, WUI intermixed, or urban area—are caused by firebrands that directly ignite structures or fuels on or adjacent to structures.

2 **Radiant heat.** Heat is transferred to fuels on or next to structures, driving temperatures to the point of combustion. In dense suburban environments, radiant heat plays a big role in wildfire spread. This is largely due to the fact that structures burn at very hot temperatures, compared to most vegetation, making homes in close proximity particularly vulnerable.

3 **Direct flame contact.** Wildfire flames light fuels directly on or adjacent to structures. This is especially likely to happen in the absence of wildfire readiness for structures and landscapes. Direct flame contact may be hastened, in part, by flame buoyancy thrusting flames forward.

- **rips in window or door screens,** which allow larger embers to enter and accumulate or become pinned to your window frame (note: all screens should be metal, not plastic mesh)

- **glass panes, trim, seals, outlets, and weather stripping** around windows and doors (including the garage door and exterior crawl space doors) that allow air from the outside to come into a structure, which can also let in embers and heated air

Rachel only learned that the seals on her windows were compromised after the Camp Fire, when she found ashes covering the windowsills. You can test for air leaks around doors, windows, and outlets by closing everything down, turning on any appliances that exhaust out of the home (for example, clothes dryer, bathroom exhaust fans), and checking for air movement using a lighted stick of incense or by feeling along seams with damp fingers, just as you might for a home energy audit.

Roofs, gutters, eaves, and decks should be cleaned of all debris and spiderwebs (on the surface as well as underneath) every year. A shop vacuum is especially handy for removing spiderwebs on structures. Moss that has accumulated anywhere on a structure can act like tinder during wildfire season so should be removed. Use either a scraper and/or a pressure washer (adding a little vinegar to the water can help kill the moss). Moss buildup on rocks or concrete is not generally a concern.

Start at the top of the structure and work your way down. In other words, clear roof litter before cleaning out your gutters. Clear all crevices where even small bits of debris might accumulate and thus where embers could alight. Pay special attention to areas where roof meets siding, siding meets

Windblown embers landing on flammable materials cause most structure loss during wildfires. Just one tiny ember igniting a few dried leaves on a roof or deck can destroy a home.

If You
Go Away During Fire Season

Consider leaving your house and yard in the condition you would leave them in if you were evacuating (with a few exceptions outlined here). Also, it may be a good idea to give a trustworthy neighbor or friend a key to your house and walk them through anything you would want them to do or know in case of emergency.

Inside the house:

- Take pictures/videos of your home for insurance purposes, especially highlighting expensive items that you may not be able to pack. This doesn't take much time and could easily be done before heading out on travel.

- Shut off the heat and/or air conditioning.

- Shut and lock all windows and doors. If you were evacuating, you would leave them unlocked (in case firefighters need to access the inside of your home).

- Remove lightweight curtains and move flammable furniture to the center of the room, away from windows and doors. If you have a lot of curtains and/or heavy furniture, this might be a bit of a stretch to prepare for going away, but in a real evacuation it's a task worth completing.

- Ensure that anyone who might be looking after the house can locate and shut off your gas (and pilot light switch), electricity, and water in case of emergency. This is something you would do in a full evacuation but don't need to do if you're just going on vacation. Note that turning gas back on at the meter must be done by professionals (and there is usually a fee for this service).

Outside the house:

- Gather up flammable items (toys, rugs, welcome mats, furniture, art/decorations) and bring them inside.

- Turn off propane tanks and move propane barbecue appliances as far away as possible from structures. Safely store small propane tanks (like those used for barbecues).

- Connect garden hoses to outside water valves or spigots and leave them coiled at least a few feet from structures. Fill water buckets and place them around the house so firefighters can use them if need be.

- Seal the house, closing vents if they have no ember screens.

deck, and roof meets chimney. All gaps should be fixed by a qualified professional as soon as possible. If you need a quick temporary fix, fill gaps with noncombustible materials such as rock wool insulation.

Part of home hardening should include consolidated, safe storage of cleaning products, poisons, light bulbs, fuels, and the like. Seriously consider reducing your stockpiles of home chemicals before fire season. Anything you don't need can be dropped off at your county hazardous household waste processing facility.

Hardening Vulnerable Parts of Structures

These parts of your home and other structures are most susceptible in a wildfire event:

- roofing
- rain gutters
- overhangs, eaves, and soffits
- vents
- siding
- exposed glass surfaces
- decks

We will consider how to address each area.

Roofing

Roofs are vulnerable to ignition not only because of accumulated debris but also because of the construction materials used. Unrated roofing material has no fire resistance. Fire-resistant roofing is classified as either Class A (the best option), Class B (the second-best option), or Class C (the third-best option). Here are some examples of materials in each of the classes:

- **Class A**—asphalt fiberglass composition shingles, clay and cement tiles (flat and barrel shaped), and slate
- **Class B**—exterior-grade pressure-impregnated fire-retardant-treated shakes or shingles
- **Class C**—recycled plastic, rubber, and aluminum roofing

Find out what type of roofing (including underlayment) you have, as well as its fire-resistance classification. If your roofing has no classification, replace it with a Class A material as soon as you are able. If your structure has roofing with a Class B or C rating, make sure to also investigate (by engaging a qualified professional) the classification of its underlayment.

In addition to checking the materials and underlayment, don't forget to check for integrity issues as a part of your annual care. This is especially important for sensitive roof materials (like clay and cement tiles) because if there are cracks, that means your underlayment becomes your only barrier (so you should be sure to check its integrity too). Before Adrienne had her roof replaced with composition shingles, it was made of fifty-year-old barrel-shaped clay tiles with limited insulation underneath. Although the roof was not leaking, there were holes large enough for a baby possum to fall through. If a baby possum can fall through your tile roof, embers can surely enter!

If you are planning to update your roofing and choose a Class A roof material like clay or concrete, make sure the underlayment is also Class A, as any cracked tile can leave your roof still vulnerable. If you choose to install Class B or C roof materials (instead of Class A), you can still achieve a "by assembly" Class A rating if additional materials that increase fire resistance are used in assembling the roof (according to manufacturers' instructions).

69

If you are not yet able to replace your roofing, there are lower-cost solutions for the short term. In areas where roof meets siding and roof meets chimney, consider installing about 6 inches of metal flashing (especially if the siding and/or the roofing are combustible). Also, inspect everything attached to or piercing the roof (such as roof vents, bathroom and kitchen exhausts, skylights, and solar panels) for places where debris can gather and/or the integrity of materials is weakened. If you think something like metal flashing should be installed to deflect debris, make sure to collaborate with a professional on its installation.

Rain gutters

Although gutters themselves are usually made of noncombustible materials, the debris that gathers in them can catch fire and ignite the roof and/or siding. Uncovered gutters accumulate debris all year long. Gutters should

The Coffey Park neighborhood of Santa Rosa, California, burned in the Tubbs Fire of 2017, touched off by embers blown from a wildfire 5 miles away. The embers landed on exposed roofs in a development with few mature trees and spread quickly from house to house. Because the development was outside the officially mapped "very severe" hazard zone in what we think of as unburnable urban spaces, it was exempt from regulations to make buildings fire resistant.

be cleaned out in the spring, right before wildfire season, and monitored throughout wildfire season to clear any debris buildup (especially if it's windy). Rachel lives where strong summer winds are common, and she has to monitor and clean out the gutters every few weeks.

Covered gutters stay free of large debris and save you cleaning time. However, they can still become clogged with debris (on top of the cover and/or inside), and in some environments (such as conifer-dominated habitats) they don't really work. Some roofing professionals do not recommend them because long-term maintenance can be more difficult than just cleaning uncovered gutters a couple of times a year. Check with gutter professionals in your region who have been in the game a long time; they will know if gutter covers work in your area, and what types of noncombustible or fire-resistant gutter covers will work best.

If your gutters are covered, they should still be checked regularly during wildfire season for structural integrity and debris buildup behind or on the gutter cover. In areas that do not have significant rainfall or where the roof design and landscaping can compensate, consider not having gutters at all.

Your Budget and Choice *of* Materials

We recommend replacing combustible with noncombustible materials (materials that don't burn, such as brick, concrete, metal, stucco, and tile) whenever possible. Although they are the best choice, they are not the only choice (especially when considering your budget). Other ignition-resistant building materials include exterior-grade fire-retardant-treated wood lumber, fire-retardant-treated wood shakes and shingles, and other materials approved by your state fire marshal. We recommend reviewing all your options, assessing the vulnerability level and costs of each option, and making the best choices you can based on that information.

Overhangs, eaves, and soffits

Standard eave construction leaves combustible materials (rafters, beams, siding) and attic vents exposed. Windborne embers and radiant heat can be trapped under overhangs or eaves, and/or enter the attic via exposed vents. The most efficient way to make sure eaves resist ignition is to install horizontal soffits made of noncombustible or fire-resistant materials. If your soffits need vents, make sure they are ember resistant. If your home already has enclosed overhangs/eaves, check that the materials are noncombustible or fire resistant and that vents are ember resistant.

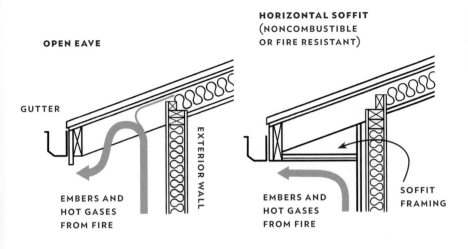

OPEN EAVE

HORIZONTAL SOFFIT
(NONCOMBUSTIBLE
OR FIRE RESISTANT)

GUTTER

EXTERIOR WALL

EMBERS AND
HOT GASES
FROM FIRE

EMBERS AND
HOT GASES
FROM FIRE

SOFFIT
FRAMING

Standard open eave construction (left) traps heat and leaves combustible materials exposed. A noncombustible or fire-resistant horizontal soffit (right) stops embers and superheated air from becoming trapped under the eaves.

Vents

Even if all the other components of your home are sealed tight, in good shape, and hardened for fire, embers can still get in through the vents. Vents are typically placed at the bottom (crawl space) and top (attic, garage) of structures to help remove excess moisture. Some vents can be closed by hand, but crawl space vents are not usually closeable. You will need to install either ember screens or ember-and-flame screens. These wire mesh screens come in a variety of mesh sizes. Here's a breakdown of the options, from worst to best:

- **¼-inch mesh, the standard gauge,** is great for air flow and therefore a huge hazard in fire season.

- **⅛-inch mesh blocks larger embers** but allows smaller embers to enter.

- **1/16-inch mesh provides the best ember defense.** However, because it is so small it can get clogged with debris and doesn't allow for easy air movement for moisture removal at other times.

- **Special mesh** designed to be both flame and ember resistant is ideal for high-hazard areas and homes in dense suburban communities.

Siding

Siding is vulnerable when it is exposed to radiant heat and/or direct flame contact during a wildfire. As with your roofing, first check what type of siding and underlayment you have. Siding that is combustible, such as wood siding, or vulnerable to warping, such as vinyl siding, which then exposes underlayment, presents a risk. If your siding is combustible or vulnerable, replace it with a non-combustible or fire-resistant siding (such as stucco, steel, and/or fiber cement) as soon as you are able. If you are not in a position to replace your siding, focus on vulnerable areas around and on your siding, such as these:

- **Areas where siding meets horizontal surfaces** (deck, roof), where debris and/or embers can gather. Keep all these areas clear of debris that could ignite, and keep an eye on them all through wildfire season, especially when it is windy in your area.

- **Decorative details or shutters** around windows and doors and/or trim on the siding that creates horizontal surfaces against the siding. Siding should allow any materials that hit it to slide to the ground and not rest against the structure. You can either decide to get rid of the trim or install angled metal flashing that would allow any debris and embers to fall to the ground.

- **At the bottom of the siding** where flames and radiant heat are more likely to be directed. Keep the 5 feet directly next to your structure(s) completely clear of combustible materials.

Exposed glass surfaces

Exposed glass surfaces such as windows, skylights, and doors (and their framing structures) are vulnerable to radiant heat and/or direct flame contact during a wildfire. Plastic and wooden frames are susceptible to failure from burning or melting, so the only viable framing option is metal. Glass can be especially vulnerable to thermal stress when exposed to heat. How much thermal stress it can tolerate before shattering is highly dependent on the type of glazing used. Glass with a low-emissivity (low-e) coating is best; tempered glass is good; laminated is okay. A proprietary fiberglass-reinforced translucent glazing for skylights is recommended. Annealed, ceramic, or plastic glazing is not recommended.

Glass is a pretty good insulator, but glass panes are thin. A single-pane window does not provide much protection from radiant heat. Double- or triple-pane windows, which have two or three panes of glass with insulating argon gas sandwiched between them, provide more protection. But like roofs, multiple-pane glass has an effective lifespan, and if the sealing is in poor condition, the glass is less able to resist radiant heat. Rachel had a window professional check her dual-pane windows and was told they were in such disrepair that they were no more protective than single-pane windows.

Check the integrity of exposed glass surfaces. Are there any cracks in the glass? Cracked glass increases the chances of shattering due to radiant heat during a wildfire. Are the weather stripping and caulk intact? Even if you cannot install new windows, maintaining the seals on existing windows is important to prevent outside air and particulates from coming into your home.

Screens can also play a role in glass hardening and can be a good alternative focus when replacing windows is not an option. Metal screens (and even fiberglass with polyvinyl chloride coating) have been found to improve the resilience of glass exposed to radiant heat (but not direct flame contact). Make sure to routinely check for screen integrity issues like tears (which can let in debris and embers) and fit (screens should fit snugly but not be impossible to remove).

To increase the resilience of your windows beyond screens (which usually cover only part of the window), you could look into noncombustible shutters. These shutters should be made of solid metal (that wouldn't melt under radiant heat) that is insulated to protect your windows from the conductive and radiant heat of the metal.

Key Terms

Embers are small, glowing pieces of superheated wood, coal, or other material that remain after (or sometimes precede) a fire; embers can glow as hot as the fire from which they arise and are light enough to be carried by the wind for long distances without being extinguished.

Firebrands are flying embers that can set additional fires ("spot fires"). Both wildland and structure fires can generate burning particles that flow in wind along with the gaseous combustion products.

Combustible materials are those that will burn. **Flammable** materials are combustible materials that ignite easily at ambient temperatures.

Noncombustible materials do not burn when subjected to fire. **Ignition-resistant** materials resist burning and withstand heat.

An **evacuation order** is a lawful order to leave immediately due to immediate threat to life. An **evacuation warning** indicates a potential threat to life and/or property, for those who require additional time to evacuate and those with pets and livestock to manage.

Fire retardant is anything that can slow down or stop the spread of fire or reduce its intensity.

A **wildfire sprinkler system** consists of sprinklers connected to a water supply by way of a water distribution system that provides adequate pressure and flow rate.

Decks

Decks pose particular challenges for keeping structures safe. They usually are made from combustible materials, have large horizontal surface areas that are vulnerable on top and bottom, and are connected to the main structure. Besides that, they tend to accumulate dead plant debris and spiderwebs, and they often have combustible items on top of them (such as furniture, toys, sunshades, and potted plants) and sometimes underneath them. Barbecues on decks may contain fire accelerants. Given these facts, decks tend to be one of the biggest structural vulnerabilities during wildfires. Although some things are not easy to change (such as the construction materials used), you can take steps to keep your deck as safe as possible.

Do not keep anything on a deck (or under the deck) that cannot be easily moved. When you are concerned about evacuation or have been given an evacuation warning, you should be able to move all items indoors or into your defensible space. If you have sunshades or shade sails, make sure you install them so they can be quickly removed. Rachel's home is very sunny on two sides, so she sets up at least eight sunshades in the summer. To make them easy to remove, she attaches them with eye hooks and carabiners at all attachment points. In some areas that aren't accessible without a ladder, she also uses quick-release knots with long ropes to release them.

Barbecues should not be kept on decks in wildfire country but should instead be placed on a concrete or gravel pad away from the house.

Do not keep barbecues on decks, especially ones that use accelerants like propane. Keep them in your defensible space and in an area with good spacing from combustible items. It is advisable to use paving stones in these areas normally anyway, to keep out weeds and provide a level noncombustible surface for barbecues.

If your deck is raised, maintain a weed-free zone underneath. A deep gravel base (4 to 6 inches) can be quite effective. Keep the deck clear of all dead plant debris and spiderwebs. Make sure to monitor areas where siding meets the deck for debris buildup and keep these areas clear.

If what you have now is redwood or cedar decking and you cannot afford to replace it yet, consider increasing the gap between boards to ¼ or ½ inch to make it easier to clean out debris that builds up and allow embers to more easily fall under the deck rather than accumulate on top of it. Think about replacing any deck boards right next to the structure with more fire-compliant material, and install 6-inch flashing against the siding both above and below the ledger board.

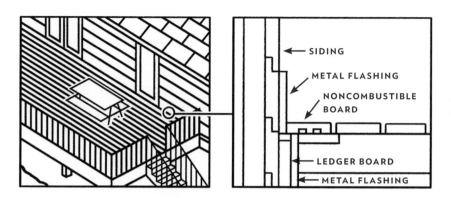

To improve fire safety without replacing an entire deck made of combustible material, replace deck boards right next to the structure and install metal flashing where the deck meets the house.

If you are in the market for a deck remodel, here are some tips to keep in mind:

- **If possible, design your deck to be at ground level.** This decreases the vulnerability of both the deck and your home (especially if combustible materials are used).

- **If your deck cannot be at ground level,** enclose the area below the deck with noncombustible materials. You can use ember- and/or flame-resistant screening or build a noncombustible wall. Enclosing the deck protects the structure the same way enclosing your eaves does, by shielding the underside (and vents) from radiant heat and embers.

- **Use fire-compliant decking materials** not only for deck boards but also for joists, posts, and railings. The best materials are metal and lightweight concrete solid surface decking. Pressure-impregnated fire-retardant-treated wood is a good choice. High-density hardwood and plastic composite decking is okay.

Extra Supports for Home and Yard Hardening

Other options that can be employed to support and enhance the main goals of yard and structure hardening include wildfire sprinkler systems, water tanks, water pumps, fire retardants, and structure wraps. By no means should these be prioritized before basic hardening practices. It's important to note that almost all of these options are expensive (if not very expensive).

An emergency wildfire sprinkler system can aid in putting out embers that land on structure(s) and help maintain humidity to decrease ignition probability. Some sprinkler systems include just the sprinklers themselves, while others include sprinklers, water pumps, and hoses. There are two very important points to remember about these systems: (1) they depend on having a large water source (like a tank, pool, or lake) that is not a municipal source, and (2) the water

This fire-resistant structure wrap by Firezat can help to protect a home if a wildfire is near. After wrapping the house, all combustible items should be removed from zone 1.

pump must work independently of grid power. Although wildfire sprinkler systems are extremely effective, they should not be connected directly to a municipal water service because they can compromise water pressure for firefighting. Therefore, if you opt to incorporate a structure sprinkler system, you need an independent water source. If your independently stored water cannot be used without a pump, and the pump motor is powered with flammable accelerants, it should be placed as far away from structures as possible to keep it from becoming a hazard in case of wildfire.

Plastic water tanks can range in storage capacity from hundreds to thousands of gallons. Their intended uses vary from everyday purposes (watering your garden) to emergency needs (fighting fire). Rachel's family has one for potential use in wildfire situations, and it also comes in really handy during power outages to access well water. You can fill such a tank by buying water (pumped in from a water tank truck) and/or by collecting rainwater during the rainy season.

If you do not have a complete sprinkler system, you can still buy a water pump (with generator/battery) and hose for use with an independent water source. Your choice of water pump and hose should correlate with the amount of water storage you have. Some homeowners choose this route so firefighters can use their system to fight fire on their property even when they have evacuated. Even though water will still come out of a tank without a pump, pumps are usually recommended, depending on the placement and how fast water should be pumped to make a difference. Again, if your pump motor is powered with flammable accelerants, you will need to be very conscious about its placement.

You can buy fire retardants for use around your home when embers are falling and/or a fire is approaching. Fire retardants will not prevent a structure from igniting in an extreme wildfire but will delay ignition. This is a great tool for folks who have vulnerable areas around structures that have not yet been retrofitted or modified for fire safety. Most residential fire retardants that you can buy connect to your garden hose and produce a gel or foam as the product is sucked out with the water. You simply spray the retardant onto the vulnerable parts of your home and/or other structures.

Retardants fall into one of two classes based on their heat-absorbing properties: Class A retardants slow the spread of flames by 75 percent or more; Class B retardants, by 25 percent to 75 percent. Another variable to consider is environmental impact. Fire retardants contain a mix of ammonium salts (nitrogen fertilizer) and trace amounts of natural thickeners, stabilizers, colorants, corrosion inhibitors, and bactericides. Although no 100 percent biodegradable retardants are available yet, nontoxic or low-toxin retardants are an option.

Structure fire blankets (also called structure wraps), made of the same material that firefighters deploy when trapped in a fire event, have been employed to save historic structures and ancient redwoods in recent years. These blankets are now more readily available and not only block embers and firebrands but also withstand up to 96 percent of radiant heat and up to 92 percent of conductive heat. However, they are expensive and can take days to install properly, so they may not be very useful when evacuation orders come suddenly. In addition, the amount of time they last under conditions of severe heat exposure and high wind is relatively brief (about ten minutes).

Your Plan for
Hardening Your Home Against Fire

Annual assessment and care

- At the beginning of wildfire season, check each part of your home and other structures for debris and spiderweb buildup (especially in crevices and places where debris naturally tends to gather) and for structural integrity issues. Leave no stone unturned. Any place where debris gathers is a place where embers can gather.

- If it's windy where you live, multiple times during wildfire season check the parts of the structure that tend to catch and gather debris.

- Finally, if you cannot safely clear all debris on your own, hire a professional to clean and check for integrity issues on a regular basis.

Hardening vulnerable parts of structures

- For each part of your home and other structures, investigate the construction materials (combustible or noncombustible) and how those materials compare to the ideal materials for structure hardening.

- If your materials are not ideal, plan how you will mitigate the risk for now, and develop priorities for future retrofits or modifications.

- If you are unsure, consult professionals to determine the materials to use and how much future retrofits or modifications will cost.

- Decide if you want to buy any nonessential add-ons that would further enhance the hardening of your yard and home.

Creating Defensible Space

Two examples of residential gardens in Palm Springs, California. The garden in the foreground is fire wise and wildlife friendly; the neighboring garden, however, with vegetation growing right next to the house in zone 1, is not.

CREATING FIRE-RESILIENT PROPERTIES depends (in part) on defensible space. How you manage the space around your home can have a tremendous influence on the behavior of embers, as well as potential sources of radiant heat or direct flame exposure. As mentioned in the previous chapter, structures most commonly burn during wildfires due to these three sources of ignition.

A major misconception about defensible space is that all vegetation (dead or alive) surrounding your home increases fire risk, so you must remove as much vegetation as possible. Unfortunately, fire risk is not that simple. Structures can burn because of (1) too much surrounding vegetation, (2) too little surrounding vegetation, or (3) completely independent of vegetation. Embers cause the majority of exterior-ignited structure fires and require no contribution from adjacent vegetation at all. Radiant heat and direct flame contact are of greater concern when too much vegetation is immediately adjacent to structures.

One ingrained sensibility that is hard to counter is the tendency to decorate our homes with foundation plantings—shrubbery tucked right next to buildings. Foundation plantings greatly increase the probability that structures will burn. We need to ingrain a new aesthetic for fire safety that includes a "noncombustible" zone next to structures, a "lean, clean, and green" zone farther out, a "wildland fuel reduction" zone appropriate to the biotic community beyond that, and a "habitat" zone even beyond that.

Keep Goldilocks in mind when planning defensible space for your property: aim for a "just right" number and placement of plants, not too many or too few. Live, healthy green vegetation can capture, block, and/or slow windborne embers from reaching structures. Considered placement of plants can decrease and change wind speeds around structures, and potentially shield structures from embers for some time. In the worst-case scenario, even if the vegetation eventually burns, that time delay may give you precious minutes for evacuation. Living vegetation around your property also improves your home's energy efficiency and helps support native wildlife.

Thinking in Terms of Zones

Defensible space can be organized into three main zones where the density of vegetation is strictly manipulated and monitored, and a fourth zone where habitat is maintained for ecological health. In the zones closer to a structure, plant density should be low; in the zones farther away from a structure, the

OPPOSITE The area from 0 to 5 feet away from a home in wildfire country should be landscaped with noncombustible materials. Plastic downspouts, combustible lighting, art, and landscaping in this zone are generally ill advised.

80

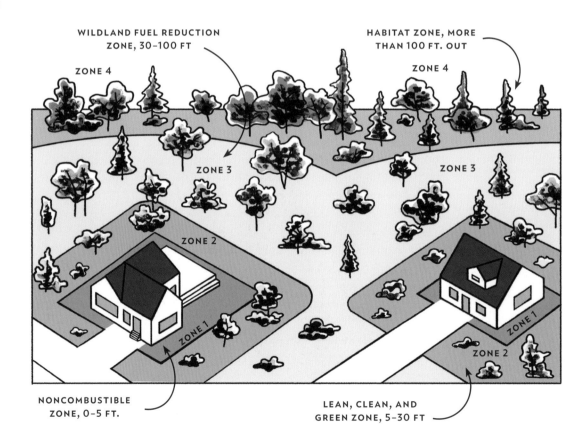

WILDLAND FUEL REDUCTION ZONE, 30–100 FT

HABITAT ZONE, MORE THAN 100 FT. OUT

ZONE 4

ZONE 4

ZONE 3

ZONE 3

ZONE 2

ZONE 1

ZONE 1

ZONE 2

NONCOMBUSTIBLE ZONE, 0–5 FT.

LEAN, CLEAN, AND GREEN ZONE, 5–30 FT

acceptable plant density increases. Each and every structure needs to have its own defensible space.

You will require the greatest fire resistance near structures, but as you move in concentric rings (zones) away from buildings, plant choices can be more diverse (in terms of fire resistance). Your goal is not to eliminate all wildfires (as that's not possible). Wildfire suppression is part of why we are seeing such devastating wildfires in many biotic communities today, specifically forests. The zone system is a strategy to help make your home resistant to fire in a landscape where plants could burn.

Consider the size of your property, the fire regime of your region, and the physical variables of where you live as you apply the zone recommendations. If the hazard level of your property is high, each zone should be tripled in size.

Zone 1 (0 to 5 feet): The noncombustible zone

Zone 1, the noncombustible zone, extends from 0 to 5 feet from each structure on your property and from anything attached to it. In other words, if you have a deck attached to your structure, consider it part of the structure and

measure the zone from there. If you live on a high-hazard property, this zone should be extended to 15 feet from structures. In this zone, you want nothing combustible.

To deter plant growth, use a noncombustible substrate like pavement, gravel, paving stones, or decomposed granite. Bare ground in seasonally dry areas is also an excellent noncombustible substrate. Do *not* use organic mulch, wood chips, or weed cloth in this zone. Obviously dead organic matter is combustible, but weed barriers can burn as well.

Because there should be no vegetation in this zone (live or dead), no living habitat (besides soil) can be provided, but many insects and reptiles can use the bare ground or inorganic mulches in this zone (with the exception of decomposed granite and concrete, which are not very wildlife friendly and have big carbon footprints). Weed barriers, particularly those made of plastic or plastic mesh, are to be avoided as they block the natural cycling of some nutrients, oxygen, and soil organisms. Besides, they lose the ability to block weed growth over time and disintegrate into microplastics.

YARD FURNITURE AND ART

It's not advisable to have yard furniture in this zone, especially pieces that cannot be moved easily. Even if the furniture isn't combustible, it could still pin flying embers (or create an ember eddy) against a structure if it is too close. It would also catch dead debris and accumulate spiderwebs. Light travel furniture can be okay, but you must be careful to put pieces away when you have finished using them or at the end of the day. Think of zone 1 as a "no overnight or long-term parking" zone.

Art in this zone can be okay if it is small (think lawn gnome size or smaller), made of noncombustible material (metal, glass, and/or concrete) without lots of nooks and crannies, and placed nearer the outer edge of the zone unless it's flat. If you really want art in this zone, consider getting creative with paving stones and/or small rock art. Medium-to-large art installations are not advisable.

SPECIAL CONSIDERATIONS

Generally speaking, nothing combustible should be stored in zone 1.

Hoses. People typically keep hoses attached to faucets in this zone to water plants in other zones (especially in summer). While hoses don't ignite easily, they can pin flying embers and melt against a house if attached flush. If they are left coiled on the ground, care should be taken to regularly clear debris. If they are coiled around a hose butler or pot, these should be constructed of metal or noncombustible material and kept free of debris.

Garbage cans. People tend to keep garbage cans in zone 1 for convenience, but this is a bad idea in wildfire country. Either keep them in a garage or store them in zone 2.

Fencing. Fencing can be a highway for fire to spread and can be very dangerous in this zone, especially if it is wood and connects to your structure. Replace wooden fencing in zone 1 with a noncombustible material. You can extend a wooden fence to structures with noncombustible metal fencing. If your fence connects to your structure, you should extend zone 1 an extra 5 feet beyond the fence (if it isn't right on your property line).

MAINTENANCE

Overall, this zone needs to be kept cleared of all vegetation and dead plant debris. Any fencing in this zone needs to be under regular surveillance to keep it clear of combustible materials , and the fencing should be noncombustible.

Zone 2 (5 to 30 feet): The lean, clean, and green zone

The lean, clean, and green zone extends from 5 to 30 feet from each structure on your property. If you live on a high-hazard property, this zone should extend from 15 to 90 feet from each structure. This is the zone where you can fine-tune your focus on balancing beauty and fire resistance by planting grasses, shrubs, and small trees.

Zone 2 of a defensible space can include grasses, shrubs, and small trees.

83

The spacing of plants on the ground can determine how readily a fire spreads from one plant to the next. Fine, interdigitating leaves will carry a fire continuously. Gaps of bare ground, rocks, flame-resistant mulches, and hardscaping (such as driveways, rock walls, and sidewalks) that are a minimum of 4 feet wide can disrupt fuels for fire, decreasing fire intensity. In an extreme wind-driven fire, no aboveground vegetation may survive. But in patchier fires, dictating the structure and distribution of plants, particularly shrubs and trees, will deprive fire of fuel.

Clusters of diverse plants create more diverse habitat and thereby support more wildlife diversity. In zone 2 you want clusters to be small, with larger spaces between clusters (creating fuel breaks), and mostly composed of herbaceous plants (those without woody stems). Spacing between clusters should be determined by fuel loads. For example, a cluster with woody plants needs to have larger spacing than one that is just herbaceous plants. Spacing between plantings should be bare dirt or nonflammable substrate (no wood chips or other organic mulch).

Shorter herbaceous perennials can be planted at low densities in the area 6 to 10 feet from structures. Moderate-height annuals and perennials at more moderate densities and heights can be placed in the area of zone 2 farther from structures.

Any shrubs in zone 2 should be spaced at least twice their height from another shrub or tree, and at least twice their height from the outer perimeter of zone 1. Clusters of a few shrubs should be spaced with similar intervening gaps of roughly twice the maximum plant height, measured from the edge of the dripline. You can plant more shrubs than trees in zone 2, but the overall density should still be low.

Smaller trees and large shrubs with mature heights of less than about 15 feet are okay to plant in this zone. Ideally, small trees and large shrubs should be far enough from structures that they wouldn't reach either zone 1 or another tree if they fell over. This results in trees at low densities placed at least 20 feet from structures.

Species with similar watering needs should be grouped together into hydrozones. Careful placement of plants requiring more water nearer to structures can optimize your use of space for fire resistance. It can also allow you to increase biodiversity at small scales. For example, you may have a dry chaparral patch north of your home, a patch of wetter riparian species east of your home, and a vegetable garden on the south side of your home.

YARD FURNITURE AND ART

You can have some furniture in this zone. If the furniture is not easily moved, it should be made of noncombustible material (metal, glass, and/or concrete). Wherever you place or store your outdoor furniture, make sure you leave adequate space from any plantings. In general, allow a distance of twice the height of the plants measured from the unoccupied furniture. Travel furniture can work here, too, but if it is made of combustible material, you will want to put it away at the end of the day. Similarly, if you use cushions on your furniture, they should be stored inside when not in use. All furnishings should be regularly cleaned of debris and spiderwebs.

Outdoor art can be positioned in zone 2 as well. As a general rule, keep larger pieces (say, a 6-foot ceramic urn) far enough away from structures that if they fell over they would still clear the structure by 5 feet. You don't want falling pieces hitting the structure and creating a damaged area vulnerable to embers, or landing close enough to create an ember eddy. Smaller to medium pieces (like a birdbath) can be okay throughout zone 2. Just like furniture, art pieces should be made of noncombustible material (metal, glass, and/or concrete).

SPECIAL CONSIDERATIONS

Raised bed gardens. Raised beds can be okay in zone 2 if they are near the outer edge of the zone (especially if your property is small and doesn't really have other zones). As they are usually made of wood planks, it is best to have them surrounded by either bare dirt or nonflammable substrate (not wood chips or mulch). When you are considering spacing to the next planter or tree or large shrub, include the height of the bed itself in figuring the height of any plants in a raised bed. For example, the height of a small specimen tree in a raised bed includes both the height of the tree and the height of the planter, even if the planter is completely noncombustible.

Children's play equipment. Play equipment can also be okay in zone 2. If it is constructed from combustible materials, it is best placed near the outer edge of zone 2 and surrounded by either bare dirt or nonflammable substrate (not wood chips or mulch). Keep at least a 5-foot buffer from other combustible items.

Emergency water tanks (usually nonpotable) and well pumps. Water tanks and pumps are typically found in zone 2, but not every property will have or need them. Keep at least a 5-foot buffer from combustible items.

Fencing. Since fences can be a highway for fire to spread, it is essential to keep them clear of dead plant debris and spiderwebs. Planting near fencing in this zone depends on three main factors: (1) whether the fencing is connected to a structure, (2) how porous the fencing is, and (3) how combustible it is.

- **For fencing that is all wood with little or no space between boards,** keep organic mulch or wood chips away from the base. If the fencing is connected to a structure, clear all plants (live and dead) and combustible material to a distance of at least 5 feet on either side. If the fencing is not connected to a structure, you can place live plants with high water content at very low densities near the fence.

85

- **For fencing that is all wood or mixed wood and metal** with spacing between boards that allows air movement, keep organic mulch or wood chips away from the fenceposts if they are made of wood. If the fencing is connected to a structure, clear all plants (live and dead) and combustible material to a distance of at least 5 feet on either side. If the fencing is not connected to a structure, you can place live plants with high water content at low densities near the fence.

- **For fencing that is noncombustible,** regardless of whether it impairs air movement, you can place live, healthy plants on either side except in zone 1. Live plant density near the fence can be low to moderate.

MAINTENANCE

In zone 2, dead plant materials should be cleared regularly, especially when conditions are dry. All trees and large shrubs should be limbed up at least 6 feet from the ground. If these plants are just getting established, they should be treated as shrubs in this zone until mature enough to be limbed up.

- **Clear dead plant debris and spiderwebs** from herbaceous plants, furniture, art, raised planting beds, and children's play structures.
- **Keep shrubs clear** of dead plant debris, spiderwebs, and dead branches.
- **Keep trees limbed up** at least 6 feet from the ground and clear of dead branches.
- **Clear spaces between clusters of plants** (or other combustible items) of weeds and dead plant debris.
- **Keep all fencing clear** of dead plant debris and spiderwebs.

Zone 3 (30 to 100 feet): The fuel reduction zone

Zone 3, the fuel reduction zone, extends from 30 to 100 feet from each structure on your property. If you live on a high-hazard property, this zone should be extended to 300 feet from each structure (although some research indicates no added structure protection to thinning beyond 100 feet). You can imagine this area as a place that could burn, but not too hot, because you actively manage the quantity and distribution of fuel.

Herbaceous plants can be placed at moderate to high densities in zone 3 as long as adequate spacing is allowed between clusters or plantings. Moderate densities are best closer in, and higher densities are okay farther out. The key is to ensure you have areas that starve a fire on the ground.

Overall tree and shrub densities should be low to moderate, depending on mature heights (and widths), fuel quantity, and adequate spacing between plants. Lower densities should occur closer in, with more moderate

densities in the outer portion of the zone. Tree canopies should be separated by at least 10 feet. Shrubs can be planted under tree canopies in this zone, but trees and shrubs need to be managed according to the horizontal and vertical spacing guidelines discussed later in this chapter.

Plant clusters in zone 3 can be larger but still need to have adequate breaks between them. On steeper slopes, this spacing should increase. Again, the space between clusters should be left bare ground or covered with a nonflammable substrate (not wood chips or mulch).

YARD FURNITURE AND ART
The same furniture rules apply here as in zone 2. Any size art piece can be installed here. The same considerations for materials and maintenance of furniture and art apply here as in zone 2.

SPECIAL CONSIDERATIONS
Wood piles. Exposed wood piles need to be placed at least 10 feet from plantings, planting clusters, or other combustible items. If you have a

This house's zone 3 defenses kept it safe during a wildfire; grasses had been mown and shrubs and burnable debris had been removed.

small property (that may extend only to zone 2), store wood the farthest you can from all structures, including your neighbors', preferably within a semi-closed, noncombustible storage area. It is unwise to store large amounts of firewood on small lots.

MAINTENANCE
Same recommendations as for zone 2.

Zone 4 (more than 100 feet out): The habitat zone

The habitat zone extends beyond the area 100 feet from each structure on your property. If you live on a high-hazard property, this zone starts at 300 feet from each structure. Generally, this zone is outside your defensible space and tends to reflect more of the wild habitat in your area. On the other hand, if zone 4 overlaps with neighbors' structures, the appropriate precautions for zone distances to structures apply. After all, your defensible space should include your neighbors, and vice versa.

This zone, farthest away from structures, likely already provides diverse habitat. What is most important in zone 4 is to maintain or increase habitat health. Healthy habitats are more fire resistant! Many forested habitats across

Chaparral habitats like this one involved in the Carlton Complex Fire in Washington state naturally burn and regenerate. They can be left alone in zone 4 of defensible space, aside from removing invasive species.

88

Summary of
Defensible Space Zones

Taking a bird's eye view from the air, no plants should be growing in the zone 0 to 5 feet from structures. Up to 70 feet from all structures (depending on specific site conditions), woody vegetation cover should be reduced by 40 to 50 percent compared to unmanaged areas. The managed garden spaces that remain help protect your home, the soil, and the community.

Zone	Standard	High Hazard
1—noncombustible	0–5 feet	0–15 feet
2—lean, clean, and green	5–30 feet	15–90 feet
3—fuel reduction	30–100 feet	90–300 feet*
4—habitat	More than 100 feet	More than 300 feet

Living plant densities can increase the farther away you get from structures. Spacing distance depends on the zone and how much fuel load each planting has.

- **Clusters of diverse species** create habitat for wildlife.

- **Spaces between items that are combustible** should be bare dirt or nonflammable substrate (not wood chips or mulch).

- **Items that are not easily moved** should be made of noncombustible material (metal, glass, and/or concrete).

- **Special care should be given to fencing,** depending on what it's made of, which zone it's in, and whether it connects to a structure.

See note on page 86

the United States have woody plant densities exceeding what is healthy due to fire suppression policies. For example, forests in the Sierra Nevada historically had tree densities that were significantly smaller but with larger trees than modern tree densities of one hundred to two hundred trees per acre.

Habitat health can be supported via density control in forests and thatch removal in grasslands, and in all habitats by getting rid of invasive species, which tend to grow rapidly and increase the amount of fuels that catch fire easily. Removing invasive species in this zone is often one of the most impactful actions you can take to reduce wildfire risk. Chaparral habitats in zone 4 can be pretty much left alone, aside from removing invasive species. If a fire comes through, chaparral will burn and regenerate. With sufficient attention to fire-resistant construction and maintenance of defensible zones closer to structures, chaparral at this distance is much less likely to ignite those structures.

You will need to do a little research to find out what healthy looks like in your local area. Do the best you can to support sustainable habitats in zone 4, depending on time and money available. That includes working within your community to apply for grants or cooperate with other landowners to manage particular habitats.

MAINTENANCE

Work to maintain healthy densities of woody species. When deciding which species to thin, focus on keeping healthy, mature individuals and fewer juveniles, but keep in mind that you need some diversity in all age classes. Get rid of invasive plants.

Shelterbelts for Protection from Embers and Fire

A powerful key to protecting your home in wildfire-prone areas is to learn how vegetation and structures affect wind patterns. Researchers are increasingly modeling wind behavior around buildings during fires. They are finding, for example, that buildings cause wind-driven flames to pulsate more, creating intermittent hot spots on structures that become more likely to ignite.

It helps to understand that air and water follow two general flow patterns, laminar and turbulent. Smooth, laminar flow occurs when there are no obstructions, while turbulent flow occurs when objects or rough surfaces disrupt the flow. When wind flows against a solid structure, turbulence spirals around and behind it, just like water flowing past a boat. So the mere presence of solid structures in wild areas causes turbulence and frictional drag on air moving over and around them. This turbulence can cause abrupt changes in wind speed and direction, and can also increase the likelihood that materials around a building will ignite. In contrast, semi-porous obstructions, like strategically placed vegetation in windbreaks or shelterbelts, can reduce both turbulence and wind velocity.

This is why it would not be a good idea to just build a solid 20-foot wall all around your property. Think about the problem of turbulence behind solid structures that we just discussed. Eddies caused by turbulence behind

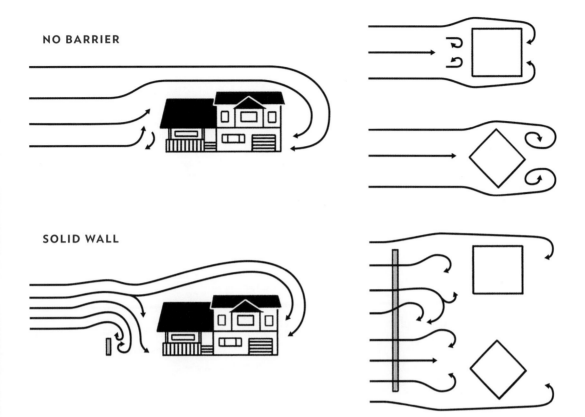

NO BARRIER

SOLID WALL

a tall solid wall could simply stir embers and debris together into an ignition free-for-all. A porous wall would reduce this effect. Trees and shrubs that allow air to pass through would also reduce this effect, plus they have the ability to cool the air and provide wildlife habitat.

Such shelterbelts can be compared to the windbreaks that are invaluable tools for reducing soil erosion and controlling snowdrifts throughout the Great Plains states. The height of a windbreak has the biggest impact on the amount of area protected. Wind speeds are reduced in front of the windbreak (the windward or upwind side) for a distance of two to five times the height of the windbreak. On the leeward, or downwind, side of a windbreak, wind speeds are reduced for a distance of up to thirty times the height of the windbreak. For example, a line of trees 20 feet high could reduce wind speeds 40 to 100 feet in front of the shelterbelt, where the wind is coming from, and up to 600 feet on the leeward side. This is assuming that the windbreak is semi-permeable—that is, not so dense that it blocks the wind completely.

If you understand the behavior of wind where you live, you can manipulate the wind to help protect your home using fire shelterbelts. Fire shelterbelts are semi-permeable barriers of trees and shrubs (or noncombustible materials)

When wind flows against a solid structure like a house or a wall, turbulence is created. The turbulence spirals around and behind the structure, increasing the likelihood that materials around it will ignite during a wildfire.

A SEMI-PERMEABLE WINDBREAK

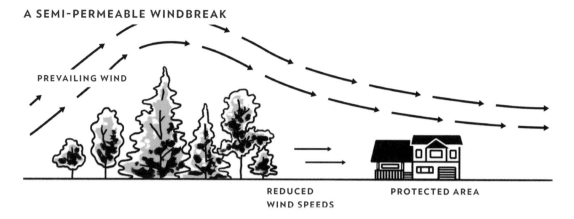

PREVAILING WIND

REDUCED WIND SPEEDS

PROTECTED AREA

A DENSE WINDBREAK

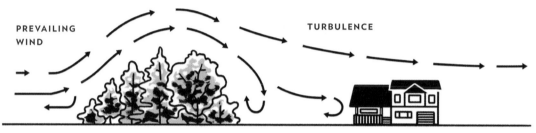

PREVAILING WIND

TURBULENCE

TURBULENCE

A windbreak that is semi-permeable breaks and lifts prevailing wind currents, protecting structures and soil on the leeward side. If the windbreak is too dense and blocks the wind completely, it will cause turbulence on the leeward side.

strategically placed to reduce wind, radiant heat, and flying embers. They should be oriented in front of prevailing winds, upwind from structures, and can be installed in zone 2 and/or zone 3 of your defensible space.

An extremely important caveat is that under severe fire conditions (such as extremely hot, dry, windy events where a wildfire is creating its own weather), wind-deflection strategies will likely buy you only a few more minutes to shut down your home and evacuate. But if fire conditions are less severe, having a fire shelterbelt of well-hydrated and properly maintained live plants as part of your defensible space may well make the difference between saving and losing your home. In contrast, if you ignore wind patterns and remove all the vegetation except perhaps green lawn around you, you will make your home a more vulnerable target for ignition.

Although little detailed information exists on the intentional use of what we're calling fire shelterbelts, a few basic guidelines based on windbreaks are instructive. Shelterbelts can have multiple layers, be staggered clusters of trees and shrubs, and be on more than one side of a property. A tree-and-shrub shelterbelt with a density of 40 to 60 percent provides the greatest area of downwind protection, although with somewhat lower wind speed reduction than a denser windbreak, while minimizing wind turbulence.

Denser windbreaks protect a smaller area but with greater wind speed reduction (and increased eddy formation). Low shrublands and desert vegetation can place some drag on wind movement, so even consistently erratic wind can be disrupted to some degree.

A corollary to this is that anywhere wind is funneled through canyons, buildings, or vegetation, wind speeds will increase (the Venturi effect). This means that any major gaps between windbreaks could allow wind to funnel through at higher velocities, so fire shelterbelts must be positioned strategically (for example, overlapping relative to wind direction) for prevailing and foehn winds during fire season.

Strategically placed plants in a fire shelterbelt form a living green barrier that contains water, decreases wind speeds, and catches embers or cinders rather than letting your home catch them. As long as your plants are well cared for and strategically spaced, the chance of their combustion is much lower than that of a standard house. Remember, houses are built with dead plants (wood), while healthy live plants are filled with water and thus naturally less combustible (and slower to ignite).

Stone and masonry walls make great shelterbelts if you don't want to use vegetation, but be sure to make them semi-permeable to allow wind flow, and keep them free of debris. Usually such walls are installed to separate plantings, protect landscapes from erosion, and/or create a more dynamic

Tracy Salcedo of Glen Ellen, California, believes that the live oak canopy over her 110-year-old wood-frame house caught embers and protected her roof from a wildfire in 2017 that burned more than four hundred homes in the Sonoma Valley.

93

Bringing Your
Property into Compliance

It's important to acknowledge that when you're first starting the process of creating defensible space, your whole yard might be out of compliance with recommendations. This can be overwhelming! Apply your efforts one zone at a time, working from zone 1 (highest risk for your structure) outward. Also, don't think that you will get everything on your list done in one season or year. It can be very helpful to keep a running list or seasonal schedule to keep track of what needs to be done and when.

It's also important to acknowledge that some property owners make decisions that go against recommendations for defensible space. Sometimes it's hard to remove plants or items that you love, that aren't easily removed, and/or that are not in your budget to remove. When this happens, it's imperative to recognize how much your decision elevates your risk and what can be done to mitigate that risk as much as possible.

landscape, but they also can serve as an effective shelterbelt with proper maintenance and use of noncombustible ground coverings at the base. More porous structures are effective at slowing wind speeds without creating strong eddies. Solid noncombustible retaining walls can disrupt airflow, creating wind eddies that can keep embers away from combustible items and structures on your property if placed in zones 2, 3, or 4 as you see fit, but you would not want solid walls creating circling embers too close to structures.

Managing Your Property's Fuel Load

In wildfire country, all fuels should be managed in landscapes that are near structures and neighbors. To become wildfire ready, you have two choices. You can either clear fuels out or thin them. Clearing gets rid of all or most combustible materials in an area, like a forest clear-cut. Thinning, in contrast, decreases combustible fuel densities by removing some vegetation or parts of vegetation to maintain healthy spacing between plants.

As we've said before, clearing all vegetation around your home is not a good idea, even if you plan to fill it with irrigated and mowed lawn. It just creates ideal conditions for unobstructed wind flow—and what Richard Halsey of the California Chaparral Institute calls the perfect "bowling alley" for embers. Clearing can also have the nasty side effect of fostering the invasion of weedy fuels—especially nonnative annual grasses—that are highly ignitable.

Instead, aim to thin the fuel load on your property. Thinning is especially critical within the zone 30 to 70 feet from your home (zone 3). The amount of thinning required will depend on your starting point. In some areas with dense populations of invasive species, such as Scotch broom (*Cytisus scoparius*) and Spanish broom (*Spartium junceum*), whole plants should be removed, roots and all, but the soil should not be left bare, particularly where there is risk of erosion

94

or landslide. We go into detail in the maintenance chapter about managing the spaces between and within plants by proper pruning.

When analyzing the fuel load on your property, it can be helpful to visualize what is available to burn by imagining how plants in the horizontal and vertical planes influence wind flow around structures.

Vertical spacing

For trees that are at least 15 feet tall or five years old, remove all tree branches to a level at least 6 feet above the ground. For taller trees, you can remove branches much higher above the ground, but roughly the upper two-thirds of the tree should have branches. If you are establishing new trees, treat them like shrubs until they develop adequate trunk taper for support, which means allowing lower branches to remain (although shortened) for several years before removing them. (When trunks are about the same diameter at the base as they are just below the crown, they lack trunk taper, which significantly weakens the trunk and slows tree growth.)

If shrubs are under trees, vertical space is needed between the shrubs and the branches above. Lack of vertical spaces between canopies of different heights can allow a fire to move from the ground to the shrubs to the treetops like a ladder. The proper vertical spacing between the highest point of a shrub and the lowest branches of a tree is three times the shrub height.

Horizontal spacing

How much horizontal space there should be between plants depends on the slope of the land and plant heights. Follow these guidelines:

- **On a flat to mild (less than 20-percent) slope,** allow 10 feet between trees, and two times the height of the shrubs for spacing between shrubs.

- **On a mild to moderate (20-to-40-percent) slope,** allow 20 feet between trees, and four times the height of the shrubs for spacing between shrubs.

- **On a moderate to steep (more than 40-percent) slope,** allow 30 feet between trees and six times the height of the shrubs for spacing between shrubs.

For all distances between shrubs and trees, make sure measurements are taken from the farthest extent of the plant width, not from the plant's center or trunk.

Key Terms

Defensible space is an area where flammable material has been cleared, reduced, or replaced with less-flammable material as a barrier to approaching wildfires.

Fire shelterbelts are windbreaks, usually made up of one or more rows of relatively fire-resistant (hydrated) trees and shrubs, managed to provide a fire screen of 40-to-60-percent density to reduce wind, flying embers, and firebrands.

The **Venturi effect** causes wind speeds to increase when wind flows through a constriction.

Fuel management is manipulating fuels to reduce the likelihood of ignition, reduce the intensity of fire, and/or lessen potential damage from a fire.

Herbaceous plants are those without persistent woody stems.

Hydrozones are groupings of plants with similar water needs. Hydrozoning is a way to conserve water and avoid overwatering or underwatering plants.

Special Concerns for Intermix and Interface WUI Communities

Defensible space concerns that are most important for you to address depend on the type of WUI community you live in.

If you live in an intermix WUI area, your driveway should be easily identifiable from its access road. Make sure your address is printed on reflective material and can be seen coming from either direction. If you have gates, make sure they open inward and are wide enough to accommodate emergency equipment. For safe evacuation and access by firefighters, driveways should meet minimum installation standards of state and local codes (regarding width, weight limits, grade, and curve radius) to allow fire and emergency vehicles to reach your home.

Your driveway should also be maintained in accordance with these same codes for clearance and passage of emergency vehicles. Trim trees and shrubs to create a minimum 10-foot horizontal clearance on either side (allowing for two-way traffic) and a 14-foot vertical clearance above the driveway. Maintain spaces where fire engines can easily turn around for access to structures. If you have a long and/or complex driveway structure, check your state and local codes for any specific guidelines for making your driveway safe for emergency vehicles.

Maintenance of evacuation routes for safe evacuation and access by firefighters isn't something you likely have control over. However, you do have the power to communicate with your county or state to advocate for regular and timely maintenance for safe evacuation.

If you live in an interface WUI area, you need to consider how your defensible zones connect with other properties with respect to the orientation and placement of structures on adjacent lots. Solid wood fences are very commonly used between properties in interface WUI areas. This increases the ability of a fire started at one home to spread quickly to other properties. Unlike with viruses and vaccines, there is no herd immunity for fire safety in at-risk communities. Even one unkempt property can cause an entire community to ignite, especially when fires can simply travel along wood fences from house to house.

Interface WUI communities with small lot sizes have higher densities of people and homes. During the 2018 Camp Fire in Paradise, California, there were so many people living in such a small area along ridgelines that traffic was impeded in all directions of potential evacuation. Advocating at the community level for safer developments and evacuation routes is paramount.

Defensible space doesn't end at your property line, but your control likely does. Being able to communicate with your neighbors is important to help motivate fire-safe behavior and get help if needed. Fire-safe community organizations can help mediate firescaping disputes.

Ensuring roads and driveways are wide enough and easily accessible to emergency vehicles can make a critical difference in a wildfire.

97

What to Plant, Where, and When

A landscape that is a mixture of native and nonnative perennials can provide desired color while supporting habitat and requiring little maintenance.

HOW DO YOU CREATE A GARDEN that brings you joy while also reducing the risks of damaging wildfires and at the same time supporting the integrity of wild places? After hardening structures and planning defensible space with fire shelterbelts, your choice of plants and their placement is paramount. This chapter focuses on plant selection, placement, planting techniques, and the timing of installation, all of which can have immense impacts on how resistant your landscape might be to wildfires and how much effort you spend maintaining your plants. Selecting the wrong plants for the wrong place or failing to maintain plants appropriately drives up fire risk to structures and personal safety.

The gift of living in the WUI is that we are surrounded to varying degrees by plants and animals and rocks and soil and water that are not manipulated into an environment so dissimilar from the region as to be unrecognizable. Drive through any city or suburban neighborhood in the United States and you can check off the same list of nonnative landscaping plants—from Asia, South Africa, Australia, South America—that have displaced the local character of the countryside. The WUI should retain some wildness as we live around and in it, but that requires care. It requires an attitude of gratitude and reciprocity for that vestige of wildness, which means tending to our wild relatives as we live among them.

Plant Starter Guide

If you are not very familiar with plants, a good starter guide for the West Coast is *The New Sunset Western Garden Book* (2012). This guide is a good starting place to get to know which plants are possible in your landscape and potentially available for purchase. It provides lists and photos of plants available in western nurseries from around the world, and their adaptability to various Sunset climate zones. When you know your Sunset climate zone, you can choose plants appropriate for your zone's heat and cold extremes, humidity, wind, ocean influence, snow cover, and length of growing season. Of course, any plants that are native in your area are naturally adapted to your climate and naturally provide services to pollinators and other wildlife!

Urban, suburban, rural, and WUI areas can be planted and managed to support wild species and allow for species movement across landscapes. If you landscape and garden not just for defensible space but for wildlife, you will be able to enjoy native host plants and the colors and movements and sounds of bugs, butterflies, and birds. As you think about what to plant, aim to grow some natives, diversify with good nonnatives, minimize the use of pesticides and dangerous chemicals, and remove invasive species. Avoid plants that are poor, bad, and noxious for wildlife, and keep the fire enablers a healthy distance from structures and other plants. Start with healthy plants and plant at the right time for your area, and then mulch with appropriate materials.

Choosing Plants for a Sustainable Landscape

Upon visiting family in Palm Springs, California, a friend once wrote a poem about petunias growing in the desert. As an entomologist and gardener, she knew that petunias don't support pollinators, and they use a lot of water for something that gives little beyond an ephemeral splash of color for humans to appreciate. Perhaps you happen to be a big fan of petunias, or you plant them every year to remind you of your grandparents. Creating more sustainable landscapes in the WUI does not have to exclude landscaping and gardening with nonnative plants. The privilege of living in the WUI should, however, come with responsibility to support the native plants and wildlife that were here before us. This means finding a balance between what was natural habitat before, what will remain, and what we add. It means thinking about how those decisions might impact the WUI.

What are the right plants for your landscape? How do you choose? One basic principle is that unless you are an active gardener or pay someone to manage your property for fire, every plant within 100 feet surrounding your structures should be low maintenance. It should require minimal water to remain hydrated and should not produce much litter or dead wood.

We recommend beginning by creating an initial plant wish list, a potential palette, with plants grouped by life form and mature size. The largest plants, or already existing plants that you want to keep, are the major scaffolding to anchor your landscaping (large trees, shrubs, cacti, depending on where you live) and should be considered first. If you don't know plants at all, you can at least list desired sizes and shapes. Then you can consult published resources or a qualified professional.

Let's say you want a large deciduous tree to reduce summer sun exposure on the west side of a building. You can create a list of potential trees appropriate to your area that could also provide the shade you desire and then decide on the particular species based on growing requirements, shape, growth rate, mature height, insect and disease susceptibility, weediness, maintenance considerations, and availability. The plant directory in the next chapter gives numerous suggestions of native species in a range of different size, shape, and function categories.

Once you have a potential palette of plants by form and mature size, excluding species that are invasive in your area, you can pare down your selections based on growing and maintenance, and what functions you want

Think about desired plant shapes as you create your initial wish list.

ROUND   SPREADING   PYRAMIDAL

OVAL   CONICAL   VASE SHAPED   COLUMNAR

OPEN   WEEPING   IRREGULAR

OPPOSITE Garden-
ing successfully
with natives often
takes just a shift
in mindset and a
little self-education;
for example, on
the West Coast,
native manzanita
is a better-adapted
shrub for evergreen
foliage than nonna-
tive boxwood.

those plants to provide. In fire landscapes, every plant choice should be tempered by how well it might protect your home from wildfires. Be aware of plant characteristics that make plants more or less ignitable, flammable, and combustible. Also, investigate how climate change is affecting your region now and into the future, and keep water conservation in mind. Choose plants that serve your purposes and also create native wildlife habitat and promote native diversity. You can use this same approach to evaluate the plants in your existing landscape. Is it the right plant in the right place?

When finalizing your decisions about what to plant in your yard, consider how much maintenance you can handle. Maintenance of your defensible space is a never-ending necessity. A caveat of plant selection is that if you put plants into cultivated habitats and they perform poorly, you should remove them and try something more appropriate that would also reduce your fire hazards. Plants are cheaper to replace than homes.

Plant some natives

Plant lovers get euphoric when surrounded by cool plants. (We are not immune!) Designers exalt in finding the mix of textures and colors to shape the mood and function of outside spaces. But gardeners and landscapers should minimize harm, like doctors taking the Hippocratic oath.

One way to minimize environmental harm is to grow native plants. When we cultivate invasive species, import pests and diseases on plants we bring in, or inadvertently facilitate hybridization between local natives and plants brought in from elsewhere, we can cause reductions in native biodiversity and lose puzzle pieces from food webs. When we cultivate species native to our local area (or species not native to our local area but good for pollinators, wildlife, and habitat), we can compensate for habitat fragmentation.

The advantages of including native plants in your garden are numerous.

- **Native plants provide shelter and food** for wildlife (rather than eliminating them).
- **Natives support local biodiversity,** including rare species that can benefit from being propagated.
- **They are better adapted to local soils,** microbes, and insects.
- **Native plants require less maintenance** (little to no watering, no fertilizer, and no pesticides).
- **They tend to be more water efficient** (and less likely to die off in drought conditions).
- **Local native plants are part of the native fire regime** (rather than augmenting it).

A bonus of planting natives is that they almost always require less water than nonnatives to stay healthy. Healthy plants that are sufficiently hydrated are less likely to ignite. And slow-growing, locally adapted plants can reduce your maintenance burdens. Plus, using more plants that are native to our West Coast states lets you celebrate our extremely high native plant diversity. However, know that certain natives have flammable plant qualities you should avoid or manage in some zones.

How can you incorporate natives into your landscape? The simplest way is to create fire-safe zones in existing wild habitat. In the built environment, you can also reduce the negative impacts of habitat fragmentation by including in your garden at least some native plants found in adjacent wildlands, thus creating a native plant stepping-stone for creatures. If at least 30 to 50 percent of your landscape consists of plants native to your area, you will certainly be providing greater continuity of wildlife resources across the WUI than if you plant 100 percent exotics. For example, native oaks provide food and habitat for hundreds of other species, shade, soil stabilization, and water and air filtration.

Whenever possible, your landscape should include diverse native trees, shrubs, grasses, and forbs where at least some blooms are available over a long time period. On the other hand, it is good to provide some large clumps (say, 3 feet by 3 feet) of the same kind of plant to make the flowers more attractive to pollinators. For example, bumblebees prefer to visit flowers in large patches, providing shorter travel distances between pollen rewards, as a way to optimize foraging time.

There is often a disconnect between plants commonly available for sale and the ecological services you may want to provide in a landscape. Only a fraction of our native plant diversity is listed in the *Sunset Western Garden Book* or available from plant nurseries. Fortunately, many other books and online resources are now available to further inform your native plant choices, whether you are grooming existing wildland plants in your landscape, purchasing native plants from nurseries, or starting native plants from seeds. Native plant societies, nurseries that feature native plants, and natural resource agencies can foster better planting choices that go beyond arranging pretty plants like furniture.

Include good nonnatives

Generally speaking, greater native plant diversity and structure can support a greater diversity of native insects and other animals. Yet adding good nonnative plants can also increase overall species diversity and abundance by increasing the variety of food and shelter resources. Some nonnative plants are exceptional pollinator and wildlife resources for food, nesting, and overwintering, and other nonnatives . . . not so much. Learning which plants are good for wildlife can make the difference between low-quality and higher-quality habitat in your fire-safe zones. Judicious use of noninvasive garden favorites can round out your defensible space designs, as long as they are planted in conditions appropriate for healthy growth.

The bottom line is that you can expand your design palette by including nonnatives that provide food for you or good wildlife value without being invasive. Do be sure to strictly monitor edible plants that have the potential to invade or affect your fire preparedness (for example, edible fig, fennel,

Online Native Plant Lists
and Information

Many excellent books and online sites provide details about native plants available for landscaping in California, Oregon, and Washington. Rather than risk missing a gem by trying to list all these resources, we highlight online sites maintained by nonprofits and state agencies. Local native plant societies can be experts on plants and conditions in your area, and native plant nurseries in your region can provide a wealth of information as well. For example, Las Pilitas Nursery (laspilitas.com) in Santa Margarita, California, has been supplying photos of and invaluable insights about native plants online for decades.

- **The California Native Plant Society's online tool Calscape (calscape.org)** lists and includes photographs of almost eight thousand plant species and varieties that are native or introduced to California. In addition, the Calscape Garden Planner (gardenplanner.calscape.org) supplies custom native plant lists and example garden designs based on the city, garden style, sun exposure, and design priority you specify.

- **Calflora (calflora.org)** maintains a collection of useful information about the wild plants of California. You can use the Planting Guide to find out what types of native wild plants will grow where you live, search Great Places to find out where to view California native plants, or go to What Grows Here? to find out what you might be seeing at your favorite state park or hiking trail.

- **Oregon State University's Extension Service** supplies native plant profiles online and has published a few guides to native plants in different growing regions, such as west of the Cascades versus central Oregon (extension.oregonstate.edu/collection/native-plant-gardening). The Native Plant Society of Oregon (npsoregon.org) supplies general advice about landscaping with native plants, and opportunities to learn more from members.

- **The Washington Native Plant Society (wnps.org)** offers plant lists and recommendations for landscaping with native plants on its website. It maintains a native plant directory with detailed photos, plant characteristics, and ethnobotanical uses for several hundred species, sortable by habitat requirements. The website is also a good place to find native plant and seed vendors in your area.

105

wild plum, and Himalayan blackberry) and remove their fruits before they can escape. By the same token, restrict horseradish and mint to pots anywhere with year-round moisture.

As you think about plants for your landscape, it can be helpful to classify them into five categories: good, poor, bad, noxious, and fire enablers.

- **Good**—noninvasive plants that provide pollinator and wildlife habitat, food, or shelter
- **Poor**—nonnative plants that provide little food or shelter value, creating empty patches devoid of much life
- **Bad**—invasive species that spread easily by seed or vegetative propagation on their own
- **Noxious**—aggressive invasive species that can crowd out other species and even change some ecosystem functions
- **Fire enablers**—plants that are especially effective at igniting and spreading fire

This good-poor-bad-noxious-fire enablers framework is useful for analyzing both the value of each plant as a resource and its combustibility. At the same time, we should recognize that all plants are good somewhere, and many plants could fit into more than one of these categories, depending on where they are growing. In general, you should avoid planting bad, noxious, and poor plants. If you find such plants on your property, you should remove them as soon as possible before they do more harm.

106

Let's look at some example plants that fit into our functional plant categories. Species in the genus *Salvia*, sage, are solidly good garden plants because of the pollinator resources they provide across a range of water availability. They produce copious nectar and pollen, and are magnets for bees, bee mimics, hummingbirds, butterflies, and moths. There are almost a thousand species worldwide adapted to a range of conditions, including many that are native to our geographic region. They are almost never invasive, with the exception of clary sages (*Salvia sclarea* and *S. pratensis*), classified as invasive in parts of Washington state, and Mediterranean sage (*Salvia aethiopis*), considered invasive in parts of California and Oregon.

In contrast, Bermuda grass (*Cynodon dactylon*) is a bad plant, and oleander (*Nerium oleander*) is a poor plant. Bermuda grass is invasive on every continent but Antarctica and spreads readily via rhizomes and seeds. Oleander, although showy when flowering, provides no nectar, has pollen that sticks in clumps and is toxic to some pollinators, and offers little to wildlife except perhaps cover. All parts of the plant are toxic, and exposure to the sap can cause skin rashes. Perhaps a good plant for highway medians, oleander can be relatively fire resistant when young but can become massive and full of dead woody debris with age.

An example of a truly noxious species is tree of heaven (*Ailanthus altissimus*), and an example of a nonnative fire enabler is pampas grass (*Cortaderia selloana*). Tree of heaven is a clonal tree that forms dense thickets and can exclude native species. (Tree of heaven is easy to identify by its rancid peanut butter smell.) It thrives in disturbed, degraded areas and resprouts

107

LEFT Many homeowners want some amount of lawn. If you must have it, strengthen your defensible space and the local ecosystem by placing native plants around the perimeter, as here in Eugene, Oregon.

OPPOSITE Salvia species are solidly good garden plants because they produce copious nectar and pollen.

vigorously after fires. The persistent seed plumes of pampas grass act like torches to carry fire. Fire enablers are flammable, combining ease of ignition and ability to sustain fire in one package.

The plant palette offered in the next chapter gives ideas about native alternatives to plants that are poor, bad, or noxious.

Plant sources and local adaptation

So you have developed a wish list of plants you want to add to your landscape. Before you rush out to buy plants for landscaping, we would be remiss if we did not emphasize the importance of choosing plants that are adapted to your area and that are unlikely to hybridize with or spread diseases to local native plants in the WUI. In practice, this means obtaining plants propagated from seeds or cuttings from similar climate areas and from not too far away. One exception might be the need to propagate and plant a rare species from populations not in your area when that species needs more viable populations or is inbred and could benefit from greater gene flow. (This would depend on research-based recommendations.)

Another consideration is that many native plants for sale in nurseries are propagated from cuttings of just a few plants, or clones from a named cultivar. Cultivars, in particular, are selected on the basis of what looks good to humans but not necessarily what might be best adapted to your environment or specialist pollinators. Planting native cultivars in small clusters in your yard is unlikely to be detrimental to the WUI, but it would be unwise to use native cultivars for large restoration plantings. Cultivars may be maladapted to local conditions and could hybridize with existing native vegetation. Be especially cautious about introducing a cultivar from somewhere else if you live near a wildland area with endemic species of manzanita (*Arctostaphylos*), wild lilac (*Ceanothus*), buckwheat (*Erigeron*), sycamore (*Platanus*), yarrow (*Achillea*), lupine (*Lupinus*), primrose (*Oenothera*), grape (*Vitis*), mahogany (*Cercocarpus*), sunflower (*Helianthus*), trefoil/deervetch (*Lotus*), yellow cress / marsh cress (*Rorippa*), poppy (*Eschscholzia*), hibiscus (*Hibiscus*), old man's beard / virgin's bower (*Clematis*), or rhododendron/azalea (*Rhododendron*) All of these are known to hybridize easily, and hybrids could spread into wildland areas, compromising species integrity.

A final word of caution about introducing nursery-grown plants into the WUI. Research has indicated that many *Phytophthora* species (including *Phytophthora ramorum*, the cause of the disease sudden oak death) have been spreading from infected restoration plantings into chaparral areas. You should not plant nursery-grown plants in the WUI outside of your defensible space, and if you notice massive die-off of plants, they should be removed and disposed of immediately—to a landfill!

Key Terms

Wildland vegetation refers to plant species growing spontaneously that are shaped by both the site and biological processes.

Sunset climate zones are hardiness zones in the West defined by average high and low temperatures, humidity, wind, ocean influence, snow cover, and length of growing season.

Herbaceous plants have stems and leaves that die back at the end of each growing season, as opposed to **woody** plants, whose stems remain year after year. **Forbs** are herbaceous flowering plants that are not grasses, sedges, or rushes. Wildflowers, for example, are forbs.

Cultivars are cultivated varieties of plants, the result of selective breeding by humans.

Flammability is a measure of ease of ignition (ignitability), ability to sustain fire, and combustion temperature. **Pyrolysis** is smoldering combustion.

Fire-retardant plants don't tend to burn. **Fire-resistant** plants are difficult to ignite.

Mulching is spreading a loose layer of organic or inorganic matter over the soil surface among and around plantings.

We encourage you to explore your own WUI "backyard" and learn more about propagating and sustaining the diversity that is in your local area. Indeed, we challenge you to learn more about the native treasures in your area by becoming involved in local native plant and wildlife groups. You could even help spur recognition and propagation of any one of our many horticulturally overlooked plant gems.

Considering Plant Flammability

Some plants are fire retardant, in that they don't tend to burn, depriving a fire of fuel, or they are fire resistant, being difficult to ignite. Fire-retardant trees also can reduce wind speeds and trap blowing embers. Fire-resistant plants and trees are able to act as radiant heat screens and absorb more of the heat of an approaching fire without burning. Fire-resistant ground covers can also capture burning embers without catching fire themselves.

Anything will burn once it has been heated to its ignition point, including any plant. When plant cells are exposed to temperatures of around 300°F, cellulose, a major component of plant cell walls, begins to break down; ignition and pyrolysis begin around 500°F. The exact conditions of the fuel can greatly modify the point at which that happens. Yet, there are qualities that make some plants more resistant to ignition than others. Conversely, some plants have characteristics that make them highly flammable under most conditions or without regular maintenance.

Relative flammability depends on many factors, including life form, growth rate, architecture, debris shed, presence of volatile compounds, and salt content.

- **Life form.** Tall, frilly grasses, and plants with needle-like leaves, flakey or shredded bark, and shallow root systems are more flammable. Low-growing grasses, forbs, and shrubs, and plants with thick green leaves, thick tight bark, and extensive, deep root systems are less flammable. Succulents, because their aboveground tissues have high water content, are also less flammable.

- **Growth rate.** Plants with a fast growth rate are more flammable than those with a slow growth rate.

- **Architecture.** Plants with lots of fuels connected to each other (leaves and branches within and between vertical layers touching) are more flammable. Plants that have been limbed up or thinned; plants with open, loose branching and a low volume of leaves; and plants with bushy or frilly structures removed or minimized are less flammable.

- **Debris buildup.** Plants with a large amount of dead or diseased material retained, lots of dead leaves and branches, are more flammable than plants with little dead or diseased material retained.

- **Volatile compounds.** Plants containing oils, resins, waxes, pitch, and aromatics like terpenes and phenols are more flammable than those without these volatile compounds.

- **High salt content.** Some plants such as saltbush (*Atriplex* species) have high salt content, which makes them somewhat fire retardant.

A study comparing the flammability of 194 native and exotic species in New Zealand found that forbs (herbaceous flowering plants that are not grasses, sedges, or rushes) were consistently the least flammable. Grasses showed flammability similar to trees and shrubs. (Succulents were not included in the study.) Still, particular species within plant types vary in flammability. For example, while it is often true that grasses can ignite and burn more easily than herbs/forbs, carefully selected and managed grasses can be safe as part of your garden palette.

You do not have to avoid all plants with more combustible characteristics, but they should be isolated, at least 30 feet away from all structures, including your neighbors'. This may mean you have no room for them in your yard.

Grasses

Recent research indicates that not all grasses are the same when it comes to fire. More flammable grasses tend to have low leaf moisture content, lots of growth aboveground, a loose or frilly canopy of grass blades, a vertical growth form, and contain tannins or volatile oils. Conversely, less flammable grasses have high leaf moisture content, less growth aboveground, leaf blades densely packed, a more horizontal growth form, and low levels of tannins or volatile oils. This helps explain why irrigated, mown lawns tend to be fire resistant.

Grasses that are less flammable also tend to be those that are more palatable to grazers, such as deer or livestock. Appropriately timed mowing or grazing can make grasses more fire resistant while allowing for flowering and seed production. Cutting grasses back after seed fall and before fire season significantly reduces their ignitability.

Certain growth forms can make grasses more or less flammable. Fire avoiders form mats with sparse aerial structures, like West Coast bentgrass (*Agrostis pallens*). Fire resistors may have aerial leaves that burn but don't kill the plant (at least in moderate fires), like purple needlegrass (*Stipa pulchra*) and California fescue (*Festuca californica*). Fire enhancers have lots of airy vertical growth, like Mexican feather grass (*Nassella tenuissima*) and pampas grass (*Cortaderia selloana*).

111

BELOW LEFT West Coast bentgrass (*Agrostis pallens*) is a fire avoider, forming mats with sparse aerial structures.

BELOW MIDDLE AND RIGHT Purple needlegrass (*Stipa pulchra*) and California fescue (*Festuca californica*) resist fire with aerial leaves that burn but don't kill the plant.

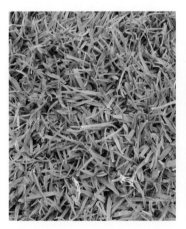

Mexican feather grass (*Nasella tenuissima*) and pampas grass (*Cortaderia selloana*) have lots of airy vertical growth that makes them fire enhancers (they are also aggressive invaders in some regions).

There is overwhelming evidence that nonnative grasses have led to increased fire occurrence and frequency in the West—specifically cheatgrass (*Bromus tectorum*), buffelgrass (*Pennisetum ciliare*), Medusahead grass (*Elymus caput-medusae*, syn. *Taeniatherum caput-medusae*), giant reed (*Arundo donax*), red brome (*Bromus rubens*), Arabian schismus (*Schismus arabicus*), and common Mediterranean grass (*Schismus barbatus*). Not surprisingly, they all tend to have low leaf moisture content, lots of dead material aboveground, loose canopies, and a vertical growth form; some contain tannins or volatile oils. Most are palatable to grazers only early in the season or not at all.

Forbs, bulbs and bulb-like plants, and succulents

The same characteristics that make some grass species less flammable also apply to forbs, bulbs and bulb-like plants, and succulents. Leaf moisture content is probably the greatest predictor of flame resistance, but compact growth, low-surface-area-to-volume leaves, little accumulation of dead material, and low levels of volatile compounds are desirable fire-resistant traits. Succulents, particularly those that aren't too furry with hairs or prickles, are the most resistant to fire (as long as dead material is removed) because they contain lots of water.

Still, succulents can be very combustible if not appropriately managed. The succulent invaders highway iceplant (*Carpobrotus edulis*) and sea fig (*C. chilensis*) can give a false sense of security. Older patches with dieback can be highly ignitable (plus they are invasive).

Shrubs and trees

Manzanitas (*Actostaphylos* species), some of our most beautiful native shrubs, have gotten a bad reputation with regard to fire. Manzanita wood is quite dense and can burn really hot. However, correctly spaced and pruned in a landscape, this shrub can actually be quite fire resistant (as well as incredibly drought tolerant and good for erosion control). The key is to let these photogenic native shrubs be isolated as individual specimens or patches, and to prune up lower branches and dead material (except for the creeping ground cover species).

The same can be said of a number of tall shrubs, including commonly planted nonnatives such as bottlebrush (*Callistemon citrinus*) and oleander (*Nerium oleander*). However, planting discretion is advised for nonnatives in the WUI. For example, although bottlebrush provides good nectar and pollen resources, oleander is practically devoid of wildlife value, and Scotch broom (*Cytisus scoparius*) not only enhances destructive wildfire risk but can generate impenetrable monocultures of itself after fire, with a stubbornly persistent bank of seeds deposited into soils every year.

Many chaparral shrubs and conifers contain oils and resins. Nonnative plants with oils and resins include ornamental junipers, Leyland cypress, rosemary, arborvitae, eucalyptus species, some acacia species, gorse, and camphor tree. Camphor tree is an example of a pretty solid fire enabler, because it produces flammable oils and is also disease-prone, resulting in lots of dead material on the ground and in the tree. (Even healthy plants rain plant litter year-round.)

In chaparral, sagebrush, and scrub desert areas, most of the brushier native shrubs (those with lots of small twigs that give a broomlike architecture to the plants) tend to be flammable. You can prune them into fire resistance only by meticulous removal of dead twigs and branches. If you are willing to invest the regular time required, most of these species can be pruned into small (less than 10 inches tall), medium (10 to 36 inches), or large (30 to 80 inches) bonsai. Examples include chemise (*Adenostoma fasciculatum*), coyote brush (*Baccharis pilularis*), big sagebrush (*Artemisia tridentata*), brittlebrush (*Encelia farinosa*), creosote bush (*Larrea tridentata*), and many of the brushier shrubs that occur with them.

Without intensive pruning, these plants should simply be spaced a safe distance away from structures. The value of these native shrubs is their innate beauty and the incredible array of wildlife they support. Bare soil between sparsely spaced plants can help keep flames in check. Occasional early-morning watering can reduce twig die-off. Placing a "nurse" boulder on the south sides of plants like these can help moderate soil temperature and moisture, and reduce drought stress and competition. What is essential for these flammable shrubs is to remove invasive weeds that can carry flames from one shrub to the next, especially nonnative grasses like cheatgrass (*Bromus tectorum*).

Just as the flammability of grasses can increase after they set seed and start dying back, the reproductive stage of shrubs can affect their flammability as the season progresses. Live fuel moisture typically declines through summer months but can vary from year to year. As fruits mature, plants become drier. Be aware of different plant stages that may indicate seasonal wildfire vulnerability.

113

Starting with Healthy Plants

As we hinted earlier, the placement, health, and maintenance of a plant are more important than its fire resistance. Healthy plants decrease flammability. Aim to start with healthy plants and root systems, know how and where to plant, and tend your plants. Just as you would nurture a child to maturity, nurturing plants requires attention to different needs at different life stages.

Seeds versus potted starts

Seeds can be the most economical way to start plants, and a great way to include natives from the WUI in your garden. If you see a lovely plant in your local WUI that is abundant and producing seed, you can always try to start the seed in your own yard. Before purchasing seeds online or at a store, make sure you have the right conditions for their establishment and are not spreading invasive species. Consult plant propagation resources for your area.

Wildflowers, like poppies and lupines, are best started from seeds scattered before the start of growing season precipitation, or before snowfall at higher elevations. Seeds know when to germinate. They remain dormant until the right temperature, moisture, and light conditions occur, or until the seed coat is sufficiently weakened (scarified; seeds can be scarified beforehand with sandpaper or a mild acid like white vinegar to speed the process).

A key to easy success is simply to make sure the area where you want to scatter seeds has been depleted of weeds like nonnative annual grasses and their seeds. These grasses tend to germinate after the very first winter or early spring rains or snowmelt and can therefore crowd out anything that germinates later. To deplete a weedy seed bank in sunnier climates, you can cover the area with clear plastic during the heat of summer for several months. If you want to avoid using plastic, you can alternately water and rake out weeds for one to three years without letting those seedlings produce seed. This has the added advantage of removing any excess fertilizers and pesticides that may have been applied in the past. A third option, if you live in a place where this is allowed, is to plant in an area you have used for burning debris or as an outdoor fire circle. The fire can kill seeds near the surface, and grass seeds in particular don't persist in soil for more than two or three years. Once you have depleted the seed bank, you may still have to do a little selective weeding to promote the desired plants, but once established your desired species can help crowd out invasive species.

Most gardeners and landscapers begin not with seeds but with potted or bare root plants. Before purchasing, you should inspect not just the aboveground portion but also the root system. Look for encircling roots at the surface, gently squeeze the pot to see how much it gives, and check for older or dead roots coming out the bottom. You can even pull the plant up by its trunk to peek at the root ball (being careful not to damage the plant). A poorly developed root system can doom a plant to being less drought tolerant and more prone to branch dieback, thus increasing your fire risk. In fact, you should avoid buying woody plants that have been marked down in price if they are root-bound (in pots too small for their size, with roots wrapped around in circles).

Furthermore, resist the temptation to buy bigger plants because you think they will give you a head start on a new landscape. Many, many studies have found that plants in smaller pots, and even bare root plants, catch up in size to larger specimens within two to three years because they develop healthier root systems. Some species will tolerate root and shoot pruning to correct for poor root structure, but in general it makes more sense to save money by buying smaller plants that will catch up in size more quickly and be more fire resilient.

Root Pruning for Plant Health

When planting new woody plants, always inspect them for healthy root structure. Root pruning may be needed to correct pot-bound plants or plants that were potted into larger pots without correcting encircling roots from the previous container. Teasing roots away from the root ball periphery encourages roots to grow away from the trunk as well. If you do significant root pruning, some of the shoots should be pruned as well, to reduce transplant shock. Failure to inspect and prune root systems can condemn a shrub or tree to unhealthy growth and an untimely death.

BELOW LEFT Poor root structure should be pruned or shaved to eliminate "containerized" roots encircling trunk and root-ball, if the plant can survive it (some native chaparral species in particular may not). Corrective pruning results in strong root development in the ground.

BELOW RIGHT Encircling roots should be cut back to the point where the pot deflects their growth—at point A, not point B.

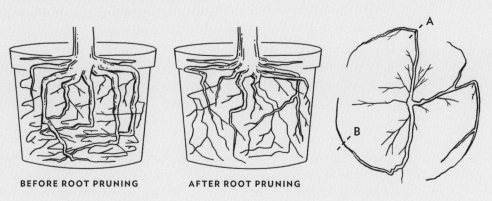

BEFORE ROOT PRUNING   AFTER ROOT PRUNING

Planting and placement

Many of us are planting incorrectly, dooming our woody plants to poor health. Copious horticultural research over the past few decades has completely debunked the notion that we should dig really deep holes and fill them full of organic amendments and fertilizer. Here's what we know now. Planting holes should be no deeper than the root ball and can be dug as much as twice as wide to loosen soil for the roots. The edges of your planting hole should be rough, not smooth like the inside of a pot. In addition, organic soil amendments should not be added to planting holes, as they only break down and cause plants to sink over time, may inhibit roots from extending out into soil, and sometimes create hollow air pockets around the central root ball that make plants more drought susceptible and fire vulnerable. Any added soil amendments are best used as dressing on top of the soil, applied under mulch.

Shrubs and trees should be planted proud—that is, with the trunk flare above the root system at or slightly above the soil surface, to avoid the accumulation of debris and mulch next to stems, which can also make plants more vulnerable to ignition. Before placement, the root ball should be loosened a bit to encourage roots to grow outward rather than in pot formation. Many native plants don't appreciate much root disturbance; gently loosening roots around the edges of the root ball without tearing them is sufficient. Finally, it's okay to create a small berm to catch water around a plant when it is getting established, but after a few years, berms should be smoothed out, again so that mulch and debris don't collect in the bowl you created adjacent to trunks.

Among the gravest mistakes homeowners and landscapers make when installing new plants is where they are placed. Avoid placing a plant in a spot that is too small for its mature size. No plant should be placed without accounting for its mature size and whether it is a species known to accept pruning without compromising plant health. When you know the mature size and pruning tolerance of a plant, you can place it a sufficient distance from walls, roofs, fences, and power lines (don't forget to look up!) to avoid becoming a source of ignition. In wildfire country, no plants should be installed right next to structures; such foundation plantings and anything else flammable should be avoided in zone 1.

When planting trees, you must keep the tree's mature height in mind to determine how far from a building to plant it. A tree that will grow to 40 feet tall should be planted at least 45 feet from the upwind side of a structure, measured from the outer dripline of the mature tree to the structure. Of course, solar panels, power structures, and fences also should be taken into account before planting. Keep in mind that many native species grow slowly the first two to three years, as their root systems develop, and then grow more rapidly once established.

A quick note about the match between plants and soils: it is always wise to pay attention to whether a particular plant requires good drainage. If so, and you plant it in heavy clay soil, it will easily die when water is abundant. If you have clay soil and still really want to grow a plant that hates clay soil, do not add sand! That is how you make bricks, literally. Instead, create mounds augmented with soil amendments such as composted woody materials or rock to improve drainage.

The right time to plant

The importance of when you plant is often overlooked. For healthier plants, you should let planting times be dictated by the biotic community and fire regime you live with. If you live in a Mediterranean or desert climate, winter and spring are the growing seasons. Moderate temperatures combined with precipitation are ideal for plant establishment. Indeed, most Mediterranean-adapted plants are dormant during summer. Planting during winter gives your plants the chance to develop more root growth before the dry season. Where there is winter snow cover, planting before the first snow gets roots growing before spring.

Fall-to-early-spring planting makes plants drought tolerant sooner, as their roots follow the soil moisture down with progressing summer heat. Ultimately, stronger root systems can make plants more resilient to fire because they tend to experience less extreme drought stress and tissue mortality.

In all but the wettest areas or where snow restricts your ability to plant, planting is best done between November and April. Conversely, planting during drier spells is preferred in the wet coastal regions of the Northwest to minimize damage to soil structure. When it's too wet to plow, it's too wet to plant.

The Magic of Mulching

Mulching—spreading a loose layer of organic or inorganic matter over the soil surface among and around plantings—is magic. Mulch reduces water loss from the soil, cools soil temperatures, smothers weeds, and helps curb soil erosion. Plant-and-manure-based mulches and compost also improve soil structure and moisture-holding capacity by adding organic matter to the soil. And they improve nutrient availability, help reduce soil compaction over time, and store carbon.

Mulching should be done when a landscape is first planted. Because organic mulches break down over time, adding to the mulch layer periodically over the years is also important. Depending on how fast it breaks down, mulch may need to be augmented annually or every three to four years. Cedar and cypress break down more slowly than other organic mulches and thus may need replenishing less often. Spread mulch in the early spring to keep weeds down, but be careful not to apply too much. A too-thick layer of dense mulch can keep rainwater from percolating into the soil, or may mildew in our wettest

Composted wood chips are the least combustible organic mulch, and they improve the soil as they break down further.

regions. Keep mulch away from stems and trunks, where it can cause rot and invite insects.

Not all mulches are created equal in terms of plant health benefits and combustibility. Obviously, nonorganic mulches like rock, brick, and concrete do little to improve soil structure or nutrient availability, but nonorganic mulches don't burn, and they do protect soil moisture and soil surfaces from temperature extremes. Nonorganic mulches can be used creatively in the garden to provide stunning design elements. Imagine crushing up old roof tiles for walkways, or recycling crushed glass or broken pots as mulch. Organic mulches are king when it comes to improving soil for plant health—although you must be vigilant about your mulch source if any pathogens (such as *Phytophthora ramorum*, the cause of sudden oak death) or insect pests are of concern in your area. But organic mulches are flammable. They should never be used in zone 1, 0 to 5 feet from the structure. In zone 2, 5 to 30 feet from structures, organic mulches are best applied discontinuously, with this fuel source interrupted by nonflammable materials such as concrete, gravel, rock, and irrigated low-stature plants.

In a comparison of organic and synthetic mulches ignited under dry conditions, shredded rubber, pine needles, and shredded bark ("gorilla hair mulch") were significantly more combustible than bark nuggets, green chipped tree waste, and chipped tree waste with fire retardant, in that order. Shredded rubber is particularly problematic. Not only has it been found to be the most combustible (producing the greatest flame height and temperatures), it also does not biodegrade (it only breaks down into smaller, dusty particles), does not enrich soil, may leach toxic chemicals and heavy metals, stores heat, and tends to be the most expensive. If you do choose to use either shredded rubber, pine needles, or shredded mulch where you live, do not place them within 30 feet of structures.

As for organic mulches, composted wood chips have been found to be the least combustible. Shredded western red cedar mulch ignites easily and produces the fastest flame spread, whereas composted wood chips burn primarily through smoldering, with very little flame and a slow rate of spread. Spray-on fire retardant does not necessarily prevent combustion, it merely buys you time by suppressing fire spread for five to ten minutes. Irrigating mulch before an impending wildfire would likely have little effect in slowing ignition and might reduce water pressure available for firefighting.

Using plastic film or weed-barrier fabrics in WUI landscapes can be something you end up regretting. First and foremost, like shredded rubber, they are highly combustible. Beyond that, plastic films choke off soil from water and nutrients normally deposited due to decomposition of organic matter. Further, in some environments they can provide ideal nesting habitat for household roaches. Weed-barrier fabrics do allow moisture to pass through to soil, but they tend to cause soil to compact over time, partly because they restrict organic inputs that add structure to soil. Although they reduce the number of weeds initially, over time weeds just pierce the fabric or grow on top. Landscape fabrics are made of plastics that may leach toxic chemicals, and they don't biodegrade, they just add nanoplastics into your soil as they break down. Plus, anywhere you put down plastic films or weed barriers, you will not be able to scatter seeds to establish plants.

In contrast, bare ground provides an excellent firebreak. More important, bare ground is essential nesting habitat for a couple thousand species of native bees and other organisms. Roughly 70 percent of native bees (which are quite docile and rarely sting, or are stingless) nest in burrows they form in bare soil; the remaining 30 percent nest in hollowed-out stems and wood. Soil should be considered a living resource that supports all sorts of biodiversity, and it should be included in your landscape along with mulched areas.

Varying the mulches you use expands the diversity of habitats around you. Generally speaking, desert plants should be mulched with rocks, and plants elsewhere can be mulched with organic or inorganic material as dictated by conditions. Long-lived shrubs and trees can be mulched with bark, or even evergreen oak mulch. Breaking up combustible mulches with nonorganic ones and bare ground can foster greater biodiversity and increase food web complexities, ultimately making plants less likely to suffer from large-scale insect or disease outbreaks. Don't forget to leave some bare ground for nesting bees and other organisms.

Desert plants should be mulched with rocks or decomposed granite.

A Native Plant Palette for Fire-Safe Gardens

This fire-wise garden in southern California features drought-tolerant native and nonnative plants with a mix of rock, bark, and bare soil.

DESPITE THE FACT THAT HALF OF THE PACIFIC COAST REGION is considered a biodiversity hot spot and our region hosts more than a hundred thousand plants and animals, we rely far too heavily on horticultural introductions from Asia, South Africa, and South America in our gardens. Our plant directory lists bad, poor, or noxious nonnative offenders and suggests native plant alternatives that share similar characteristics but are better for habitat sustainability and fire resilience. Many great nonnative plants support wildlife, put on wonderful displays, and are well behaved, but with our abundant native plant diversity and increasing habitat fragmentation in the WUI, native plants should be used whenever possible. Native alternatives are suggested for all vegetation groups except evergreen conifers, because we did not find any invasive evergreen conifers to list. (Regardless of whether they are native or exotic, needle-leaved evergreen conifers are often more ignitable due to their fine foliage and resin content, so they should not be planted near structures.)

Know Your
Sunset
Climate Zone

Sunset climate zone maps take into account a number of factors besides winter low temperatures, which are the basis for the USDA hardiness zone maps. Sunset's zones help you see not just where a plant might survive the winter but also where that plant will thrive year-round. They consider latitude, elevation, ocean influence, continental air influence, mountains and valleys, and local microclimates. To find out which Sunset climate zone you live in, go to sunsetwesterngardencollection.com/climate-zones/.

Remember: bad plants are those invasive species that spread easily by seed or vegetative propagation on their own, and noxious plants are aggressive invasive species that can crowd out other species and even change some ecosystem functions. Do not plant these, and if you see them on your property, remove them if possible. Poor plants are nonnatives that provide little food or shelter value, creating empty patches devoid of much life. Avoid filling space with these.

This is only a partial list of native plants you could substitute for species that may be invasive where you live. Whether a plant is invasive depends on habitats in your area. Suggested replacements are native to some portion of our three states, but their appropriateness to replace a given bad or poor plant depends on your local growing conditions. Many of the bad and noxious plants are invasive in only a portion of our Pacific Coast states (often in riparian areas, desert washes, and the wetter coast ranges, as is the case, for example, with butterfly bush, *Buddleja davidii*) and are well behaved in other areas. Some of the bad species included in this list are notable because they tend to invade wild areas from roads and human activities around the WUI. These same species may be less impactful in an urban environment. Conversely, just because a plant is native in one portion of our range does not mean it is appropriate for another.

We encourage you to use this directory as a starting point, a preliminary palette of possibilities. We did not include subspecies, varieties, or hybrids, whether naturally occurring or human-selected. Augment this information with expert knowledge in your region—from native plant growers, native plant societies, and local naturalists/botanists. Use online and print resources to learn more about particular native species and to check which species are invasive in your area.

Large Broadleaf Evergreen Trees

These trees reach 40 feet or more at maturity. All prefer sun or part shade.

BAD OR NOXIOUS PLANTS	PLANT INSTEAD

Eucalyptus camaldulensis (RIVER RED GUM)
Eucalyptus globulus (BLUE GUM)
	Arbutus menziesii (PACIFIC MADRONE)
	Chrysolepis chrysophylla
	    (GIANT/GOLDEN/WESTERN CHINQUAPIN)
	Notholithocarpus densiflorus (TANBARK OAK)
	Quercus agrifolia (COAST LIVE OAK)
	Quercus chrysolepis (CANYON LIVE OAK,
	    GOLDEN-CUP OAK)
	Quercus engelmannii (ENGELMANN OAK)
	Quercus wislizeni (INTERIOR LIVE OAK)
	Umbellularia californica
	    (CALIFORNIA BAY, OREGON MYRTLE)

Arbutus menziesii

Chrysolepis chrysophylla

PACIFIC MADRONE
Arbutus menziesii

Sunset zones 4–7, 14–19
Water needs: none to occasional once established; does not tolerate alkaline water
Soil preferences: well drained
Maintenance: some debris shed year-round; susceptible to sudden oak death; prune after blooming and when dry

GIANT/GOLDEN/WESTERN CHINQUAPIN
Chrysolepis chrysophylla

Sunset zones 4–7, 14–18
Water needs: none to occasional once established
Soil preferences: well drained; in dry, poor soils and at high elevation may not exceed small tree size
Maintenance: susceptible to sudden oak death; prune late fall when dry

TANBARK OAK
Notholithocarpus densiflorus, syn.
Lithocarpus densiflorus

Sunset zones 4–7, 14–24
Water needs: moderate but tolerates some drought
Soil preferences: rich, well drained
Maintenance: highly suceptible to sudden oak death; prune late summer when dry

Notholithocarpus densiflorus

Quercus engelmannii

Umbellularia californica

COAST LIVE OAK
Quercus agrifolia

Sunset zones 7–9, 14–24
Water needs: none to occasional once established
Soil preferences: adaptable, well drained
Maintenance: susceptible to sudden oak death; prune late summer

CANYON LIVE OAK, GOLDEN-CUP OAK
Quercus chrysolepis

Sunset zones 3–11, 14–24
Water needs: none to occasional once established
Soil preferences: adaptable, well drained
Maintenance: susceptible to sudden oak death; prune late summer

ENGELMANN OAK
Quercus engelmannii

Sunset zones 3, 5, 7–9, 14–24
Water needs: none to occasional once established
Soil preferences: adaptable, well drained
Maintenance: susceptible to sudden oak death; prune late summer

INTERIOR LIVE OAK
Quercus wislizeni

Sunset zones 7–9, 14–16, 18-21
Water needs: none to occasional once established
Soil preferences: adaptable, well drained
Maintenance: prune late summer; saplings can be gangly but mature trees handsome

CALIFORNIA BAY, OREGON MYRTLE
Umbellularia californica

Sunset zones 1–9, 14–24
Water needs: none to occasional once established
Soil preferences: adaptable, well drained; tolerates both serpentine and clay
Maintenance: some debris cleanup in fall; prune to size in late summer/fall; resistant carrier of sudden oak death, so plants in Pacific Coast Range with confirmed infections should be removed

Large Deciduous Trees

These trees reach 40 feet or more at maturity. All prefer sun or part shade.

BAD OR NOXIOUS PLANTS	PLANT INSTEAD
Acer platanoides (NORWAY MAPLE)	*Acer macrophyllum* (BIG LEAF MAPLE)
Juglans nigra (BLACK WALNUT), Eastern US species can hybridize with western species but can be safely used as rootstock for grafting	*Juglans californica* (CALIFORNIA BLACK WALNUT) *Juglans hindsii* (HINDS' BLACK WALNUT)
Paulownia tomentosa (PRINCESS TREE) invasive in riparian areas	*Acer macrophyllum* (BIG LEAF MAPLE) *Platanus racemosa* (CALIFORNIA SYCAMORE) *Populus angustifolia* (NARROWLEAF POPLAR) *Populus fremontii* (FREMONT/WESTERN COTTONWOOD) *Populus trichocarpa* (BLACK COTTONWOOD)
Platanus ×acerifolia (LONDON PLANE TREE)	*Platanus racemosa* (CALIFORNIA SYCAMORE)
Populus alba (WHITE/SILVERLEAF POPLAR)	*Populus tremuloides* (QUAKING ASPEN)
Robinia pseudoacacia (BLACK LOCUST) seeds toxic to birds and other animals	*Fraxinus latifolia* (OREGON ASH) *Juglans californica* (CALIFORNIA BLACK WALNUT) *Juglans hindsii* (HINDS' BLACK WALNUT) *Quercus garryana* (OREGON WHITE OAK) *Quercus kelloggii* (BLACK OAK) *Quercus lobata* (VALLEY OAK)
Ulmus pumila (SIBERIAN ELM)	*Alnus rhombifolia* (WHITE ALDER) *Alnus rubra* (RED ALDER) *Betula papyrifera* (PAPERBARK BIRCH) *Quercus douglasii* (BLUE OAK) *Quercus garryana* (OREGON WHITE OAK) *Quercus lobata* (VALLEY OAK)

BIG LEAF MAPLE
Acer macrophyllum

Sunset zones 1–9, 14–24
Water needs: moderate to regular
Soil preferences: deep alluvial soils
Maintenance: seasonal debris cleanup; susceptible to sudden oak wilt, prune after leaf fall but before significant rains

Acer macrophyllum

WHITE ALDER
Alnus rhombifolia

Sunset zones 1b–10, 14–19, 22–24
Water needs: moderate
Soil preferences: acid, sandy or silty loams; tolerates clay
Maintenance: seasonal debris cleanup and thinning; prune winter

RED ALDER
Alnus rubra

Sunset zones 2–7, 14–24
Water needs: moderate, but more drought tolerant with less frequent deep watering
Soil preferences: acid, sandy or silty loams; tolerates slow drainage and saline soils
Maintenance: seasonal debris cleanup and thinning; prune winter; prune out mistletoe

Fraxinus latifolia

Juglans californica

PAPERBARK BIRCH
Betula papyrifera

Sunset zones 1–6
Water needs: moderate
Soil preferences: acid, sandy or silty loams
Maintenance: seasonal debris cleanup and thinning; prune winter

OREGON ASH
Fraxinus latifolia

Sunset zones 3–9, 14–24
Water needs: little to no water once established
Soil preferences: variable
Maintenance: seasonal debris cleanup and thinning; prune late summer

CALIFORNIA BLACK WALNUT
Juglans californica

Sunset zones 18–24
Water needs: low once established
Soil preferences: deep alluvial soils
Maintenance: some debris cleanup year-round; prune winter

HINDS' BLACK WALNUT
Juglans hindsii

Sunset zones 5–9, 14–20
Water needs: low once established
Soil preferences: deep alluvial soils
Maintenance: some debris cleanup year-round; prune winter

CALIFORNIA SYCAMORE
Platanus racemosa

Sunset zones 4–24
Water needs: moderate to regular
Soil preferences: deep alluvial soils
Maintenance: some debris cleanup year-round; prune winter

NARROWLEAF POPLAR
Populus angustifolia

Sunset zones 1–11, 14–21
Water needs: moderate water or shallow groundwater
Soil preferences: riparian habitats (even California palm oases)
Maintenance: seasonal debris cleanup and thinning in summer to early winter when dry

Platanus racemosa   *Quercus douglasii*   *Quercus lobata*

FREMONT/WESTERN COTTONWOOD
Populus fremontii

Sunset zones 1–12, 14–21
Water needs: moderate, best near perennial water source
Soil preferences: adaptable, sandy to clay
Maintenance: seasonal debris cleanup and thinning; prune winter

QUAKING ASPEN
Populus tremuloides

Sunset zones 1–7, 14–19
Water needs: moderate, best near perennial water source
Soil preferences: adaptable, sandy to clay
Maintenance: seasonal debris cleanup and thinning; prune winter; forms clonal stands

BLACK COTTONWOOD
Populus trichocarpa

Sunset zones 1–9, 14–24
Water needs: moderate; moderate drought tolerance once established
Soil preferences: well drained
Maintenance: seasonal debris cleanup and thinning; prune winter

BLUE OAK
Quercus douglasii

Sunset zones 1–11, 14–24
Water needs: little to moderate water, as needed
Soil preferences: well drained
Maintenance: seasonal debris cleanup and thinning summer to fall

OREGON WHITE OAK
Quercus garryana

Sunset zones 2a–11, 14–23
Water needs: little to no water once established
Soil preferences: variable
Maintenance: seasonal debris cleanup and thinning; prune late summer

BLACK OAK
Quercus kelloggii

Sunset zones 6, 7, 9, 14–21
Water needs: little to no water once established
Soil preferences: variable
Maintenance: seasonal debris cleanup and thinning; prune late summer

VALLEY OAK
Quercus lobata

Sunset zones 3b–9, 11–24
Water needs: little to no water once established
Soil preferences: variable
Maintenance: seasonal debris cleanup and thinning; prune late summer

Medium Evergreen to Semi-Evergreen Trees

These trees or tall shrubs reach 15 to 40 feet tall at maturity. All prefer sun or part shade.

BAD OR NOXIOUS PLANTS	PLANT INSTEAD
Acacia baileyana (COOTAMUNDRA WATTLE) *Acacia cyclops* (COASTAL WATTLE) *Acacia dealbata* (SILVER WATTLE) *Acacia longifolia* (GOLDEN WATTLE) *Acacia melanoxylon* (BLACK ACACIA) *Acacia paradoxa* (KANGAROO THORN) *Acacia pycnantha* (GOLDEN WATTLE) *Acacia saligna* (ORANGE WATTLE)	*Arbutus menziesii* (PACIFIC MADRONE) *Arctostaphylos columbiana* (HAIRY MANZANITA) *Arctostaphylos glauca* (BIG BERRY MANZANITA) *Arctostaphylos manzanita* (COMMON MANZANITA) *Ceanothus megacarpus* (BIG POD CEANOTHUS) *Ceanothus spinosus* (GREEN BARK CEANOTHUS) *Cercocarpus betuloides* (BIRCH-LEAF MOUNTAIN MAHOGANY) *Cerocarpus ledifolius* (CURL-LEAF MOUNTAIN MAHOGANY) *Fremontodendron californicum, F. mexicanum* (FLANNEL BUSH) *Umbellularia californica* (CALIFORNIA BAY, OREGON MYRTLE)
Ilex aquifolium (ENGLISH HOLLY), invasive in riparian areas and irrigated landscapes	*Heteromeles arbutifolia* (TOYON) *Prunus ilicifolia* (HOLLYLEAF CHERRY)
Myoporum laetum (FALSE SANDLEWOOD / NGAIO)	*Comarostaphylis diversifolia* (SUMMER HOLLY) *Lyonothanmus floribundus* (CATALINA IRONWOOD) *Morella californica*, syn. *Myrica californica* (CALIFORNIA WAX MYRTLE) *Umbellularia californica* (CALIFORNIA BAY, OREGON MYRTLE)
Olea europaea (EUROPEAN EDIBLE OLIVE), invasive in riparian areas	*Arctostaphylos columbiana* (HAIRY MANZANITA) *Arctostaphylos glauca* (BIG BERRY MANZANITA) *Arctostaphylos manzanita* (COMMON MANZANITA) *Ceanothus arboreus* (ISLAND CEANOTHUS) *Ceanothus parryi* (PARRY'S CEANOTHUS) *Ceanothus thyrsiflorus* (BLUE BLOSSOM CEANOTHUS) *Quercus chrysolepis* (CANYON LIVE OAK, GOLDEN-CUP OAK) *Umbellularia californica* (CALIFORNIA BAY, OREGON MYRTLE) *Xylococcus bicolor* (MISSION MANZANITA)

PACIFIC MADRONE
Arbutus menziesii

See entry under Large Broadleaf Evergreen Trees.

HAIRY MANZANITA
Arctostaphylos columbiana

Sunset zones 4, 5, 7, 14–17
Water needs: no added water once established
Soil preferences: well drained; tolerant of clay or alluvial soil
Maintenance: prune after flowering when dry

HAIRY MANZANITA
Arctostaphylos glauca

Sunset zones 7, 11, 14–24
Water needs: no added water once established
Soil preferences: well drained; tolerant of clay or alluvial soil
Maintenance: prune after flowering when dry

COMMON MANZANITA
Arctostaphylos manzanita

Sunset zones 4–9, 14–24

Water needs: no added water once established
Soil preferences: well drained; tolerant of clay or alluvial soil
Maintenance: prune after flowering when dry

ISLAND CEANOTHUS
Ceanothus arboreus

Sunset zones 7–9, 14–17, 19–24
Water needs: none to occasional once established
Soil preferences: adaptable, well drained
Maintenance: some debris cleanup in fall; prune to size in late summer/fall; resistant carrier of sudden oak death, so plants in Pacific Coast Range with confirmed infections should be removed

BIG POD CEANOTHUS
Ceanothus megacarpos

Sunset zones 20–24
Water needs: none to occasional once established
Soil preferences: adaptable, well drained
Maintenance: some debris cleanup in fall; prune to size in late summer/fall

PARRY'S CEANOTHUS
Ceanothus parryi

Sunset zones 7, 14–17
Water needs: none to occasional once established
Soil preferences: adaptable, well drained
Maintenance: some debris cleanup in fall; prune to size in late summer/fall; assumed carrier of sudden oak death, so plants in Pacific Coast Range with confirmed infections should be removed

GREEN BARK CEANOTHUS
Ceanothus spinosus

Sunset zones 7–9, 14–24
Water needs: none to occasional once established
Soil preferences: adaptable, well drained
Maintenance: some debris cleanup in fall; prune to size in late summer/fall; assumed carrier of sudden oak death, so plants in Pacific Coast Range with confirmed infections should be removed

BLUE BLOSSOM CEANOTHUS
Ceanothus thyrsiflorus

Sunset zones 6–9, 14–24
Water needs: none to occasional once established
Soil preferences: adaptable, well drained
Maintenance: some debris cleanup in fall; prune to size in late summer/fall; carrier of sudden oak death, so plants in Pacific Coast Range with confirmed infections should be removed

Cercocarpus betuloides

BIRCH-LEAF MOUNTAIN MAHOGANY
Cercocarpus betuloides

Sunset zones 3, 5, 7–10, 13–24 (*C. ledifolius* is adapted to higher elevations, western ranges)
Water needs: no added water once established
Soil preferences: fast draining
Maintenance: prune late summer to early fall

CURL-LEAF MOUNTAIN MAHOGANY
Cerocarpus ledifolius

Sunset zones 1–3, 7–10, 14–24
Water needs: no added water once established
Soil preferences: fast draining
Maintenance: prune late summer to early fall

SUMMER HOLLY
Comarostaphylis diversifolia

Sunset zones 7–9, 14–24
Water needs: little to no water once established
Soil preferences: well drained
Maintenance: debris cleanup mostly in late fall and winter; prune to size in late summer to fall

FLANNEL BUSH
Fremontodendron californicum, F. mexicanum

Sunset zones 4–12 (*F. mexicanum*, 13), 14–24
Water needs: no added water once established
Soil preferences: fast draining
Maintenance: prune late summer to early fall; wear gloves and long sleeves when pruning and locate away from foot traffic to avoid irritating hairs

TOYON
Heteromeles arbutifolia

Sunset zones 5–19, 14–24
Water needs: low to little added water once established

Heteromeles arbutifolia

Morella californica

Washingtonia filifera

Xylococcus bicolor

Soil preferences: adaptable; tolerates serpentine
Maintenance: seasonal debris cleanup; prune late summer to winter

CATALINA IRONWOOD
Lyonothanmus floribundus

Sunset zones 14–17, 19–24
Water needs: little to regular
Soil preferences: adaptable, but deeper soils best
Maintenance: debris cleanup mostly in late fall to winter; prune to size in late summer to fall

CALIFORNIA WAX MYRTLE
Morella californica, syn. *Myrica californica*

Sunset zones 5–9, 14–24
Water needs: little to regular
Soil preferences: adaptable, but deeper soils best
Maintenance: debris cleanup mostly in late fall to winter; prune to size in late summer to fall

HOLLYLEAF CHERRY
Prunus ilicifolia

Sunset zones 5–9, 12–24
Water needs: little to no water once established
Soil preferences: adaptable, well drained; grows fastest in fertile, coarse, fast-draining soil
Maintenance: seasonal debris cleanup; prune late summer to winter

CANYON LIVE OAK, GOLDEN-CUP OAK
Quercus chrysolepis

See entry under Large Broadleaf Evergreen Trees.

CALIFORNIA BAY, OREGON MYRTLE
Umbellularia californica

See entry under Large Broadleaf Evergreen Trees.

CALIFORNIA FAN PALM
Washingtonia filifera

Generally not recommended in high-risk fire areas
Sunset zones 8–10, 11–24
Water needs: little to regular
Soil preferences: adaptable
Maintenance: regular debris cleanup, plus must keep dead "skirt" of leaves pruned up

MISSION MANZANITA
Xylococcus bicolor

Sunset zones 14–17, 19–24
Water needs: little to no water once established
Soil preferences: well drained
Maintenance: some debris cleanup year-round; prune midsummer to fall

Medium Deciduous Trees

These trees reach 15 to 40 feet tall at maturity. All prefer sun or part shade; *Acer circinatum* prefers afternoon shade.

BAD OR NOXIOUS PLANTS	PLANT INSTEAD
Ailanthus altissima (TREE OF HEAVEN)	*Acer circinatum* (OREGON VINE MAPLE) *Acer negundo* (BOX ELDER) *Chilopsis linearis* (DESERT WILLOW) *Prosopis glandulosa* var. *torreyana* (HONEY MESQUITE) *Prosopis pubescens* (SCREWBEAN, TORNILLO)
Catalpa bignonioides (SOUTHERN CATALPA) *Catalpa speciosa* (NORTHERN CATALPA) *Catalpa ×erubescens* (HYBRID CATALPA), invasive in riparian areas	*Acer circinatum* (OREGON VINE MAPLE) *Aesculus californica* (CALIFORNIA BUCKEYE) *Chilopsis linearis* (DESERT WILLOW)
Crataegus monogyna (ENGLISH/COMMON HAWTHORNE)	*Acer circinatum* (OREGON VINE MAPLE) *Alnus incana* subsp. *tenuifolia* (MOUNTAIN/THIN-LEAVED/GRAY ALDER) *Amelanchier alnifolia* (WESTERN/PACIFIC SERVICEBERRY, JUNEBERRY, WESTERN SHADBUSH) *Celtis reticulata* (WESTERN/NET-LEAVED HACKBERRY) *Crataegus douglasii* (DOUGLAS HAWTHORN) *Malus fusca* (WESTERN/OREGON CRABAPPLE)
Nicotiana glauca (TREE TOBACCO), seeds toxic to birds and other animals, plants toxic to some insects	*Parkinsonia florida*, syn. *Cercidium floridum* (BLUE PALO VERDE) *Parkinsonia microphylla*, syn. *Cercidium microphyllum* (LITTLE-LEAF PALO VERDE) *Prosopis glandulosa* var. *torreyana* (HONEY MESQUITE) *Prosopis pubescens* (SCREWBEAN, TORNILLO)
Prunus cerasifera (CHERRY PLUM), invasive in riparian areas and irrigated landscapes	*Frangula purshiana*, syn. *Rhamnus purshiana* (CASCARA SAGRADA, CASCADE BUCKTHORN) *Prunus emarginata* (BITTER CHERRY)
Tamarix species and hybrids (TAMARISK / SALT CEDAR), invasive in riparian areas; all quite ignitable	*Prosopis glandulosa* var. *torreyana* (HONEY MESQUITE) *Prosopis pubescens* (SCREWBEAN, TORNILLO) *Salix* species native to your area
Triadica sebifera, syn. *Sapium sebiferum* (CHINESE TALLOW TREE)	*Aesculus californica* (CALIFORNIA BUCKEYE) *Frangula purshiana*, syn. *Rhamnus purshiana* (CASCARA SAGRADA, CASCADE BUCKTHORN) *Psorothamnus spinosus*, syn. *Dalea spinosa* (SMOKE TREE)

Acer circinatum

132

Celtis reticulata

OREGON VINE MAPLE
Acer circinatum

Sunset zones 1–9, 14–20
Water needs: moderate to regular
Soil preferences: adaptable, well drained
Maintenance: seasonal debris cleanup and thinning in winter when dry

BOX ELDER
Acer negundo

Sunset zones 1–10, 12–24
Water needs: moderate water or shallow groundwater
Soil preferences: riparian habitats (even California palm oases)
Maintenance: seasonal debris cleanup and thinning in summer to early winter when dry

CALIFORNIA BUCKEYE
Aesculus californica

Sunset zones 3–10, 14–24
Water needs: little to no water, as needed
Soil preferences: well drained
Maintenance: seasonal debris cleanup and thinning summer to fall; summer through winter deciduous

MOUNTAIN/THIN-LEAVED/GRAY ALDER
Alnus incana subsp. *tenuifolia*

Sunset zones 1–3, 7, 10, 14–24
Water needs: moderate to regular
Soil preferences: adaptable, well drained; often found on nutrient-poor soils, which limits height
Maintenance: seasonal debris cleanup and thinning in winter when dry

WESTERN/PACIFIC SERVICEBERRY, JUNEBERRY, WESTERN SHADBUSH
Amelanchier alnifolia

Sunset zones 1–6
Water needs: moderate, low moisture
Soil preferences: adaptable, prefers loamy soils
Maintenance: fall/winter debris cleanup, regular pruning

WESTERN/NET-LEAVED HACKBERRY
Celtis reticulata

Sunset zones 1–24
Water needs: moderate to regular
Soil preferences: adaptable
Maintenance: seasonal debris cleanup and thinning in winter when dry

DESERT WILLOW
Chilopsis linearis

Sunset zones 3B, 7–14, 18–23
Water needs: little to moderate water once established
Soil preferences: well drained
Maintenance: seasonal debris cleanup and thinning summer/fall when dry

DOUGLAS HAWTHORN
Crataegus douglasii

Sunset zones 1, 2, 4–7, 14–18
Water needs: moderate to regular
Soil preferences: deep, moist, fine-textured soil
Maintenance: seasonal debris cleanup and thinning in winter when dry

CASCARA SAGRADA, CASCADE BUCKTHORN
Frangula purshiana, syn. *Rhamnus purshiana*

Sunset zones 1–7, 14–17
Water needs: low
Soil preferences: adaptable
Maintenance: seasonal debris cleanup and thinning in winter when dry; carrier of sudden oak death, so plants in Pacific Coast Range with confirmed infections should be removed

WESTERN/OREGON CRABAPPLE
Malus fusca

Sunset zones 4–5, 14–17
Water needs: moderate to regular
Soil preferences: sandy or loamy soils; does not grow well in clay soils
Maintenance: seasonal debris cleanup and thinning in winter when dry

BLUE PALO VERDE
Parkinsonia florida, syn. *Cercidium floridum*

Sunset zones 7–14, 19–20
Water needs: no water once established
Soil preferences: fast draining
Maintenance: seasonal debris cleanup; prune summer/fall when dry

LITTLE-LEAF PALO VERDE
Parkinsonia microphylla, syn. *Cercidium microphyllum*

Sunset zones 8–14, 18–20
Water needs: no water once established
Soil preferences: fast draining
Maintenance: seasonal debris cleanup; prune summer/fall when dry

HONEY MESQUITE
Prosopis glandulosa var. *torreyana*

Sunset zones 10–13, 18–24
Water needs: little to moderate
Soil preferences: adaptable, well drained
Maintenance: seasonal debris cleanup and thinning in winter

SCREWBEAN, TORNILLO
Prosopis pubescens

Sunset zones 10–13, 18–24
Water needs: little to moderate
Soil preferences: adaptable, well drained
Maintenance: seasonal debris cleanup and thinning in winter

BITTER CHERRY
Prunus emarginata

Sunset zones 1–10, 14–23
Water needs: moderate to regular
Soil preferences: tolerates clay but best in loamy soils
Maintenance: seasonal debris cleanup and thinning in winter

SMOKE TREE
Psorothamnus spinosus, syn. *Dalea spinosa*

Sunset zones 12, 13
Water needs: little to no water once established
Soil preferences: well drained
Maintenance: seasonal debris cleanup and thinning summer to fall

WILLOW
Salix species native to your area

Sunset zones depend on geographic ranges of species; check with local nurseries
Water needs: moderate water or shallow groundwater
Soil preferences: riparian habitats (even California palm oases)
Maintenance: seasonal debris cleanup and thinning in summer to early winter when dry; always check for bird nests before pruning

Malus fusca

Salix gooddingii

Small Trees / Large Shrubs, Evergreen

These trees and shrubs reach 5 to 15 feet tall at maturity. All prefer sun or part shade.

BAD OR NOXIOUS PLANTS	PLANT INSTEAD
Cordyline australis (NEW ZEALAND CABBAGE TREE)	*Yucca brevifolia* (WESTERN JOSHUA TREE) *Yucca jaegeriana* (EASTERN JOSHUA TREE) *Yucca schidigera* (MOJAVE YUCCA); all provide great habitat but should not be planted close to structures
Cotoneaster franchetii (ORANGE/FRANCHETTI COTONEASTER) *Cotoneaster lacteus*, syn. *Cotoneaster parneyi* (MILKFLOWER/LATE COTONEASTER) *Cotoneaster pannosus* (SILVERLEAF/VELVET COTONEASTER) *Cotoneaster simonsii* (HIMALAYAN COTONEASTER); all members of this genus tend to become invasive	*Arctostaphylos glandulosa* (EASTWOOD MANZANITA) and others *Ceanothus crassifolius* (HOARY-LEAVED CEANOTHUS), *C. cuneatus* (BUCKBRUSH), *C. velutinus* (TOBACCO BRUSH), and others *Eriogonum arborescens* (SANTA CRUZ ISLAND BUCKWHEAT) *Frangula californica*, syn. *Rhamnus californica* (COFFEEBERRY) *Heteromeles arbutifolia* (TOYON) *Rhamnus ilicifolia* (HOLLYLEAF REDBERRY)
Cytisus scoparius (SCOTCH BROOM) *Cytisus striatus* (PORTUGUESE BROOM) *Genista canariensis*, syn. *Cytisus canariensis* (CANARY ISLAND BROOM) *Genista monspessulana* (FRENCH BROOM) *Spartium junceum* (SPANISH BROOM); all regenerate vigorously after fire from long-lived seed bank, crowd out other species; seeds toxic to livestock and birds	*Asclepias albicans* (WHITESTEM MILKWEED) *Dendromecon rigida* (BUSH POPPY) *Dendromecon harfordii* (ISLAND BUSH POPPY) *Eriogonum umbellatum* (SULPHUR BUCKWHEAT)
Elaeagnus angustifolia (RUSSIAN OLIVE)	*Atriplex polycarpa* (ALLSCALE, CATTLE SALTBUSH) *Baccharis pilularis* (COYOTE BRUSH) *Baccharis salicifolia* (MULE FAT) *Ceanothus integerrimus* (DEER BRUSH), *C. papillosus* (WARTLEAF CEANOTHUS), *C. verrucosus* (WHITE COAST CEANOTHUS), and others *Erica lusitanica* (PORTUGUESE/SPANISH HEATH) *Eriogonum arborescens* (SANTA CRUZ ISLAND BUCKWHEAT), *E. fasciculatum* (CALIFORNIA BUCKWHEAT), *E. giganteum* (ST. CATHERINE'S LACE), and others *Morella californica*, syn. *Myrica californica* (PACIFIC WAX MYRTLE)
Erica lusitanica (PORTUGUESE/SPANISH HEATH)	*Adenostoma fasciculatum* (CHAMISE) *Carpenteria californica* (BUSH ANEMONE) *Ceanothus foliosus* (WAVY-LEAVED CEANOTHUS)

BAD OR NOXIOUS PLANTS	PLANT INSTEAD
Erica lusitanica (PORTUGUESE/SPANISH HEATH), Cont.	*Ceanothus integerrimus* (DEER BRUSH) *Eriogonum giganteum* (ST. CATHERINE'S LACE) and others *Gambelia speciosa*, syn. *Galvezia speciosa* (ISLAND BUSH SNAPDRAGON) *Lepechinia calycina* (WHITE PITCHER SAGE) *Lepechinia fragrans* (FRAGRANT PITCHER SAGE) *Pickeringia montana* (CHAPARRAL PEA) *Shepherdia argentea* (SILVER BUFFALO BERRY)
Ilex aquifolium (ENGLISH HOLLY) and varieties	*Heteromeles arbutifolia* (TOYON) *Prunus ilicifolia* (HOLLYLEAF CHERRY) *Rhamnus crocea* (HOLLYLEAF REDBERRY) *Rhamnus ilicifolia* (HOLLYLEAF REDBERRY)
Ligustrum japonicum (JAPANESE PRIVET) *Ligustrum lucidum* (GLOSSY PRIVET) *Ligustrum ovalifolium* (OVAL-LEAF PRIVET) *Ligustrum sinense* (CHINESE PRIVET) *Ligustrum vulgare* (EUROPEAN PRIVET); all members of this genus tend to become invasive	*Arctostaphylos nummularia* (GLOSSY-LEAVED MANZANITA), and others *Baccharis pilularis* (COYOTE BRUSH) *Frangula californica*, syn. *Rhamnus californica* (COFFEEBERRY) *Garrya elliptica* (COAST SILKTASSEL) *Garrya fremontii* (FREMONT SILKTASSEL) *Gaultheria shallon* (SALAL) *Heteromeles arbutifolia* (TOYON) *Morella californica*, syn. *Myrica californica* (PACIFIC WAX MYRTLE)
Olea europaea (EUROPEAN EDIBLE OLIVE), invasive in riparian areas	*Arctostaphylos insularis* (ISLAND MANZANITA), *A. viscida* (WHITELEAF MANZANITA), and others *Atriplex breweri* (BREWER SALTBUSH), *A. canescens* (SHADSCALE), *A. lentiformis* (BIG SALTBUSH), and others *Condea emoryi*, syn. *Hyptis emoryi* (DESERT LAVENDER, BUSHMINT) *Forestiera neomexicana* (DESERT OLIVE) *Garrya elliptica* (COAST SILKTASSEL) *Garrya fremontii* (FREMONT SILKTASSEL) *Simmondsia chinensis* (JOJOBA)
Pittosporum undulatum (VICTORIAN BOX)	*Garrya elliptica* (COAST SILKTASSEL) *Garrya fremontii* (FREMONT SILKTASSEL) *Morella californica*, syn. *Myrica californica* (PACIFIC WAX MYRTLE) *Prunus ilicifolia* (HOLLYLEAF CHERRY) *Quercus durata* (LEATHER OAK) *Xylococcus bicolor* (MISSION MANZANITA)

135

BAD OR NOXIOUS PLANTS	PLANT INSTEAD
Prunus lusitanica (PORTUGUESE LAUREL CHERRY)	*Frangula californica*, syn. *Rhamnus californica* (COFFEEBERRY) *Gaultheria shallon* (SALAL) *Heteromeles arbutifolia* (TOYON) *Prunus ilicifolia* (HOLLYLEAF CHERRY)
Pyracantha angustifolia (NARROWLEAF FIRETHORN) *Pyracantha coccinea* (SCARLET FIRETHORN) *Pyracantha crenulata* (NEPALESE FIRETHORN) *Pyracantha crenatoserrata* (BROAD-LEAF FIRETHORN) *Pyracantha fortuneana* (CHINESE FIRETHORN) *Pyracantha koidzumii* (FORMOSAN FIRETHORN); all members of this species tend to become invasive	*Arctostaphylos pajaroensis* (PAJARO MANZANITA) and others *Frangula californica*, syn. *Rhamnus californica* (COFFEEBERRY) *Heteromeles arbutifolia* (TOYON) *Prunus ilicifolia* (HOLLYLEAF CHERRY) *Rhus integrifolia* (LEMONADE BERRY) *Rhamnus crocea* (HOLLYLEAF REDBERRY)
Rhamnus alaternus (ITALIAN BUCKTHORN)	*Ceanothus cuneatus* (BUCKBRUSH), *C. leucodermis* (CHAPARRAL WHITETHORN), and others *Chrysolepis sempervirens* (SIERRA CHINQUAPIN) *Frangula californica*, syn. *Rhamnus californica* (COFFEEBERRY) *Heteromeles arbutifolia* (TOYON) *Prunus ilicifolia* (HOLLYLEAF CHERRY) *Rhus integrifolia* (LEMONADE BERRY)
Ricinus communis (CASTOR BEAN/OIL PLANT), whole plant toxic; seeds toxic to birds if eaten	*Berberis aquifolium*, syn. *Mahonia aquifolium* (TALL OREGON GRAPE) *Gaultheria shallon* (SALAL)
Ulex europaeus (GORSE)	*Chrysothamnus viscidiflorus* (YELLOW RABBITBRUSH) *Ericameria nauseosa*, syn. *Chrysothamnus nauseosus* (GRAY RABBITBRUSH) *Frangula californica*, syn. *Rhamnus californica* (COFFEEBERRY) *Larrea tridentata* (CREOSOTE BUSH) *Lycium californicum* (CALIFORNIA BOXTHORN) *Malosma laurina*, syn. *Rhus laurina* (LAUREL SUMAC) *Rhus integrifolia* (LEMONADE BERRY) *Rhus ovata* (SUGAR BUSH) *Rhus trilobata* (SKUNKBUSH)
Nerium oleander (OLEANDER), toxic to pets and most livestock, nectarless, no pollinator visitation	*Arctostaphylos bakeri* (BAKER'S MANZANITA), *A. pajaroensis* (PAJARO MANZANITA), and others *Atriplex canescens* (FOUR-WING SALTBUSH) *Dendromecon rigida* (BUSH POPPY) *Dendromecon harfordii* (ISLAND BUSH POPPY) *Fremontodendron californicum*, *F. mexicanum* (FLANNEL BUSH)

BAD OR NOXIOUS PLANTS	PLANT INSTEAD
Nerium oleander (OLEANDER), toxic to pets and most livestock, nectarless, no pollinator visitation, Cont.	*Garrya congdonii* (INTERIOR SILKTASSEL) *Garrya elliptica* (COAST SILKTASSEL) *Garrya flavescens* (ASHY/YELLOWLEAF SILKTASSEL) *Garrya fremontii* (FREMONT SILKTASSEL) *Garrya veatchii* (CANYON SILKTASSEL) *Lycium brevipes* (BAJA DESERT THORN) *Pluchea sericea* (ARROW WEED, ARROWLEAF) *Xylococcus bicolor* (MISSION MANZANITA)
Camelia japonica, C. sasanqua (DOUBLE CAMELIA VARIETIES), no pollinator resources	*Malocothamnus fasciculatus* (CHAPARRAL BUSHMALLOW) *Rhododendron macrophyllum*, syn. *Rhododendron californicum* (COAST RHODODENDRON) *Rhododendron occidentale* (WESTERN AZALEA)
Nandina domestica (HEAVENLY BAMBOO), berries contain cyanide when ripe and may harm/kill some birds	*Berberis aquifolium*, syn. *Mahonia aquifolium* (OREGON GRAPE) *Berberis nevinii*, syn. *Mahonia nevinii* (NEVIN'S BARBERRY) *Berberis nervosa*, syn. *Mahonia nervosa* (LONGLEAF MAHONIA) *Berberis pinnata* (COAST BARBERRY) *Carpenteria californica* (BUSH ANEMONE) *Eriogonum giganteum* (ST. CATHERINE'S LACE) *Gambelia speciosa*, syn. *Galvezia speciosa* (ISLAND BUSH SNAPDRAGON) *Lepechinia calycina, L. fragrans* (PITCHER SAGE) *Malocothamnus densiflorus* (YELLOW STEM BUSH MALLOW) *Malocothamnus fremontii* (FREMONT'S BUSHMALLOW) *Malocothamnus jonesii* (JONES'S BUSH MALLOW) *Malocothamnus palmeri* (SANTA LUCIA BUSH MALLOW) *Malosma laurina*, syn. *Rhus laurina* (LAUREL SUMAC) *Rhamnus crocea* (SPINY REDBERRY) *Rhus aromatica* (FRAGRANT SUMAC) *Rhus integrifolia* (LEMONADE BERRY) *Rhus ovata* (SUGAR BUSH)

137

CHAMISE
Adenostoma fasciculatum

Sunset zones 6–9, 14–24
Water needs: little to no water once established
Soil preferences: gravelly, rocky; tolerant of clay or alluvial soil if very well drained
Maintenance: debris cleanup and dead tissue removal; thin summer/fall; intensive pruning required for fire safety

BAKER'S MANZANITA
Arctostaphylos bakeri

Sunset zones 4–9, 14–17
Water needs: none to low
Soil preferences: adaptable, moderately to well drained; tolerant of sand or clay and serpentine

Atriplex canescens

Berberis aquifolium

EASTWOOD MANZANITA
Arctostaphylos glandulosa

Sunset zones 7, 9, 14–24
Water needs: none to low
Soil preferences: well drained, gravelly

ISLAND MANZANITA
Arctostaphylos insularis

Sunset zones 16–24
Water needs: none to low
Soil preferences: adaptable, tolerant of sand or clay

GLOSSY-LEAVED MANZANITA
Arctostaphylos nummularia

Sunset zones 5, 14–17
Water needs: none to low
Soil preferences: deep, high organic content, acidic

PAJARO MANZANITA
Arctostaphylos pajaroensis

Sunset zones 7–9, 14–24
Water needs: none to moderate
Soil preferences: adaptable, sand to clay

WHITELEAF MANZANITA
Arctostaphylos viscida

Sunset zones 1a, 7–16, 18–23
Water needs: none to low
Soil preferences: adaptable; tolerates clay with good drainage; tolerates serpentine

WHITESTEM MILKWEED
Asclepias albicans

Sunset zones 7, 10–13
Water needs: none to moderate
Soil preferences: well drained

BREWER SALTBUSH
Atriplex breweri

Sunset zones 8, 9, 12–24
Water needs: little to no water once established
Soil preferences: adaptable, well drained; high salt tolerance
Maintenance: remove dead or crowded stems annually

SHADSCALE
Atriplex canescens

Sunset zones 1–3, 7–24
Water needs: little to no water once established
Soil preferences: adaptable, well drained; high salt tolerance
Maintenance: remove dead or crowded stems annually

BIG SALTBUSH
Atriplex lentiformis

Sunset zones 1–3, 7–24
Water needs: little to no water once established
Soil preferences: adaptable, well drained; high salt and alkaline tolerance
Maintenance: remove dead or crowded stems as needed

ALLSCALE, CATTLE SALTBUSH
Atriplex polycarpa

Sunset zones 8, 9, 11–22
Water needs: low
Soil preferences: sandy or loamy, does not tolerate clay
Maintenance: remove dead or crowded stems as needed

COYOTE BRUSH
Baccharis pilularis

Sunset zones 5, 7–9, 14–24
Water needs: occasional once established, riparian
Soil preferences: clay, sandy or loamy, but well drained
Maintenance: debris cleanup and dead tissue removal; thin summer/fall; cut back to ground after bloom periodically when dry

MULE FAT
Baccharis salicifolia

Sunset zones 1–10, 16–24, 26
Water needs: little to regular
Soil preferences: loamy, moist
Maintenance: debris cleanup and dead tissue removal; thin summer/fall; cut back to ground after bloom periodically when dry

OREGON GRAPE
Berberis aquifolium, syn. *Mahonia aquifolium*

Sunset zones 2–12, 14–24
Water needs: little to no water once established
Soil preferences: adaptable, well drained
Maintenance: debris cleanup and dead tissue removal; thin summer/fall, or shape in winter after berries gone

LONGLEAF MAHONIA
Berberis nervosa, syn. *Mahonia nervosa*

Sunset zones 2–10, 14–24
Water needs: low
Soil preferences: well drained, acidic
Maintenance: prune after flower, or summer/fall

NEVIN'S BARBERRY
Berberis nevinii, syn. *Mahonia nevinii*

Sunset zones 2b–10, 14–24
Water needs: moderate to regular
Soil preferences: adaptable, prefers coarse and well drained
Maintenance: prune after flowering, or summer/fall

COAST BARBERRY
Berberis pinnata, syn. *Mahonia pinnata*

Sunset zones 4–9, 14–24

Water needs: moderate to regular
Soil preferences: adaptable
Maintenance: prune after flowering, or summer/fall

BUSH ANEMONE
Carpenteria californica

Sunset zones 5–9, 14–24
Water needs: little added water once established
Soil preferences: adaptable
Maintenance: very little debris shed in fall, can be pruned for size and narrow spaces

HOARYLEAF CEANOTHUS
Ceanothus crassifolius

Sunset zones 7–9, 14–24
Water needs: little to no water once established
Soil preferences: well drained, gravelly soils
Maintenance: debris cleanup and dead tissue removal; thin summer/ fall, or shape in winter after berries gone

BUCKBRUSH
Ceanothus cuneatus

Sunset zones 7–9, 14–24
Water needs: little to no water once established
Soil preferences: well drained; tolerates serpentine
Maintenance: debris cleanup and dead tissue removal; thin summer/fall, or shape in winter after berries gone

WAVY LEAVED CEANOTHUS
Ceanothus foliosus

Sunset zones 3, 7, 14–21
Water needs: no water once established
Soil preferences: fast draining
Maintenance: prune late summer to early fall

DEER BRUSH
Ceanothus integerrimus

Sunset zones 1–7, 14–21
Water needs: none to little added water once established
Soil preferences: gravelly, rocky; tolerant of clay or alluvial soil if very well drained
Maintenance: debris cleanup and dead tissue removal; thin summer/fall

CHAPARRAL WHITETHORN
Ceanothus leucodermis

Sunset zones 7, 14–18
Water needs: no added water once established
Soil preferences: fast draining, rocky
Maintenance: prune late summer to early fall

WARTLEAF CEANOTHUS
Ceanothus papillosus

Sunset zones 5, 7, 14–19, 20–24
Water needs: little to regular
Soil preferences: loamy, moist
Maintenance: debris cleanup and dead tissue removal;
thin summer/fall

SNOWBRUSH
Ceanothus velutinus

Sunset zones 1, 2, 6, 7, 15–17
Water needs: low once established
Soil preferences: well drained
Maintenance: seasonal debris cleanup and thinning
summer/fall when dry

WHITE COAST CEANOTHUS
Ceanothus verrucosus

Sunset zones 19–24
Water needs: little to regular
Soil preferences: loamy, moist
Maintenance: debris cleanup and dead tissue removal;
thin summer/fall

SIERRA CHINQUAPIN
Chrysolepis sempervirens

Sunset zones 1–7, 14–17
Water needs: none to occasional once established
Soil preferences: well drained; depending on soil condi-
tions may stay small or grow large
Maintenance: susceptible to sudden oak death; prune
late fall when dry

YELLOW RABBITBRUSH
Chrysothamnus viscidiflorus

Sunset zones 1–3, 10, 11
Water needs: little to no water once established
Soil preferences: well drained
Maintenance: debris cleanup and dead tissue removal;
thin summer/fall

DESERT LAVENDER, BUSHMINT
Condea emoryi, syn. *Hyptis emoryi*

Sunset zones 8–17, 19–24
Water needs: low
Soil preferences: well drained, sandy or gravelly
Maintenance: debris cleanup and dead tissue removal;
thin summer/fall

ISLAND BUSH POPPY
Dendromecon harfordii

Sunset zones 7–9, 14–24
Water needs: little to no added water once established
Soil preferences: well drained
Maintenance: debris cleanup and dead tissue removal;
thin summer/fall; can cut to ground to refresh

BUSH POPPY
Dendromecon rigida

Sunset zones 4–12, 14–24
Water needs: little to no added water once established
Soil preferences: well drained
Maintenance: debris cleanup and dead tissue removal;
thin summer/fall; can cut to ground to refresh

Ceanothus velutinus

Dendromecon rigida

GRAY RABBITBRUSH
Ericameria nauseosa, syn.
Chrysothamnus nauseosus

Sunset zones 1–3, 10, 11
Water needs: little to no water once established
Soil preferences: well drained
Maintenance: debris cleanup and dead tissue removal; thin summer/fall

SANTA CRUZ ISLAND BUCKWHEAT
Eriogonum arborescens

Sunset zones 5, 7–9, 14–24
Water needs: low once established
Soil preferences: well drained
Maintenance: remove dead tissue summer/fall

CALIFORNIA BUCKWHEAT
Eriogonum fasciculatum

Sunset zones 7–9, 12–24
Water needs: low once established
Soil preferences: adaptable, well drained
Maintenance: debris cleanup and dead tissue removal; thin summer/fall; prune oldest stems to ground occasionally

ST. CATHERINE'S LACE
Eriogonum giganteum

Sunset zones 5, 7–9, 14–24
Water needs: little to no water once established
Soil preferences: gravelly, rocky; tolerant of clay or alluvial soil if very well drained
Maintenance: debris cleanup and dead tissue removal; thin summer/fall

SULPHUR BUCKWHEAT
Eriogonum umbellatum

Sunset zones 1–24
Water needs: low once established
Soil preferences: well drained, sandy or gravelly
Maintenance: remove dead tissue summer/fall; prune oldest stems to ground occasionally

DESERT OLIVE
Forestiera neomexicana

Sunset zones 1–3, 7–24
Water needs: little to no water once established
Soil preferences: adaptable, well drained
Maintenance: remove dead or crowded stems annually

COFFEEBERRY
Frangula californica, syn. *Rhamnus californica*

Sunset zones 3a–10, 14–24
Water needs: little to no water once established
Soil preferences: adaptable, well drained
Maintenance: very little debris shed in fall, can be pruned for size and narrow spaces

ISLAND BUSH SNAPDRAGON
Gambelia speciosa, syn. *Galvezia speciosa*

Sunset zones 14–24
Water needs: little to no water once established
Soil preferences: gravelly, rocky; tolerant of clay or alluvial soil if very well drained
Maintenance: debris cleanup and dead tissue removal; thin summer/fall

INTERIOR SILKTASSEL
Garrya congdonii

Sunset zones 7, 14–21
Water needs: low once established
Soil preferences: will tolerate heavy soils if well drained
Maintenance: debris cleanup and dead tissue removal; thin summer/fall

COAST SILKTASSEL
Garrya elliptica

Sunset zones 4–9, 14–24
Water needs: low once established
Soil preferences: adaptable; will tolerate sand but also heavy soils and serpentine
Maintenance: debris cleanup and dead tissue removal; thin summer/fall

141

Frangula californica

ASHY/YELLOWLEAF SILKTASSEL
Garrya flavescens

Sunset zones 7–11; 14–24
Water needs: low once established
Soil preferences: will tolerate heavy soils if well drained
Maintenance: debris cleanup and dead tissue removal; thin summer/fall

FREMONT SILKTASSEL
Garrya fremontii

Sunset zones 1–7, 9, 14–23
Water needs: low once established
Soil preferences: will tolerate heavy soils if well drained
Maintenance: debris cleanup and dead tissue removal; thin summer/fall

CANYON SILKTASSEL
Garrya veatchii

Sunset zones 7, 14–21
Water needs: low once established
Soil preferences: will tolerate heavy soils if well drained
Maintenance: debris cleanup and dead tissue removal; thin summer/fall

SALAL
Gaultheria shallon

Sunset zones 4–7, 14–17, 20–24
Water needs: moderate to regular
Soil preferences: loamy, moist
Maintenance: dead tissue removal; thin or cut back to ground after bloom and periodically

TOYON
Heteromeles arbutifolia

See entry under Medium Evergreen to Semi-Evergreen Trees.

CREOSOTE BUSH
Larrea tridentata

Sunset zones 7–14, 18–23
Water needs: little to no water once established
Soil preferences: well drained, rocky, sandy, or gravelly
Maintenance: debris cleanup and dead tissue removal; thin summer/fall

PITCHER SAGE
Lepechinia calycina, L. fragrans

Sunset zones 7–9, 14–24
Water needs: little to no water once established
Soil preferences: gravelly, rocky; tolerant of clay or alluvial soil if very well drained

CALIFORNIA BOXTHORN
Lycium californicum

Sunset zones 8, 9, 14–17, 19–24
Water needs: little to no water once established
Soil preferences: well drained
Maintenance: debris cleanup and dead tissue removal; thin summer/fall

YELLOW STEM BUSHMALLOW
Malocothamnus densiflorus

Sunset zones 7, 11, 18, 19, 21–24
Water needs: low
Soil preferences: adaptable but well drained
Maintenance: debris cleanup and dead tissue removal; thin summer/fall; can cut back to ground to refresh

CHAPARRAL BUSHMALLOW
Malocothamnus fasciculatus

Sunset zones 7, 11, 14–24
Water needs: low
Soil preferences: adaptable
Maintenance: debris cleanup and dead tissue removal; thin summer/fall; can cut back to ground to refresh

FREMONT'S BUSHMALLOW
Malocothamnus fremontii

Sunset zones 6, 7, 14–24
Water needs: low
Soil preferences: adaptable
Maintenance: debris cleanup and dead tissue removal; thin summer/fall; can cut back to ground to refresh

JONES'S BUSH MALLOW
Malocothamnus jonesii

Sunset zones 7–9, 14–17, 19–24
Water needs: low once established
Soil preferences: well drained, sandy loam
Maintenance: debris cleanup and dead tissue removal; thin summer/fall; can cut back to ground to refresh

SANTA LUCIA BUSH MALLOW
Malocothamnus palmeri

Sunset zones 7–9, 14–24
Water needs: low
Soil preferences: moderately drained, clay
Maintenance: debris cleanup and dead tissue removal; thin summer/fall; can cut back to ground to refresh

Larrea tridentata

LAUREL SUMAC
Malosma laurina, syn. *Rhus laurina*

Sunset zones 14–17, 19–24
Water needs: little to no water once established
Soil preferences: well drained
Maintenance: remove dead or crowded stems annually

PACIFIC WAX MYRTLE
Morella californica, syn. *Myrica californica*

See entry under Medium Evergreen to Semi-Evergreen Trees.

ARROW WEED, ARROWLEAF
Pluchea sericea

Sunset zones 7, 11, 13, 21–24
Water needs: low once established
Soil preferences: adaptable, prefers medium to coarse textured; will tolerate heavy soils if well drained
Maintenance: debris cleanup and dead tissue removal; thin summer/fall

HOLLYLEAF CHERRY
Prunus ilicifolia

See entry under Medium Evergreen to Semi-Evergreen Trees.

LEATHER OAK
Quercus durata

Sunset zones 5, 7–10, 14–24
Water needs: little to no water once established
Soil preferences: well drained
Maintenance: prune in summer

SPINY REDBERRY
Rhamnus crocea

Sunset zones 7, 14–24
Water needs: little to no water once established
Soil preferences: adaptable, well drained
Maintenance: debris cleanup and dead tissue removal; shape in winter after berries gone

COAST RHODODENDRON
Rhododendron macrophyllum,
syn. *Rhododendron californicum*

Sunset zones 4–7; 14–17; 19–24
Water needs: moderate to regular
Soil preferences: rich, well drained, loamy
Maintenance: removal of dead tissues; thin or cut back to ground after bloom periodically

WESTERN AZALEA
Rhododendron occidentale

Sunset zones 3–7; 14–17; 19–24
Water needs: moderate to regular
Soil preferences: rich, well drained, loamy
Maintenance: removal of dead tissues; thin or cut back to ground after bloom periodically

FRAGRANT SUMAC
Rhus aromatica

Sunset zones 1–10, 14–24
Water needs: little to no water once established
Soil preferences: well drained
Maintenance: remove dead or crowded stems annually

LEMONADE BERRY
Rhus integrifolia

Sunset zones 8, 9, 14–17, 19–24
Water needs: little to no water once established
Soil preferences: adaptable, well drained
Maintenance: debris cleanup and dead tissue removal; thin summer/fall, or shape in winter after berries gone

SUGAR BUSH
Rhus ovata

Sunset zones 9–12, 14–24
Water needs: little to no water once established
Soil preferences: adaptable, moderately to well drained
Maintenance: remove dead or crowded stems annually

SKUNKBUSH
Rhus trilobata

Sunset zones 1–12, 14–21
Water needs: little to no water once established
Soil preferences: well drained
Maintenance: remove dead or crowded stems annually

JOJOBA
Simmondsia chinensis

Sunset zones 7–24
Water needs: little to no water once established
Soil preferences: adaptable, well drained
Maintenance: remove dead or crowded stems annually

MISSION MANZANITA
Xylococcus bicolor

See entry under Medium Evergreen to Semi-Evergreen Trees.

WESTERN JOSHUA TREE
Yucca brevifolia

Sunset zones 8–24
Water needs: little to no water once established
Soil preferences: well drained, coarse
Maintenance: remove dead leaves, flower stalks, and stems whenever present; trunks should be kept trimmed, limbed up, and free of adjacent vegetation; do not plant in zones 1 or 2

EASTERN JOSHUA TREE
Yucca jaegeriana

Sunset zones 10–13
Water needs: little to no water once established
Soil preferences: well drained, coarse
Maintenance: remove dead leaves, flower stalks, and stems whenever present; trunks should be kept trimmed, limbed up, and free of adjacent vegetation; do not plant in zones 1 or 2

MOJAVE YUCCA
Yucca schidigera

Sunset zones 2, 3, 7–12, 14–16, 18–24
Water needs: little to no water once established
Soil preferences: well drained, sandy and rocky
Maintenance: remove dead leaves, flower stalks, and stems whenever present; trunks should be kept trimmed, limbed up, and free of adjacent vegetation; do not plant in zones 1 or 2

144

Small Trees / Large Shrubs, Deciduous

These trees and shrubs reach 5 to 15 feel tall at maturity. All prefer sun or part shade.

BAD OR NOXIOUS PLANTS	PLANT INSTEAD
Buddleja davidii (BUTTERFLY BUSH), invasive in riparian areas	*Philadelphus lewisii* (MOCK ORANGE) *Physocarpus capitatus* (PACIFIC NINEBARK) *Ribes sanguineum* (RED-FLOWERING CURRANT) *Sambucus nigra* subsp. *cerulea* (BLUE ELDERBERRY) *Sambucus racemosa* (RED ELDERBERRY)
Calicotome spinosa (THORNY BROOM) *Cytisus multiflorus* (WHITE SPANISH BROOM) *Genista linifolia* (NEEDLE-LEAVED/FLAX BROOM) *Genista monosperma*, syn. *Retama monosperma* (BRIDAL VEIL BROOM); all regenerate vigorously after fire from long-lived seed bank, crowd out other species; seeds toxic to livestock and birds	*Ribes aureum* (GOLDEN CURRANT) *Romneya coulteri* (MATILIJA POPPY)
Corylus avellana (EUROPEAN FILBERT) *Corylus colurna* (TURKISH HAZEL) *Corylus maxima* (LARGE FILBERT), import and sale restricted in Pacific Northwest as these are disease vectors for eastern filbert blight	*Corylus cornuta* var. *californica* (WESTERN HAZELNUT) *Philadelphus lewisii* (MOCK ORANGE) *Ptelea crenulata* (WESTERN HOP TREE)
Ficus carica (EDIBLE FIG)	*Sambucus nigra* subsp. *cerulea* (BLUE ELDERBERRY) *Sambucus racemosa* (RED ELDERBERRY)
Ligustrum sinensis (CHINESE PRIVET); all members of this genus tend to become invasive	*Holodiscus discolor* (OCEAN SPRAY, CREAMBUSH) *Holodiscus dumosus* (MOUNTAIN SPRAY, ROCK-SPIREA) *Styrax redivivus* (CALIFORNIA SNOWDROP)
Lonicera maackii (AMUR HONEYSUCKLE) *Lonicera tartarica* (TARTAR HONEYSUCKLE), invasive in riparian areas and irrigated landscapes	*Calycanthus occidentalis* (SPICE BUSH) *Cephalanthus occidentalis* (BUTTONBUSH) *Diplacus longiflorus* (SOUTHERN BUSH MONKEYFLOWER) *Lonicera conjugialis* (DOUBLE HONEYSUCKLE) *Lonicera subspicata* (SOUTHERN HONEYSUCKLE) *Oemleria cerasiformis* (OSO BERRY, INDIAN PLUM) *Spirea douglasii* (WESTERN SPIREA) *Symphoricarpos albus* (COMMON SNOWBERRY) *Vaccinium parvifolium* (RED HUCKLEBERRY)

BAD OR NOXIOUS PLANTS	PLANT INSTEAD
Sesbania punicea (RED SESBANIA / SCARLET WISTERIA)	*Cercis occidentalis* (WESTERN REDBUD) *Ribes aureum* (GOLDEN CURRANT) *Ribes cereum* (WAX CURRANT) *Ribes viburnifolium* (CATALINA CURRANT) *Sorbus californica* (CALIFORNIA MOUNTAIN ASH) *Sorbus scopulina* (WESTERN MOUNTAIN ASH) *Sorbus sitchensis* (SITKA/WESTERN MOUNTAIN ASH)
Tecoma capensis (CAPE HONEYSUCKLE)	*Ribes sanguineum* (RED-FLOWERING CURRANT) *Ribes speciosum* (FUCHSIA-FLOWERING CURRANT) *Sambucus nigra* subsp. *cerulea* (BLUE ELDERBERRY)
Vitex agnus-castus (CHASTE TREE)	*Amelanchier alnifolia* (WESTERN/PACIFIC SERVICEBERRY, JUNEBERRY, WESTERN SHADBUSH) *Chilopsis linearis* (DESERT WILLOW) *Cornus nuttalii* (WESTERN DOGWOOD) *Robinia neomexicana* (DESERT LOCUST)

POOR PLANTS	PLANT INSTEAD
Rosa (ROSE) varieties with double flowers that have lost pollen and nectar resources	*Ribes aureum* (GOLDEN CURRANT) *Ribes indecorum* (WHITE-FLOWERING CURRANT) *Ribes malvaceum* (CHAPARRAL CURRANT) *Ribes sanguineum* (RED-FLOWERING CURRANT) *Ribes speciosum* (FUCHSIA-FLOWERING CURRANT) *Romneya coulteri* (MATILIJA POPPY)

146

WESTERN/PACIFIC SERVICEBERRY, JUNEBERRY, WESTERN SHADBUSH
Amelanchier alnifolia

See entry under Medium Deciduous Trees.

SPICE BUSH
Calycanthus occidentalis

Sunset zones 4–9, 14–24
Water needs: moderate
Soil preferences: loamy clay
Maintenance: remove suckers and old, dead, or diseased tissues; prune after blooming; cut down to ground every few years to refresh

BUTTONBUSH
Cephalanthus occidentalis

Sunset zones 2–10, 14–21
Water needs: moderate

Soil preferences: loamy clay
Maintenance: remove suckers and old, dead, or diseased tissues; prune after blooming; cut down to ground every few years to refresh

WESTERN REDBUD
Cercis occidentalis

Sunset zones 1–9, 12, 14–24
Water needs: low
Soil preferences: adaptable
Maintenance: remove dead tissues, thin summer/winter; can periodically cut back to ground in winter

DESERT WILLOW
Chilopsis linearis

See entry under Medium Deciduous Trees.

Cephalanthus occidentalis

Holodiscus discolor

WESTERN DOGWOOD
Cornus nuttalii

Sunset zones 3b–9, 14–20
Water needs: little to no water once established
Soil preferences: well drained
Maintenance: debris cleanup and dead tissue removal; thin summer/fall

WESTERN HAZELNUT
Corylus cornuta var. *californica*

Sunset zones 2–7
Water needs: moderate
Soil preferences: loamy, well drained
Maintenance: remove suckers and old, dead, or diseased tissues; prune after blooming

SOUTHERN BUSH MONKEYFLOWER
Diplacus longiflorus

Sunset zones 4–12, 14–24
Water needs: moderate
Soil preferences: loamy clay
Maintenance: remove suckers and old, dead, or diseased tissues; prune after blooming; cut down to ground every few years to refresh

OCEAN SPRAY, CREAMBUSH
Holodiscus discolor

Sunset zones 1–9, 14–24
Water needs: little to regular
Soil preferences: adaptable, well drained; tolerates serpentine
Maintenance: debris cleanup and dead tissue removal; thin summer/fall

MOUNTAIN SPRAY, ROCK-SPIREA
Holodiscus dumosus

Sunset zones 1–3, 10
Water needs: low once established
Soil preferences: adaptable, well drained, neutral to alkaline; tolerates serpentine
Maintenance: debris cleanup and dead tissue removal; thin summer/fall

147

DOUBLE HONEYSUCKLE
Lonicera conjugialis

Sunset zones 1, 2, 4–7, 15, 16
Water needs: moderate to regular
Soil preferences: adaptable
Maintenance: cut back to control size

TWINBERRY
Lonicera involucrata

Sunset zones 5–9, 14–24
Water needs: moderate water once established
Soil preferences: adaptable, well drained
Maintenance: debris cleanup and dead tissue removal; thin summer/fall

SOUTHERN HONEYSUCKLE
Lonicera subspicata

Sunset zones 1–24
Water needs: moderate to regular
Soil preferences: adaptable
Maintenance: cut back to control size

Ribes aureum

Robinia neomexicana

OSO BERRY, INDIAN PLUM
Oemleria cerasiformis

Sunset zones 4–9, 14–24
Water needs: moderate
Soil preferences: loamy clay
Maintenance: remove suckers and old, dead, or diseased tissues; prune after blooming; cut down to ground every few years to refresh

MOCK ORANGE
Philadelphus lewisii

Sunset zones 1–10, 14–24
Water needs: little to occasional added water once established
Soil preferences: well drained
Maintenance: debris cleanup and dead tissue removal; prune after blooming; thin suckers and old, dead, or diseased tissues in winter and spring; can cut to ground every few years to refresh

PACIFIC NINEBARK
Physocarpus capitatus

Sunset zones 2b, 3–9, 14–19
Water needs: little to occasional added water once established
Soil preferences: well drained; tolerant of heavier soils
Maintenance: debris cleanup and dead tissue removal; thin suckers and old, dead, or diseased tissues in winter and spring; can cut to ground every few years to refresh

WESTERN HOP TREE
Ptelea crenulata

Sunset zones 7–9, 14–24
Water needs: occasional deep summer watering once established
Soil preferences: adaptable
Maintenance: fall/winter debris cleanup

GOLDEN CURRANT
Ribes aureum

Sunset zones 1–2, 14–23
Water needs: low to moderate to regular
Soil preferences: adaptable, medium to slow drainage
Maintenance: remove suckers and dead tissues; can cut to ground every few years to refresh

WAX CURRANT
Ribes cereum

Sunset zones 1–7, 14–18
Water needs: low to moderate
Soil preferences: adaptable, well drained
Maintenance: remove dead tissues; thin summer/winter

WHITE-FLOWERING CURRANT
Ribes indecorum

Sunset zones 7–9, 11, 14–24
Water needs: little to occasional water once established
Soil preferences: medium to slow drainage
Maintenance: debris cleanup and dead tissue removal; thin summer/fall

Sorbus scopulina

CHAPARRAL CURRANT
Ribes malvaceum

Sunset zones 6–9, 14–24
Water needs: little to occasional water once established
Soil preferences: well drained
Maintenance: debris cleanup and dead tissue removal; thin summer/fall

RED-FLOWERING CURRANT
Ribes sanguineum

Sunset zones 7–9, 14–24
Water needs: little to occasional water once established
Soil preferences: adaptable, medium drainage
Maintenance: debris cleanup and dead tissue removal; thin winter, prune after blooming; can cut to ground every few years to refresh

FUCHSIA-FLOWERING CURRANT
Ribes speciosum

Sunset zones 7–9, 14–24
Water needs: little to occasional water once established
Soil preferences: adaptable, medium to slow drainage
Maintenance: debris cleanup and dead tissue removal; thin winter, prune after blooming; can cut to ground every few years to refresh

CATALINA CURRANT
Ribes viburnifolium

Sunset zones 5, 7–9, 14–17, 19–24
Water needs: little to no water once established

Soil preferences: adaptable, medium drainage
Maintenance: debris cleanup and dead tissue removal; thin winter; can cut to ground every few years to refresh

DESERT LOCUST
Robinia neomexicana

Sunset zones 1–3, 7–11, 14–24
Water needs: low to occasional water once established
Soil preferences: adaptable
Maintenance: remove dead tissues; thin summer/winter

MATILIJA POPPY
Romneya coulteri

Sunset zones 4–12, 14–24
Water needs: little to occasional water once established
Soil preferences: well drained
Maintenance: debris cleanup and dead tissue removal; thin summer/fall

BLUE ELDERBERRY
Sambucus nigra subsp. *cerulea*

Sunset zones 2–24
Water needs: little to occasional water once established
Soil preferences: loamy clay with medium to fast drainage
Maintenance: debris cleanup and dead tissue removal; thin winter; can cut to ground every few years to refresh

RED ELDERBERRY
Sambucus racemosa

Sunset zones 1–6
Water needs: moderate to high once established
Soil preferences: loamy sand and silt with good drainage
Maintenance: debris cleanup and dead tissue removal; thin winter; can cut to ground every few years to refresh

CALIFORNIA MOUNTAIN ASH
Sorbus californica

Sunset zones 1, 2, 4–7, 15, 16
Water needs: occasional to regular
Soil preferences: sandy or loamy
Maintenance: remove dead tissues; thin summer/winter

WESTERN MOUNTAIN ASH
Sorbus scopulina

Sunset zones 1, 2, 4–7, 15–17
Water needs: moderate
Soil preferences: sandy or loamy
Maintenance: remove dead tissues; thin summer/winter

SITKA/WESTERN MOUNTAIN ASH
Sorbus sitchensis

Sunset zones 1, 2, 4–7, 15–17
Water needs: moderate
Soil preferences: sandy or loamy, well drained
Maintenance: remove dead tissues; thin summer/winter

WESTERN SPIREA
Spirea douglasii

Sunset zones 1–9, 14–24
Water needs: moderate
Soil preferences: loamy clay
Maintenance: remove suckers and old, dead, or diseased tissues; prune after blooming; cut down to ground every few years to refresh

CALIFORNIA SNOWDROP
Styrax redivivus

Sunset zones 6–10, 14–24 (best in 14–16, 18–24)
Water needs: low to regular
Soil preferences: loamy, well drained, nonalkaline
Maintenance: debris cleanup and dead tissue removal; thin winter

COMMON SNOWBERRY
Symphoricarpos albus

Sunset zones 1–11, 14–21
Water needs: moderate
Soil preferences: loamy clay
Maintenance: remove suckers and old, dead, or diseased tissues; prune after blooming; cut down to ground every few years to refresh

RED HUCKLEBERRY
Vaccinium parvifolium

Sunset zones 2–7, 14–17
Water needs: moderate
Soil preferences: loamy clay
Maintenance: remove suckers and old, dead, or diseased tissues; prune after blooming; cut down to ground every few years to refresh

Low Shrubs

These shrubs generally reach less than 5 feel tall at maturity. All prefer sun or part shade.

BAD OR NOXIOUS PLANTS	PLANT INSTEAD
Calicotome spinosa (THORNY BROOM) *Cytisus multiflorus* (WHITE SPANISH BROOM) *Genista linifolia* (NEEDLE-LEAVED / FLAX BROOM) *Genista monosperma*, syn. *Retama monosperma* (BRIDAL VEIL BROOM), regenerate vigorously after fire from long-lived seed bank, crowd out other species; seeds toxic to livestock and birds	*Cneoridium dumosum* (BUSH RUE) *Dasiphora fruticosa*, syn. *Potentilla fruticosa* (SHRUBBY CINQUEFOIL) *Diplacus aurantiacus*, syn. *Mimulus aurantiacus* (STICKY MONKEY FLOWER) *Encelia actoni* (MOUNTAIN BUSH SUNFLOWER) *Encelia californica* (CALIFORNIA BRITTLEBUSH) *Encelia farinosa* (BRITTLEBUSH) *Encelia frutescens* (BUTTON BRITTLEBUSH) *Keckiella antirrhinoides*, *K. cordifolia* (KECKIELLA) *Peritoma arborea*, syn. *Isomeris arborea* (BLADDERPOD)
Cistus monspeliensis (MONTPELIER ROCKROSE)	*Arctostaphylos cruzensis* (ARROYO DE LA CRUZ MANZANITA), *A. densiflora* (VINE HILL MANZANITA), and others *Ceanothus cordulatus* (MOUNTAIN WHITETHORN) *Ceanothus lemmonii* (LEMMON'S CEANOTHUS) *Gambelia speciosa*, syn. *Galvezia speciosa* (ISLAND BUSH SNAPDRAGON) *Justicia californica* (CHUPAROSA) *Rosa nutkana* (NOOTKA ROSE) *Sphaeralcea ambigua* (DESERT MALLOW)
Daphne laureola (SPURGE LAUREL) (*Daphne odora*, WINTER DAPHNE, is not at all invasive)	*Arctostaphylos edmundsii* (LITTLE SUR MANZANITA), *A. pumila* (SANDMAT MANZANITA), *A. uva ursi* (KINNICKINNICK), and several named varieties *Eriogonum grande* var. *rubescens*, syn. *Eriogonum rubescens* (RED-FLOWERED BUCKWHEAT, SAN MIGUEL ISLAND BUCKWHEAT) *Kalmiopsis leachiana* (KALMIOPSIS) *Leucothoe davisiae* (SIERRA LAUREL) *Paxistima myrsinites* (OREGON BOXWOOD) *Symphoricarpos mollis* (CREEPING SNOWBERRY)
Echium candicans (PRIDE OF MADEIRA)	*Lupinus albifrons* (SILVER BUSH LUPINE) *Salvia apiana* (WHITE SAGE) *Salvia clevelandii* (CLEVELAND SAGE) *Salvia mellifera* (BLACK SAGE) *Scutellaria mexicana* (MEXICAN BLADDERSAGE) *Sidalcea malviflora* (CHECKERBLOOM)

BAD OR NOXIOUS PLANTS	PLANT INSTEAD
Echium candicans (PRIDE OF MADEIRA), Cont.	*Sphaeralcea ambigua* (DESERT GLOBEMALLOW)
	Thamnosma montana (TURPENTINE BROOM)
	Trichostema lanatum (WOOLLY BLUE CURLS)
Perovskia atriplicifolia × *P. abrotanoides* (RUSSIAN SAGE)	*Atriplex confertifolia* (SHADSCALE)
Salvia aethiopsis (MEDITERRANEAN SAGE)	*Atriplex hymenelytra* (DESERT HOLLY)
Salvia pratensis, S. sclarea (CLARY SAGE)	*Atriplex lentiformis* (BIG SALTBUSH)
	Atriplex parryi (PARRY'S SALTBUSH)
	Ceanothus divergens (CALISTOGA CEANOTHUS)
	Ceanothus maritimus (MARITIME CEANOTHUS)
	Eriogonum fasciculatum (CALIFORNIA BUCKWHEAT)
	Fallugia paradoxa (CPACHE PLUME)
	Ruellia californica (WILD PETUNIA)
	Salvia brandegeei (BRANDEGEE SAGE, SANTA ROSA ISLAND SAGE)
	Salvia apiana (WHITE SAGE)
	Salvia clevelandii (CLEVELAND SAGE)
	Salvia dorrii (DESERT SAGE)
	Salvia leucophylla (PURPLE SAGE)
	Solanum xanti (PURPLE NIGHTSHADE)
Rubus armeniacus (HIMALAYAN BLACKBERRY)	*Berberis repens,* syn. *Mahonia repens* (CREEPING MAHONIA)
	Cornus sericea (RED TWIG DOGWOOD)
	Lonicera involucrata (TWINBERRY)
	Lonicera utahensis (RED TWINBERRY)
	Rubus laciniatus, R. leucodermis, R. ursinus (NATIVE BLACKBERRIES AND RASPBERRIES)
	Rubus parviflorus (THIMBLEBERRY)
	Spirea densiflora (MOUNTAIN SPIREA)
	Symphoricarpos albus (SNOWBERRY)

POOR PLANTS	PLANT INSTEAD
Euryops acraeus, E. pectinatus (AFRICAN BUSH DAISY, EURYOPS), may not attract native bees but only honeybees and flies; more research needed	*Eriogonum cinereum* (ASHYLEAF BUCKWHEAT)
	Eriogonum crocatum (SAFFRON BUCKWHEAT)
	Eriogonum fasciculatum (CALIFORNIA BUCKWHEAT)
	Eriogonum wrightii (WRIGHT'S BUCKWHEAT)
	Lupinus arboreus (YELLOW BUSH LUPINE)

ARROYO DE LA CRUZ MANZANITA
Arctostaphylos cruzensis

Sunset zones 23–24
Water needs: low
Soil preferences: adaptable, sandy but tolerates clay; tolerates saline soils
Maintenance: debris cleanup and dead tissue removal; thin after flowering when dry

VINE HILL MANZANITA
Arctostaphylos densiflora

Sunset zones 7–9, 14–21
Water needs: low
Soil preferences: adaptable, prefers loan
Maintenance: debris cleanup and dead tissue removal; thin after flowering when dry

LITTLE SUR MANZANITA
Arctostaphylos edmundsii

Sunset zones 6–9, 14–24
Water needs: low
Soil preferences: sandy but tolerates clay
Maintenance: debris cleanup and dead tissue removal; thin after flowering when dry

SANDMAT MANZANITA
Arctostaphylos pumila

Sunset zones 16–17
Water needs: low, adapted to coastal fog; with moderate water will get larger than normal
Soil preferences: sandy but tolerates clay; tolerates saline soils
Maintenance: debris cleanup and dead tissue removal; thin after flowering when dry

KINNICKINNICK
Arctostaphylos uva-ursi

Sunset zones 1, 4–7, 14–17, 19–24
Water needs: low
Soil preferences: rocky/sandy but tolerates clay and serpentine
Maintenance: debris cleanup and dead tissue removal; thin after flowering when dry

SHADSCALE
Atriplex confertifolia

Sunset zones 1a, 2b, 8, 9, 11, 13
Water needs: low
Soil preferences: adaptable, well drained
Maintenance: debris cleanup and dead tissue removal; thin summer/fall

Arctostaphylos uva-ursi

DESERT HOLLY
Atriplex hymenelytra

Sunset zones 7–13
Water needs: low
Soil preferences: adaptable, well drained
Maintenance: debris cleanup and dead tissue removal; thin summer/fall

PARRY'S SALTBUSH
Atriplex parryi

Sunset zones 7–9, 11–14
Water needs: low
Soil preferences: adaptable, well drained
Maintenance: debris cleanup and dead tissue removal; thin summer/fall

CREEPING MAHONIA
Berberis repens, syn. *Mahonia repens*

Sunset zones 2b–9, 14–24
Water needs: little to no water once established
Soil preferences: adaptable
Maintenance: very little debris shed

MOUNTAIN WHITETHORN
Ceanothus cordulatus

Sunset zones 1–3, 6, 7, 14–18
Water needs: low
Soil preferences: well drained, sandy or loamy; does not tolerate clay
Maintenance: remove dead tissues and fruiting heads

CALISTOGA CEANOTHUS
Ceanothus divergens

Sunset zones 14–17
Water needs: low
Soil preferences: well drained, rocky
Maintenance: remove dead tissues and fruiting heads

Cornus sericea

Encelia californica

LEMMON'S CEANOTHUS
Ceanothus lemmonii

Sunset zones 7, 14–17
Water needs: low once established
Soil preferences: adaptable
Maintenance: debris cleanup and dead tissue removal; thin summer/fall

MARITIME CEANOTHUS
Ceanothus maritimus

Sunset zones 5–9, 14–24
Water needs: low once established
Soil preferences: well drained
Maintenance: remove dead tissues and fruiting heads

BUSH RUE
Cneoridium dumosum

Sunset zones 8, 9, 14–24
Water needs: low once established
Soil preferences: well drained
Maintenance: remove dead tissues and fruiting heads

RED TWIG DOGWOOD
Cornus sericea

Sunset zones 1–7
Water needs: moderate to regular
Soil preferences: adaptable
Maintenance: prune after flowering, or summer/fall

SHRUBBY CINQUEFOIL
Dasiphora fruticosa, syn. *Potentilla fruticosa*

Sunset zones 1–11, 14–21
Water needs: low once established
Soil preferences: well drained
Maintenance: remove dead tissues and fruiting heads

STICKY MONKEY FLOWER
Diplacus aurantiacus, syn.
Mimulus aurantiacus

Sunset zones 4–9, 14–24
Water needs: none once established
Soil preferences: adaptable
Maintenance: cut back to ground in late fall

MOUNTAIN BUSH SUNFLOWER
Encelia actoni

Sunset zones 7–24
Water needs: low once established
Soil preferences: well drained
Maintenance: remove dead tissues and fruiting heads

CALIFORNIA BRITTLEBUSH
Encelia californica

Sunset zones 7–12, 14–24
Water needs: low once established
Soil preferences: well drained
Maintenance: remove dead tissues and fruiting heads

BRITTLEBUSH
Encelia farinosa

Sunset zones 8–24
Water needs: low once established
Soil preferences: well drained
Maintenance: remove dead tissues and fruiting heads

BUTTON BRITTLEBUSH
Encelia frutescens

Sunset zones 7–24
Water needs: low once established
Soil preferences: well drained
Maintenance: remove dead tissues and fruiting heads

Eriogonum cinereum

Fallugia paradoxa

ASHYLEAF BUCKWHEAT
Eriogonum cinereum

Sunset zones 5, 14–17, 19–24
Water needs: low once established
Soil preferences: well drained
Maintenance: remove dead tissues summer/fall; prune oldest stems to ground occasionally

SAFFRON BUCKWHEAT
Eriogonum crocatum

Sunset zones 14–24
Water needs: low once established
Soil preferences: well drained
Maintenance: remove dead tissues summer/fall

CALIFORNIA BUCKWHEAT
Eriogonum fasciculatum

See entry under Small Trees / Large Shrubs, Evergreen.

SAN MIGUEL ISLAND BUCKWHEAT
Eriogonum grande var. *rubescens,*
syn. *Eriogonum rubescens*

Sunset zones 5, 14–24
Water needs: low once established
Soil preferences: slow drainage, rocky, yet tolerant of clay and alkaline
Maintenance: remove dead tissues, fruiting heads summer/fall; prune oldest stems to ground occasionally

WRIGHT'S BUCKWHEAT
Eriogonum wrightii

Sunset zones 7–11, 14–24
Water needs: low once established
Soil preferences: well drained, sandy or loamy but no clay
Maintenance: remove dead tissues summer/fall; prune oldest stems to ground occasionally

APACHE PLUME
Fallugia paradoxa

Sunset zones 2–23
Water needs: low once established
Soil preferences: adaptable, well drained
Maintenance: debris cleanup and dead tissue removal; thin summer/fall

ISLAND BUSH SNAPDRAGON
Gambelia speciosa, syn. *Galvezia speciosa*

See entry under Small Trees / Large Shrubs, Evergreen.

CHUPAROSA
Justicia californica

Sunset zones 12–14, 18–24
Water needs: low once established
Soil preferences: adaptable
Maintenance: debris cleanup and dead tissue removal; thin summer/fall

KALMIOPSIS
Kalmiopsis leachiana

Sunset zones 4–6, 14–17
Water needs: moderate
Soil preferences: loamy, well drained
Maintenance: remove dead tissues, fruiting heads summer/fall; prune oldest stems to ground occasionally

KECKIELLA
Keckiella antirrhinoides, K. cordifolia

Sunset zones 4–6, 14–17
Water needs: moderate
Soil preferences: loamy, well drained
Maintenance: remove dead tissues, fruiting heads summer/fall; prune oldest stems to ground occasionally

Lupinus albifrons

Rubus parviflorus

SIERRA LAUREL
Leucothoe davisiae

Sunset zones 2, 4–7, 15–17
Water needs: moderate
Soil preferences: loamy, well drained
Maintenance: remove dead tissues, fruiting heads summer/fall; prune oldest stems to ground occasionally

TWINBERRY
Lonicera involucrata

See entry under Small Trees / Large Shrubs, Deciduous.

RED TWINBERRY
Lonicera utahensis

Sunset zones 1–3
Water needs: moderate to regular
Soil preferences: adaptable
Maintenance: prune after fruiting, or summer/fall; prune oldest stems to ground

SILVER BUSH LUPINE
Lupinus albifrons

Sunset zones 5–9, 14–24
Water needs: low once established
Soil preferences: well drained
Maintenance: remove dead tissues and fruiting heads summer/fall

YELLOW BUSH LUPINE
Lupinus arboreus

Sunset zones 4, 5, 14–17, 19–24
Water needs: low once established
Soil preferences: well drained
Maintenance: remove dead tissue summer/fall

OREGON BOXWOOD
Paxistima myrsinites, syn. *Paxistima myrtifolia*

Sunset zones 2–7, 15–16
Water needs: moderate
Soil preferences: well drained
Maintenance: remove dead tissues

BLADDERPOD
Peritoma arborea, syn. *Isomeris arborea*

Sunset zones 8–9, 12–17, 19–24
Water needs: little to no water once established
Soil preferences: fast draining, neutral to basic; tolerates saline soil
Maintenance: debris cleanup and dead tissue removal; thin summer/fall

NOOTKA ROSE
Rosa nutkana

Sunset zones 1–11, 14–21
Water needs: low once established
Soil preferences: adaptable
Maintenance: debris cleanup and dead tissue removal; thin summer/fall; can cut to ground to refresh

Salvia clevelandii

NATIVE BLACKBERRIES AND RASPBERRIES
Rubus laciniatus, R. leucodermis, R. ursinus

Sunset zones 1–9, 14–24
Water needs: moderate to regular
Soil preferences: adaptable
Maintenance: prune after flowering, or summer/fall

THIMBLEBERRY
Rubus parviflorus

Sunset zones 1–2, 4–7, 14–18
Water needs: moderate to regular
Soil preferences: adaptable
Maintenance: prune after flowering, or summer/fall; remove old canes

WILD PETUNIA
Ruellia californica

Sunset zones 12, 13
Water needs: low once established
Soil preferences: adaptable, well drained
Maintenance: debris cleanup and dead tissue removal; thin summer/fall

WHITE SAGE
Salvia apiana

Sunset zones 7, 9, 11, 13–24
Water needs: little to no water once established
Soil preferences: adaptable, well drained
Maintenance: remove dead or crowded stems annually

BRANDEGEE SAGE, SANTA ROSA ISLAND SAGE
Salvia brandegeei

Sunset zones 15–17, 19–24
Water needs: low once established
Soil preferences: adaptable, well drained
Maintenance: debris cleanup and dead tissue removal; thin summer/fall

CLEVELAND SAGE
Salvia clevelandii

Sunset zones 8, 9, 12–24
Water needs: little to no water once established
Soil preferences: well drained
Maintenance: debris cleanup and dead tissue removal; thin summer/fall; remove dead or crowded stems annually

DESERT SAGE
Salvia dorrii

Sunset zones 2, 3, 10–13, 18, 19
Water needs: low once established
Soil preferences: adaptable, well drained
Maintenance: debris cleanup and dead tissue removal; thin summer/fall

PURPLE SAGE
Salvia leucophylla

Sunset zones 8, 9, 14–17, 19–24
Water needs: low once established
Soil preferences: adaptable, well drained
Maintenance: debris cleanup and dead tissue removal; thin summer/fall

BLACK SAGE
Salvia mellifera

Sunset zones 7–9, 14–24
Water needs: low once established
Soil preferences: well drained
Maintenance: remove dead tissues and fruiting heads summer/fall

MEXICAN BLADDERSAGE
Scutellaria mexicana

Sunset zones 7–23
Water needs: low once established
Soil preferences: well drained
Maintenance: remove dead tissues and fruiting heads summer/fall

CHECKERBLOOM
Sidalcea malviflora

Sunset zones 2–9, 14–24
Water needs: low once established
Soil preferences: well drained
Maintenance: remove dead tissues and fruiting heads summer/fall

PURPLE NIGHTSHADE
Solanum xanti

Sunset zones 7–9, 11, 14–24
Water needs: low once established
Soil preferences: adaptable, well drained
Maintenance: debris cleanup and dead tissue removal; thin summer/fall

DESERT GLOBEMALLOW
Sphaeralcea ambigua

Sunset zones 3, 7–24
Water needs: low once established
Soil preferences: well drained
Maintenance: remove dead tissues and fruiting heads summer/fall; can cut to ground to refresh

MOUNTAIN SPIREA
Spirea densiflora

Sunset zones 1–9, 14–21
Water needs: moderate to regular
Soil preferences: adaptable
Maintenance: prune after flowering, or summer/fall; can cut to ground to refresh

COMMON SNOWBERRY
Symphoricarpos albus

See entry under Small Trees / Large Shrubs, Deciduous.

CREEPING SNOWBERRY
Symphoricarpos mollis

Sunset zones 1–11, 14–21
Water needs: moderate
Soil preferences: loamy, well drained
Maintenance: remove dead tissues, fruiting heads summer/fall; can prune to ground to refresh

TURPENTINE BROOM
Thamnosma montana

Sunset zones 7–24
Water needs: low once established
Soil preferences: well drained
Maintenance: remove dead tissues and fruiting heads summer/fall

WOOLLY BLUE CURLS
Trichostema lanatum

Sunset zones 14–24
Water needs: low once established
Soil preferences: well drained
Maintenance: remove dead tissues and fruiting heads summer/fall

Perennial Forbs

Perennial forbs are herbaceous plants (meaning they do not have stems that persist aboveground through the winter) other than grasses. These perennial forbs prefer sun or part shade. Woodland forbs prefer shade. Maintenance is the same for all perennial forbs: remove dead tissues summer/fall.

BAD OR NOXIOUS PLANTS	PLANT INSTEAD
Acaena novae-zelandiae (BIDDY-BIDDY)	*Acaena pinnatifida* (CALIFORNIA SHEEP BURR)
Arctotheca calendula (CAPEWEED) *Gazania linearis* (GAZANIA)	*Balsamorhiza sagittata* (ARROWLEAF BALSAMROOT) *Rudbeckia californica* (CALIFORNIA CONE FLOWER) *Wyethia amplexicaulis* (NORTHERN MULE'S EARS) *Wyethia angustifolia* (NARROWLEAF MULE'S EARS) *Wyethia glabra* (SHINING MULE'S EARS) *Wyethia longicaulis* (HUMBOLDT COUNTY WYETHIA) *Wyethia mollis* (WOOLLY MULE'S EARS) *Wyethia ovata* (SOUTHERN MULE'S EARS)
Asparagus densiflorus (ASPARAGUS FERN)	*Achillea millefolium* (YARROW) *Lomatium utriculatum* (COMMON LOMATIUM)
Atriplex semibaccata (AUSTRALIAN SALTBUSH)	*Atriplex watsonii* (MATSCALE)
Cynara cardunculus ssp. *flavescens* (CARDOON) *Cynara cardunculus* ssp. *scolymus* (ARTICHOKE) *Foeniculum vulgare* (FENNEL) *Tetragonia teragonioides* (NEW ZEALAND SPINACH) *Torilis arvensis* (HEDGEPARSLEY)	*Balsamorhiza deltoidea* (DELTOID BALSAMROOT), *B. sagittata* (ARROW-LEAVED BALSAMROOT), and others *Perideridia californica* (YAMPAH), *P. montana* (MOUNTAIN YAMPAH), and others *Salvia spathacea* (HUMMINGBIRD SAGE) *Wyethia* species
Cynoglossum officinale (COMMON HOUNDSTONGUE)	*Adelinia grandis*, syn. *Cynoglossum grande* (WESTERN HOUNDSTONGUE) *Solanum xanti* (PURPLE NIGHTSHADE)
Dicentra eximia (FRINGED BLEEDING HEART), hybridizes with western bleeding heart	*Aquilegia formosa* (WESTERN COLUMBINE) *Dicentra formosa* (WESTERN BLEEDING HEART)
Digitalis purpurea (FOXGLOVE)	*Campanula rotundifolia* (BLUEBELL BELLFLOWER) *Campanula scabrella* (ROUGH BELLFLOWER) *Chamerion angustifolium* (FIREWEED) *Delphinium glaucum* (GLAUCUS LARKSPUR, SIERRA LARKSPUR), *D. menziesii* (MENZIES' LARKSPUR), *D. trolliofolium* (COLUMBIAN LARKSPUR), and others *Lepechinia fragrans* (PITCHER SAGE) *Lupinus polyphyllus* (BIGLEAF LUPINE)

BAD OR NOXIOUS PLANTS	PLANT INSTEAD
Digitalis purpurea (FOXGLOVE), Cont.	*Penstemon heterophyllus* (FOOTHILL PENSTEMON) *Phacelia californica* (ROCK PHACELIA) *Sidalcea oregana* (OREGON CHECKERMALLOW) and others
Euphorbia oblongata (OBLONG SPURGE)	*Asclepias fascicularis* (NARROWLEAF MILKWEED) *Epilobium canum,* syn. *Zauschneria canum* (CALIFORNIA FUCHSIA) *Grindelia nana* (IDAHO GUMPLANT) and others *Solidago canadensis, S. velutina* (GOLDENROD)
Helichrysum petiolare (LICORICE PLANT) *Leucanthemum vulgare* (MARGUERITE, OX-EYE DAISY) *Tanacetum parthenium* (FEVERFEW) *Tussilago farfara* (COLTSFOOT)	*Achillea millefolium* (YARROW) *Anaphalis margaritacea* (PEARLY EVERLASTING) *Eurybia radulina,* syn. *Aster radulinus* (ROUGHLEAF ASTER) *Helianthella californica* (CALIFORNIA HELIANTHELLA) *Grindelia nana* (PUGET SOUND GUMWEED) *Heterotheca sessiliflora* (FALSE GOLDENASTER) *Symphiotrichum chilense* (PACIFIC/CALIFORNIA ASTER) *Symphyotrichum foliaceum* (LEAFY ASTER) *Symphyotrichum hallii* (HALL'S ASTER) *Symphyotrichum subspicatum* (DOUGLAS' ASTER) *Thymophylla pentachaeta,* syn. *Dyssodia pentachaeta* (GOLDEN DYSSODIA) *Viguiera deltoidea,* syn. *Viguiera parishii* (GOLDENEYE) *Viguiera multiflora* (MULTIFLOWERED GOLDENEYE) *Wyethia helenoides* (WHITE MULE'S EARS)
Heuchera sanguinea (RED ALUM ROOT) hybridizes easily	*Heuchera maxima* (ISLAND ALUM ROOT) *Heuchera micrantha* (SMALL-FLOWERED ALUM ROOT) *Thalictrum fenderli* (MEADOW RUE) *Tiarella trifoliata* var. *unifoliata* (FOAMFLOWER) *Tolmiea menziesii* (PIGGYBACK PLANT)
Knotweeds: *Fallopia sachalinensis,* syn. *Polygonum sachalinense* (GIANT KNOTWEED) *Persicaria wallichii,* syn. *Polygonum polystachyum* (HIMALAYAN KNOTWEED) *Reynoutria japonica,* syn. *Fallopia japonica, Polygonum cuspidatum* (JAPANESE KNOTWEED) *Reynoutria ×bohemica,* syn. *Polygonum ×bohemicum* (BOHEMIAN KNOTWEED)	*Aralia californica* (ELK CLOVER) *Aruncus dioicus* (GOAT'S BEARD)
Lantana camara (LARGELEAF LANTANA)	*Epilobium canum,* syn. *Zauschneria canum* (CALIFORNIA FUCHSIA) *Mirabilis laevis,* syn. *Mirabilis californica* (CALIFORNIA FOUR O'CLOCK)

BAD OR NOXIOUS PLANTS	PLANT INSTEAD
Lantana camara (LARGELEAF LANTANA), Cont.	*Prunella vulgaris* subsp. *lanceolata* (SELFHEAL) *Sidalcea malviflora* (CHECKERBLOOM) and others
Lathyrus latifolius (PERENNIAL PEAVINE) *Trifolium hirtum* (ROSE CLOVER)	*Acmispon glaber*, syn. *Lotus scoparius* (DEERWEED) *Corethrogyne filaginifolia* (CALIFORNIA ASTER) *Prunella vulgaris* subsp. *lanceolata* (SELFHEAL) *Trifolium wormskioldii* (COW'S CLOVER) *Viola beckwithii* (GREAT BASIN VIOLET)
Lepidium latifolium (PERENNIAL PEPPERWEED)	*Iva hayesiana* (SAN DIEGO MARSH ELDER, POVERTY WEED) *Solidago lepida* (WESTERN GOLDENROD) *Solidago spathulata* (COAST GOLDENROD) *Solidago velutina* subsp. *californica* (CALIFORNIA GOLDENROD)
Limonium ramosissimum (STATICE, SEA LAVENDER)	*Linum lewisii* (BLUE FLAX) *Lupinus polyphyllus* (BIGLEAF LUPINE) *Penstemon centranthifolius* (SCARLET BUGLER) *Penstemon davidsonii* (DAVIDSON'S PENSTEMON) *Penstemon heterophyllus* (FOOTHILL PENSTEMON) *Penstemon newberryi* (MOUNTAIN PRIDE) *Penstemon pseudospectabilis* (DESERT BEARD PENSTEMON) *Penstemon richardsonii* (RICHARDSON'S PENSTEMON) *Penstemon rupicola* (ROCK PENSTEMON) *Penstemon rydbergii* (RYDBERG'S PENSTEMON) *Penstemon spectabilis* (ROYAL BEARDSTONGUE) *Prunella vulgaris* subsp. *lanceolata* (SELFHEAL)
Linaria dalmatica (DALMATIAN TOADFLAX) *Linaria vulgaris* (YELLOW TOADFLAX)	*Asclepias fascicularis* (NARROWLEAF MILKWEED) *Delphinium cardinale* (SCARLET LARKSPUR) *Delphinium nudicaule* (RED LARKSPUR) *Dicentra chrysantha* (GOLDEN EARDROPS) *Lupinus polyphyllus* (BIGLEAF LUPINE) *Mentzelia laevicaulis* (BLAZING STAR) *Viola adunca* (WESTERN DOG VIOLET)
Lobularia maritima (SWEET ALYSSUM)	*Tellima grandiflora* (FRINGE CUPS)
Myosotis latifolia (FORGET-ME-NOT)	*Dodecatheon* species (SHOOTING STAR) native to your area *Maianthemum dilatatum* (FALSE LILY-OF-THE-VALLEY) *Maianthemum racemosa* (FALSE SOLOMON'S SEAL) *Myosotis asiatica* (ALPINE FORGET-ME-NOT)

161

BAD OR NOXIOUS PLANTS	PLANT INSTEAD
Myosotis latifolia (FORGET-ME-NOT), Cont.	*Sisyrinchium bellum* (WESTERN BLUE-EYED GRASS) *Viola adunca* (WESTERN DOG VIOLET)
Oxalis pes-caprae (AFRICAN WOOD-SORREL, BUTTERCUP OXALIS, SOURGRASS)	*Aquilegia eximia* (SERPENTINE COLUMBINE) *Aquilegia formosa* (WESTERN COLUMBINE) *Oxalis californica* (CALIFORNIA WOOD SORREL) *Oxalis oregana* (REDWOOD SORREL) *Viola bakeri* (BAKER'S VIOLET) *Viola douglasii* (DOUGLAS' VIOLET) *Viola pedunculata* (JOHNNY JUMP UP) *Viola purpurea* (MOUNTAIN VIOLET) *Viola sempervirens* (REDWOOD VIOLET)
Salvia aethiopis (MEDITERRANEAN SAGE)	*Monardella australis*, syn. *Monardella odoratissima* (DESERT MINT) *Monardella macrantha* (RED MONARDELLA) *Monardella villosa* (COYOTE MINT) *Salvia spathacea* (HUMMINGBIRD SAGE)
Verbena bonariensis (TALL VERBENA)	*Monardella purpurea* (SISKIYOU MONARDELLA) *Monardella villosa* (COYOTE MINT) *Pycnanthemum californicum* (MOUNTAIN MINT) *Sanicula bipinnatifida* (SNAKEROOT)
Weedy mustards, grasses, and thistles	*Asclepias albicans* (WHITESTEM MILKWEED) *Asclepias asperula* (SPIDER MILKWEED) *Asclepias erosa* (DESERT MILKWEED) *Asclepias linaria* (PINE NEEDLE MILKWEED) *Asclepias nyctaginifolia* (MOJAVE MILKWEED) *Asclepias subulata* (RUSH/SKELETON MILKWEED, AJAMETE) *Asclepias vestita* (WOOLLY MILKWEED)

POOR PLANTS	PLANT INSTEAD
Asclepias curassavica (TROPICAL MILKWEED), may be harmful to monarch butterflies	*Asclepias californica* (CALIFORNIA MILKWEED) *Asclepias eriocarpa* (KOTOLO MILKWEED) *Asclepias speciosa* (SHOWY MILKWEED) *Silene californica* (CALIFORNIA INDIAN PINK) *Silene laciniata* (CARDINAL CATCHFLY)
Chrysanthemum ×morifolium (HARDY GARDEN MUMS)	*Achillea millefolium* (YARROW) *Bahiopsis parishii*, syn. *Viguiera deltoidea* (GOLDENEYE) *Calylophus hartwegii, C. drummondianus* (SUNDROPS) *Grindelia stricta* (GUMWEED) *Heterotheca sessiliflora* (FALSE GOLDENASTER)

POOR PLANTS	PLANT INSTEAD
Chrysanthemum ×morifolium (HARDY GARDEN MUMS), Cont.	*Symphiotrichum* (ASTER) species *Venegasia carpesioides* (CANYON SUNFLOWER) *Viguiera multiflora* (MULTIFLOWERED GOLDENEYE) *Wyethia glabra* (SHINING MULE'S EARS) *Wyethia mollis* (WOOLLY MULE'S EARS)
Dianthus species, doubled carnations and sweet Williams	*Achillea millefolium* (YARROW) *Sidalcea* (CHECKERMALLOW) species *Symphiotrichum* (ASTER) species
Dietes bicolor, D. grandiflora, D. iridioides, and hybrids (FORTNIGHT LILY, AFRICAN IRIS) *Phormium cookianum, P. tenax,* and hybrids (PHORMIUM), many of these are invasive	*Epilobium canum,* syn. *Zauschneria canum* (CALIFORNIA FUCHSIA) *Hesperoyucca whipplei* (CHAPARRAL YUCCA) *Iris macrosiphon* (LONG TUBED IRIS)
Gomphocarpus physocarpus, syn. *Asclepias physocarpus* (HAIRY BALLS, BALLOONPLANT), may be harmful to monarch butterflies, but more research needed	*Asclepias californica* (CALIFORNIA MILKWEED) *Asclepias cordifolia* (HEART LEAF MILKWEED) *Asclepias cryptoceras* (PALLID MILKWEED) *Asclepias eriocarpa* (KOTOLO MILKWEED) *Asclepias speciosa* (SHOWY MILKWEED)
Paeonia lactiflora (CHINESE PEONIES), doubled hybrids	*Paeonia brownii* (WESTERN PEONY) *Paeonia californica* (CALIFORNIA PEONY) *Sidalcea campestris* (MEADOW CHECKERMALLOW)

CALIFORNIA SHEEP BURR
Acaena pinnatifida

Sunset zones 4, 5, 14–18, 19–24
Water needs: low once established
Soil preferences: good drainage

YARROW
Achillea millefolium

Sunset zones 1–24
Water needs: low once established
Soil preferences: adaptable, well drained

DEERWEED
Acmispon glaber, syn. *Lotus scoparius*

Sunset zones 7–9, 14–24
Water needs: none to moderate
Soil preferences: adaptable

WESTERN HOUNDSTONGUE
Adelinia grandis, syn. *Cynoglossum grande*

Sunset zones 4–9, 14–24
Water needs: low once established
Soil preferences: good drainage

Anaphalis margaritacea

Asclepias erosa

Balsamorhiza sagittata

PEARLY EVERLASTING
Anaphalis margaritacea

Sunset zones 1–11, 14–24
Water needs: low once established
Soil preferences: adaptable, well drained

SERPENTINE COLUMBINE
Aquilegia eximia

Sunset zones 4–7, 14–24
Water needs: moderate
Soil preferences: loamy

WESTERN COLUMBINE
Aquilegia formosa

Sunset zones 1–9, 14–24
Water needs: moderate
Soil preferences: loamy

ELK CLOVER
Aralia californica

Sunset zones 4–10, 14–24
Water needs: little to moderate once established
Soil preferences: loamy

GOAT'S BEARD
Aruncus dioicus

Sunset zones 1–9, 14–17
Water needs: little to moderate once established
Soil preferences: loamy

SPIDER MILKWEED
Asclepias asperula

Sunset zone 2a and likely other warm desert areas
Water needs: none to moderate once established
Soil preferences: well drained

CALIFORNIA MILKWEED
Asclepias californica

Sunset zones 6–9, 14–24
Water needs: none to moderate once established
Soil preferences: well drained

HEART LEAF MILKWEED
Asclepias cordifolia

Sunset zones 14–24
Water needs: none to moderate once established
Soil preferences: well drained

PALLID MILKWEED
Asclepias cryptoceras

Sunset zone 1a and likely other warm desert areas
Water needs: none to moderate once established
Soil preferences: well drained

KOTOLO MILKWEED
Asclepias eriocarpa

Sunset zones 7–10, 14–24
Water needs: none to moderate once established
Soil preferences: well drained

DESERT MILKWEED
Asclepias erosa

Sunset zones 10–13 and likely other warm desert areas
Water needs: none to moderate once established
Soil preferences: well drained

NARROWLEAF MILKWEED
Asclepias fascicularis

Sunset zones 3, 7–10, 14–24
Water needs: none to moderate once established
Soil preferences: adaptable; tolerates saline soil

MOJAVE MILKWEED
Asclepias nyctaginifolia

Sunset zones 10–13
Water needs: none to moderate once established
Soil preferences: well drained

SHOWY MILKWEED
Asclepias speciosa

Sunset zones 1–10, 14–24
Water needs: none to moderate once established
Soil preferences: well drained
Note: May contain levels of cardenilids that are too toxic for monarch larvae.

RUSH/SKELETON MILKWEED, AJAMETE
Asclepias subulata

Sunset zones 7, 10–13
Water needs: none to moderate once established
Soil preferences: well drained

WOOLLY MILKWEED
Asclepias vestita

Sunset zones 19–24
Water needs: none to moderate once established
Soil preferences: well drained

MATSCALE
Atriplex watsonii

Sunset zones 22–24
Water needs: variable, low to high
Soil preferences: sandy, saline soils; tolerant of high boron and high pH

GOLDENEYE
Bahiopsis parishii, syn. *Viguiera deltoidea*

Sunset zones 10–24
Water needs: low once established
Soil preferences: well drained

DELTOID BALSAMROOT
Balsamorhiza deltoidea
ARROWLEAF BALSAMROOT
Balsamorhiza sagittata

Sunset zones 1–24
Water needs: low once established
Soil preferences: adaptable

BLUEBELL BELLFLOWER
Campanula rotundifolia
ROUGH BELLFLOWER
Campanula scabrella

Sunset zones 1–10, 14–24
Water needs: moderate
Soil preferences: loamy

FIREWEED
Chamerion angustifolium

Sunset zones 7–24
Water needs: low once established
Soil preferences: loamy, well-drained

CALIFORNIA ASTER
Corethrogyne filaginifolia

Sunset zones 7–9, 14–24
Water needs: none to moderate
Soil preferences: adaptable

SCARLET LARKSPUR
Delphinium cardinale

Sunset zones 7, 14–23
Water needs: low once established
Soil preferences: well drained

GLAUCUS LARKSPUR, SIERRA LARKSPUR
Delphinium glaucum

Sunset zones 1–7
Water needs: low once established
Soil preferences: well drained

MENZIES' LARKSPUR
Delphinium menziesii

Sunset zones 4–6
Water needs: moderate moisture
Soil preferences: loamy

Dicentra formosa

Epilobium canum

RED LARKSPUR
Delphinium nudicaule

Sunset zones 5–7, 14–17
Water needs: low once established
Soil preferences: well drained

COLUMBIAN LARKSPUR
Delphinium trolliofolium

Sunset zones 4–6, 16, 17
Water needs: moderate moisture
Soil preferences: loamy

GOLDEN EARDROPS
Dicentra chrysantha

Sunset zones 1–9, 14–24
Water needs: low once established
Soil preferences: well drained

WESTERN BLEEDING HEART
Dicentra formosa

Sunset zones 1–9, 14–24
Water needs: moderate
Soil preferences: loamy

SHOOTING STAR
Dodecatheon species native to your area

Sunset zones 7–9, 14–24
Water needs: moderate
Soil preferences: loamy, well drained

HUMMINGBIRD FUCHSIA
Epilobium californica, syn. *Zauschneria californica*

Sunset zones 2–11, 14–24

Water needs: low once established
Soil preferences: loamy, well-drained

CALIFORNIA FUCHSIA
Epilobium canum, syn. *Zauschneria canum*

Sunset zones 2–11, 14–24
Water needs: low once established
Soil preferences: adaptable; tolerates clay, sand, serpentine

ROUGHLEAF ASTER
Eurybia radulina, syn. *Aster radulinus*

Sunset zones 1–10, 14–24
Water needs: low once established
Soil preferences: adaptable

IDAHO GUMPLANT
Grindelia nana

Sunset zones 1a, 10–11
Water needs: low once established
Soil preferences: adaptable

GUMWEED
Grindelia stricta

Sunset zones 4–8, 14–24
Water needs: adaptable
Soil preferences: well drained

CALIFORNIA HELIANTHELLA
Helianthella californica

Sunset zones 14–24
Water needs: low once established
Soil preferences: well drained

Heuchera maxima

Linum lewisii

CHAPARRAL YUCCA
Hesperoyucca whipplei

Sunset zones 1–3, 7–12, 14–24
Water needs: low once established
Soil preferences: well drained

FALSE GOLDENASTER
Heterotheca sessiliflora

Sunset zones 8–24
Water needs: low once established
Soil preferences: well drained

ISLAND ALUM ROOT
Heuchera maxima

Sunset zones 15–24
Water needs: moderate
Soil preferences: loamy

SMALL-FLOWERED ALUM ROOT
Heuchera micrantha

Sunset zones 1–10, 14–24
Water needs: moderate
Soil preferences: loamy

LONG TUBED IRIS
Iris macrosiphon

Sunset zones 6–9, 14–18
Water needs: seasonally damp, tolerates low water in summer
Soil preferences: loamy, medium drainage

SAN DIEGO MARSH ELDER, POVERTY WEED
Iva hayesiana

Sunset zones 20–24
Water needs: moderate
Soil preferences: adaptable; tolerates alkaline and saline conditions

PITCHER SAGE
Lepechinia fragrans

Sunset zones 7–9, 14–24
Water needs: low once established
Soil preferences: loamy, well drained

BLUE FLAX
Linum lewisii

Sunset zones 1–9, 14–24
Water needs: low once established
Soil preferences: well drained

COMMON LOMATIUM
Lomatium utriculatum

Sunset zones 1–24
Water needs: low once established
Soil preferences: well drained

BIGLEAF LUPINE
Lupinus polyphyllus

Sunset zones 3–7, 14–21
Water needs: little to no water once established
Soil preferences: well drained

FALSE LILY-OF-THE-VALLEY
Maianthemum dilatatum

Sunset zones 2–9, 14–17
Water needs: moderate
Soil preferences: loamy, well drained

FALSE SOLOMON'S SEAL
Maianthemum racemosa

Sunset zones 1–7, 14–17
Water needs: moderate
Soil preferences: loamy, well drained

BLAZING STAR
Mentzelia laevicaulis

Sunset zones 1–3, 7–9, 14–24
Water needs: low once established
Soil preferences: well drained

CALIFORNIA FOUR O'CLOCK
Mirabilis laevis, syn. *Mirabilis californica*

Sunset zones 8, 9, 14–24
Water needs: low once established
Soil preferences: well drained

DESERT MINT
Monardella australis, syn. *Monardella odoratissima*

Sunset zones 1–3, 7–10, 14–24
Water needs: low once established
Soil preferences: well drained

RED MONARDELLA
Monardella macrantha

Sunset zones 7–9, 14–24

Mirabilis laevis

Water needs: low once established
Soil preferences: well drained

SISKIYOU MONARDELLA
Monardella purpurea

Sunset zones 6–9, 14–18
Water needs: little to no water once established
Soil preferences: rocky, gravelly, well drained

COYOTE MINT
Monardella villosa

Sunset zones 7–9, 14–24
Water needs: little to no water once established
Soil preferences: rocky, gravelly, well drained

ALPINE FORGET-ME-NOT
Myosotis asiatica

Sunset zones 1–24
Water needs: moderate
Soil preferences: loamy, well drained

CALIFORNIA WOOD SORREL
Oxalis californica

Sunset zones 21–24
Water needs: moderate
Soil preferences: loamy

REDWOOD SORREL
Oxalis oregana

Sunset zones 4–9, 14–17, 19–24
Water needs: moderate
Soil preferences: loamy

WESTERN PEONY
Paeonia brownii

Sunset zones 1–2, 7
Water needs: low
Soil preferences: well drained

CALIFORNIA PEONY
Paeonia californica

Sunset zones 7, 9, 14–24
Water needs: low
Soil preferences: well drained

SCARLET BUGLER
Penstemon centranthifolius

Sunset zones 7–23
Water needs: low once established
Soil preferences: well drained

DAVIDSON'S PENSTEMON
Penstemon davidsonii

Sunset zones 1–7, 14–15
Water needs: low once established
Soil preferences: well drained

FOOTHILL PENSTEMON
Penstemon heterophyllus

Sunset zones 7–24
Water needs: low once established
Soil preferences: well drained

MOUNTAIN PRIDE
Penstemon newberryi

Sunset zones 1–9, 14–19
Water needs: low once established
Soil preferences: well drained

DESERT BEARD PENSTEMON
Penstemon pseudospectabilis

Sunset zones 2, 3, 10, 12–21
Water needs: low once established
Soil preferences: well drained

RICHARDSON'S PENSTEMON
Penstemon richardsonii

Sunset zones 2–10, 14–21
Water needs: low once established
Soil preferences: well drained

ROCK PENSTEMON
Penstemon rupicola

Sunset zones 2–7, 14–17
Water needs: low once established
Soil preferences: well drained

RYDBERG'S PENSTEMON
Penstemon rydbergii

Sunset zones 1–7, 14–16
Water needs: low once established
Soil preferences: well drained

ROYAL BEARDSTONGUE
Penstemon spectabilis

Sunset zones 7, 14–23
Water needs: low once established
Soil preferences: well drained

Penstemon newberryi

YAMPAH
Perideridia californica, P. gairdneri

Sunset zones 7, 14–24
Water needs: seasonally wet to moderate
Soil preferences: adaptable

MOUNTAIN YAMPAH
Perideridia montana

Sunset zones 1a, 2a, 2b, 3a
Water needs: seasonally wet
Soil preferences: adaptable

ROCK PHACELIA
Phacelia californica

Sunset zones 7, 14–17
Water needs: low once established
Soil preferences: loamy, well drained

SELFHEAL
Prunella vulgaris subsp. *lanceolata*

Sunset zones 2–24
Water needs: low once established
Soil preferences: well drained

MOUNTAIN MINT
Pycnanthemum californicum

Sunset zones 1, 4–9, 14–24
Water needs: little to no water once established
Soil preferences: rocky, gravelly, well drained

CALIFORNIA CONE FLOWER
Rudbeckia californica

Sunset zones 1–10, 14–19
Water needs: low once established
Soil preferences: adaptable

HUMMINGBIRD SAGE
Salvia spathacea

Sunset zones 5, 7–9, 14–24
Water needs: low once established
Soil preferences: well drained

SNAKEROOT
Sanicula bipinnatifida

Sunset zones 4–9, 14–24
Water needs: none to little
Soil preferences: rocky, gravelly, well drained

CHECKER BLOOM
Sidalcea malviflora

Sunset zones 4–9, 14–24
Water needs: seasonal moisture, low during summer
Soil preferences: adaptable, well drained; tolerates serpentine

OREGON CHECKERMALLOW
Sidalcea oregana

Sunset zones 1–16
Water needs: regular moisture
Soil preferences: sandy, loamy

CARDINAL CATCHFLY
Silene laciniata

Sunset zones 7, 14–17, 19–24
Water needs: low once established
Soil preferences: well drained, prefers sandy

WESTERN BLUE-EYED GRASS
Sisyrinchium bellum

Sunset zones 3–11, 14–24
Water needs: seasonal once established
Soil preferences: loamy
Note: *this is actually an iris*

PURPLE NIGHTSHADE
Solanum xanti

See entry under Low Shrubs.

WESTERN GOLDENROD
Solidago lepida

Sunset zones 1–24
Water needs: moderate
Soil preferences: adaptable

COAST GOLDENROD
Solidago spathulata

Sunset zones 5, 14–17, 19–24
Water needs: moderate
Soil preferences: adaptable

CALIFORNIA GOLDENROD
Solidago velutina subsp. *californica*

Sunset zones 1–9, 14–23
Water needs: moderate
Soil preferences: adaptable

PACIFIC/CALIFORNIA ASTER
Symphiotrichum chilense

Sunset zones 1–11, 14–24
Water needs: low once established
Soil preferences: well drained

LEAFY ASTER
Symphyotrichum foliaceum

Sunset zones 1–10, 20–24
Water needs: low once established
Soil preferences: well drained

DOUGLAS' ASTER
Symphyotrichum subs*picatum*

Sunset zones 1–10, 20–24
Water needs: low once established
Soil preferences: well drained

FRINGE CUPS
Tellima grandiflora

Sunset zones 2–9, 14–24
Water needs: moderate
Soil preferences: loamy

MEADOW RUE
Thalictrum fenderli

Sunset zones 1–9, 14–24
Water needs: moderate
Soil preferences: loamy

GOLDEN DYSSODIA
Thymophylla pentachaeta, syn.
Dyssodia pentachaeta

Sunset zones 8–14, 18–23
Water needs: little to moderate
Soil preferences: adaptable, well drained

FOAMFLOWER
Tiarella trifoliata var. *unifoliata*

Sunset zones 1–7, 14–17
Water needs: moderate
Soil preferences: loamy

PIGGYBACK PLANT
Tolmiea menziesii

Sunset zones 4–9, 14–17, 20–24
Water needs: moderate
Soil preferences: loamy

COW'S CLOVER
Trifolium wormskioldii

Sunset zones 1–9, 14–17
Water needs: none to moderate
Soil preferences: adaptable

CANYON SUNFLOWER
Venegasia carpesioides

Sunset zones 14–17, 19–24
Water needs: low once established
Soil preferences: well drained

GOLDENEYE
Viguiera deltoidea, syn. *Viguiera parishii*

Sunset zones 10–24
Water needs: low once established
Soil preferences: adaptable to well drained

MULTIFLOWERED GOLDENEYE
Viguiera multiflora

Sunset zones 2, 3, 10–13
Water needs: low once established
Soil preferences: adaptable to well drained

WESTERN DOG VIOLET
Viola adunca

Sunset zones 1–7, 14–24
Water needs: moderate
Soil preferences: loamy, well drained

Tellima grandiflora

BAKER'S VIOLET
Viola bakeri

Sunset zones 1–7, 15–17
Water needs: moderate
Soil preferences: loamy

GREAT BASIN VIOLET
Viola beckwithii

Sunset zones 1–3, 6, 7, 15–18
Water needs: low
Soil preferences: adaptable

DOUGLAS' VIOLET
Viola douglasii

Sunset zones 1–3, 7–9
Water needs: moderate
Soil preferences: loamy

Wyethia mollis

JOHNNY JUMP UP
Viola pedunculata

Sunset zones 5, 7–9, 15–24
Water needs: moderate
Soil preferences: loamy

MOUNTAIN VIOLET
Viola purpurea

Sunset zones 1–9, 14–24
Water needs: moderate
Soil preferences: adaptable

REDWOOD VIOLET
Viola sempervirens

Sunset zones 4–6, 14–17, 24
Water needs: moderate
Soil preferences: loamy

NORTHERN MULE'S EARS
Wyethia amplexicaulis

Sunset zones 1, 4–9, 14–24
Water needs: low to moderate once established
Soil preferences: adaptable

NARROWLEAF MULE'S EARS
Wyethia angustifolia

Sunset zones 1, 4–9, 14–24
Water needs: low to moderate once established
Soil preferences: adaptable

SHINING MULE'S EARS
Wyethia glabra

Sunset zones 4–9, 14–24
Water needs: low to moderate once established
Soil preferences: adaptable

WHITE MULE'S EARS
Wyethia helenoides

Sunset zones 7–9, 14–17, 19–24
Water needs: low to moderate once established
Soil preferences: adaptable

HUMBOLDT COUNTY WYETHIA
Wyethia longicaulis

Sunset zones 1–7, 14
Water needs: low to moderate once established
Soil preferences: adaptable

WOOLLY MULE'S EARS
Wyethia mollis

Sunset zones 1–7
Water needs: low to moderate once established
Soil preferences: adaptable

SOUTHERN MULE'S EARS
Wyethia ovata

Sunset zones 7–11, 21–23
Water needs: low to moderate once established
Soil preferences: adaptable

Annuals and Biennials

These plants prefer sun or part shade. Grassland species prefer full sun, while woodland species prefer some shade. Maintenance is the same for all annuals and biennials: rake up after plants go to seed and dry.

BAD OR NOXIOUS PLANTS	PLANT INSTEAD
Adonis aestivalis (PHEASANT'S EYE)	*Clarkia amoena* (FAREWELL TO SPRING) *Clarkia concinna* (RED RIBBONS) *Clarkia rubicunda* (RUBY CHALICE) *Clarkia speciosa* (RED-SPOTTED CLARKIA) *Clarkia unguiculata* (ELEGANT CLARKIA) *Clarkia williamsonii* (FORT MILLER CLARKIA)
Chrysanthemum coronarium (ANNUAL CROWN DAISY)	*Eschscholzia caespitosa* (SUNCUPS) *Eschscholzia californica* (CALIFORNIA POPPY) *Layia platyglossa* (COMMON TIDYTIPS)
Echium plantagineum (PATERSON'S CURSE)	*Argemone corymbosa* (MOJAVE PRICKLY POPPY) *Argemone munita* (CHICALOTE) *Clarkia gracilis* (SLENDER CLARKIA) *Gilia capitata* (GLOBE GILIA) *Gilia tricolor* (BIRD'S-EYES) *Ipomopsis rubra*, syn. *Gilia rubra* (SCARLET GILIA) *Lupinus nanus* (SKY LUPINE) *Phacelia campanularia* (CALIFORNIA BLUEBELL)
Impatiens glandulifera (POLICEMAN'S HELMET)	*Clarkia* species *Gilia* species *Phacelia tanacetifolia* (LACY PHACELIA)
Misopates orontium, syn. *Antirrhinum orontium* (LESSER SNAPDRAGON)	*Abronia villosa* (HAIRY SAND VERBENA) *Antirrhinum multiflorum* (WITHERED SNAPDRAGON) and others *Clarkia amoena* (FAREWELL TO SPRING) *Clarkia gracilis* (SLENDER CLARKIA) *Collomia grandiflora* (LARGE-FLOWERED COLLOMIA) *Linanthus grandiflorus* (LARGEFLOWER PHLOX) *Lupinus nanus* (SKY LUPINE) *Lupinus succulentus* (SUCCULENT LUPINE) and others
Oenothera glazioviana (RED SEPAL EVENING PRIMROSE)	*Clarkia bottae* (PUNCH BOWL GODETIA) *Clarkia breweri* (FAIRY FANS) *Clarkia purpurea* (WINECUP CLARKIA) *Eschscholzia caespitosa* (SUNCUPS) *Eschscholzia californica* (CALIFORNIA POPPY) *Oenothera elata* (HOOKER'S EVENING PRIMROSE)

173

BAD OR NOXIOUS PLANTS	PLANT INSTEAD
Oncosiphon pilulifer (GLOBE CHAMOMILE)	*Eschscholzia caespitosa* (SUNCUPS) *Eschscholzia californica* (CALIFORNIA POPPY) *Kallstroemia californica* (CALIFORNIA CALTROP) *Leptosyne calliopsidea*, syn. *Coreopsis calliopsidea* (LEAFSTEM TICKSEED)

POOR PLANTS	PLANT INSTEAD
Geranium lucidum (SHINING GERANIUM) and others	*Collinsia herophylla*, syn. *Collinsia bicolor* (PURPLE CHINESE HOUSES) *Gilia tricolor* (BIRD'S-EYES) *Nemophila maculata* (FIVESPOT) *Nemophila menziesii* (BABY BLUE EYES) *Trifolium wildenovii* (TOMCAT CLOVER) and others
Helianthus annuus (ANNUAL SUNFLOWER), pollenless varieties	*Eschscholzia caespitosa* (SUNCUPS) *Eschscholzia californica* (CALIFORNIA POPPY) *Helianthus annuus* (ANNUAL SUNFLOWER) and others *Lupinus luteolus* (PALE YELLOW LUPINE)
Impatiens hawkeri (NEW GUINEA IMPATIENS) hybrids *Petunia*, most hybrids	*Collinsia heterophylla*, syn. *Collinsia bicolor* (PURPLE CHINESE HOUSES) *Lupinus microcarpus* (CHICK LUPINE, DENSE-FLOWERED PLATYCARPOS) and others *Nemophila maculata* (FIVESPOT) *Nemophila menziesii* (BABY BLUE EYES) *Trifolium albopurpureum* (RANCHERIA CLOVER) *Trifolium ciliolatum* (FOOTHILL CLOVER)
Tagetes erecta (AFRICAN MARIGOLD)	*Layia platyglossa* (COMMON TIDYTIPS) *Trifolium fucatum* (SOUR CLOVER) and others

174

HAIRY SAND VERBENA
Abronia villosa

Sunset zones 11–24
Water needs: low once established
Soil preferences: well drained

WITHERED SNAPDRAGON
Antirrhinum multiflorum

Sunset zones 7–10, 14–24, vary by species
Water needs: low once established
Soil preferences: well drained, rocky

MOJAVE PRICKLY POPPY
Argemone corymbosa

Sunset zones 1a, 7, 11, 13, 18–22
Water needs: low once established
Soil preferences: well drained, sandy

CHICALOTE
Argemone munita

Sunset zones 1–3, 7–11, 14–24
Water needs: low once established
Soil preferences: well drained

Abronia villosa

Clarkia amoena

FAREWELL TO SPRING
Clarkia amoena

Sunset zones 1–9, 14–24
Water needs: low once established
Soil preferences: well drained

PUNCH BOWL GODETIA
Clarkia bottae

Sunset zones 6–9, 14–24
Water needs: low once established
Soil preferences: well drained

FAIRY FANS
Clarkia breweri

Sunset zones 7–9, 14–17, 19–24
Water needs: low once established
Soil preferences: well drained

RED RIBBONS
Clarkia concinna

Sunset zones 7–9, 14–17, 19–24
Water needs: low once established
Soil preferences: well drained

SLENDER CLARKIA
Clarkia gracilis

Sunset zones 1–9, 14–24
Water needs: low
Soil preferences: well drained

WINECUP CLARKIA
Clarkia purpurea
RUBY CHALICE
Clarkia rubicunda

Sunset zones 7–9, 14–17, 22–24
Water needs: low
Soil preferences: well drained

RED-SPOTTED CLARKIA
Clarkia speciosa
ELEGANT CLARKIA
Clarkia unguiculata

Sunset zones 1–9, 14–24
Water needs: low
Soil preferences: well drained

FORT MILLER CLARKIA
Clarkia williamsonii

Sunset zones 1–3, 6, 7, 14–24
Water needs: low once established
Soil preferences: well drained

PURPLE CHINESE HOUSES
Collinsia heterophylla, syn. *Collinsia bicolor*

Sunset zones 1–24
Water needs: moderate
Soil preferences: well drained

Collomia grandiflora

Eschscholzia caespitosa

Gilia capitata

Helianthus annuus

LARGE-FLOWERED COLLOMIA
Collomia grandiflora

Sunset zones 1–10, 14–24
Water needs: low once established
Soil preferences: well drained

SUNCUPS
Eschscholzia caespitosa

Sunset zones 2, 3, 7–24
Water needs: low once established
Soil preferences: well drained

CALIFORNIA POPPY
Eschscholzia californica

Sunset zones 2, 3, 7–24
Water needs: low once established
Soil preferences: well drained

GLOBE GILIA
Gilia capitata
BIRD'S-EYES
Gilia tricolor

Sunset zones 1–24
Water needs: low once established
Soil preferences: well drained

ANNUAL SUNFLOWER
Helianthus annuus

Sunset zones 1–24
Water needs: low once established
Soil preferences: well drained

Layia platyglossa

Nemophila menziesii

SCARLET GILIA
Ipomopsis rubra, syn. *Gilia rubra*

Sunset zones 1–24
Water needs: low once established
Soil preferences: well drained

CALIFORNIA CALTROP
Kallstroemia californica

Sunset zones 20–23
Water needs: low once established
Soil preferences: well drained

COMMON TIDYTIPS
Layia platyglossa

Sunset zones 1–10, 14–24
Water needs: low once established
Soil preferences: well drained

BIGELOW'S TICKSEED
Leptosyne begelovii, syn. *Coreopsis begelovii*

Sunset zones 7–16, 18–24
Water needs: little or no water
Soil preferences: adaptable

LEAFSTEM TICKSEED
Leptosyne calliopsidea,
syn. *Coreopsis calliopsidea*

Sunset zones 7–24
Water needs: little or no water
Soil preferences: well drained

LARGEFLOWER PHLOX
Linanthus grandiflorus

Sunset zones 4–9, 14–24
Water needs: low once established
Soil preferences: well drained

PALE YELLOW LUPINE
Lupinus luteolus

Sunset zones 1–24
Water needs: none to moderate
Soil preferences: adaptable

DENSE-FLOWERED PLATYCARPOS
Lupinus microcarpus

Sunset zones 1–24
Water needs: none to moderate
Soil preferences: adaptable

SKY LUPINE
Lupinus nanus

Sunset zones 3–24
Water needs: none needed except in desert
Soil preferences: well drained

SUCCULENT LUPINE
Lupinus succulentus

Sunset zones 7–12, 14–24
Water needs: none needed except in desert
Soil preferences: medium to slow drainage; best in
moist clay

FIVESPOT
Nemophila maculata

Sunset zones 1–9, 12–24
Water needs: moderate
Soil preferences: well drained

Phacelia campanularia

BABY BLUE EYES
Nemophila menziesii

Sunset zones 1–24
Water needs: moderate
Soil preferences: well drained

CALIFORNIA BLUEBELL
Phacelia campanularia

Sunset zones 1–3, 7–24
Water needs: little or no water
Soil preferences: sandy, gravelly

LACY PHACELIA
Phacelia tanacetifolia

Sunset zones 7–24
Water needs: low water once established
Soil preferences: well drained

RANCHERIA CLOVER
Trifolium albopurpureum

Sunset zones 1–3, 5–9, 14–24

Water needs: moderate
Soil preferences: well drained

FOOTHILL CLOVER
Trifolium ciliolatum

Sunset zones 5–9, 14–24
Water needs: moderate
Soil preferences: well drained

SOUR CLOVER
Trifolium fucatum

Sunset zones 5–9, 14–24
Water needs: low once established
Soil preferences: well drained

TOMCAT CLOVER
Trifolium wildenovii

Sunset zones 1–9, 14–24
Water needs: moderate
Soil preferences: well drained

High Perennial Grasses and Sedges

These plants reach more than 3 feet tall and prefer sun or part shade. (Beach species prefer full sun.) Maintenance is the same for all: remove dead leaves and cut stalks after seed shed in the summer. Many more native species can be used in addition to those listed.

BAD OR NOXIOUS PLANTS	PLANT INSTEAD
Ammophila arenaria (EUROPEAN BEACH GRASS) *Ammophila breviligulata* (AMERICAN BEACH GRASS) *Ampelodesmos mauritanicus* (MAURITANIAN GRASS)	*Calamagrostis nutkaensis* (PACIFIC REEDGRASS) *Carex spissa* (SAN DIEGO SEDGE) *Eleocharis macrostachya* (COMMON SPIKERUSH) *Elymus mollis* (AMERICAN DUNEGRASS) *Juncus acutus* (SPINY RUSH) *Schoenoplectus californicus* (CALIFORNIA BULRUSH)
Andropogon virginicus (BROOMSEDGE)	*Melica californica* (CALIFORNIA MELICGRASS) *Sporobolus airoides* (ALKALI SACATON) *Stipa pulchra* (PURPLE NEEDLEGRASS) and others
Arundo donax (GIANT REED)	*Salix* (WILLOW) species native to your area, like *S. exigua* (SANDBAR WILLOW)
Cenchrus ciliaris, syn. *Pennisetum ciliare* (BUFFEL GRASS) *Pennisetum clandestinum* (KIKUYU GRASS) *Pennisetum setaceum* (CRIMSON FOUNTAINGRASS)	*Carex spissa* (SAN DIEGO SEDGE) *Melica subulata* (ALASKA ONION GRASS) *Muhlenbergia emersleyi* (BULL GRASS) *Muhlenbergia lindheimeri* (LINDHEIMER'S MUHLY GRASS)
Cortaderia jubata (PURPLE PAMPAS GRASS) *Cortaderia selloana* (PAMPAS GRASS) *Ehrharta calycina, E. erecta* (VELDT GRASSES) *Miscanthus sinensis* (CHINESE SILVERGRASS) *Phalaris arundinacea* (REED CANARY GRASS)	*Carex spissa* (SAN DIEGO SEDGE) *Elymus condensatus,* syn. *Leymus condensatus* (GIANT WILD RYE) *Elymus mollis,* syn. *Leymus mollis* (AMERICAN DUNEGRASS) *Festuca californica* (CALIFORNIA FESCUE) *Muhlenbergia rigens* (DEER GRASS) *Nolina bigelovii* (BIGELOW'S BEARGRASS) *Xerophyllum tenax* (BEAR GRASS, INDIAN BASKET GRASS)

179

Festuca californica

Muhlenbergia rigens

PACIFIC REEDGRASS
Calamagrostis nutkaensis

Sunset zones 4–9, 14–17, 19–24
Water needs: standing water
Soil preferences: adaptable

SAN DIEGO SEDGE
Carex spissa

Sunset zones 7–9, 14–17, 19–24
Water needs: none to seasonal once established
Soil preferences: adaptable, slow draining; tolerates serpentine

COMMON SPIKERUSH
Eleocharis macrostachya

Sunset zones 1–24
Water needs: regular to flooded, freshwater to brackish
Soil preferences: slow draining to standing water

GIANT WILD RYE
Elymus condensatus, syn. *Leymus condensatus*

Sunset zones 7–12, 14–24
Water needs: none to seasonal once established
Soil preferences: adaptable

AMERICAN DUNEGRASS
Elymus mollis, syn. *Leymus mollis*

Sunset zones 1–24

Water needs: regular to flooded, freshwater to brackish
Soil preferences: adaptable, fast draining sand to standing water

CALIFORNIA FESCUE
Festuca californica

Sunset zones 17–24
Water needs: seasonal once established
Soil preferences: adaptable

SPINY RUSH
Juncus acutus

Sunset zones 13, 23, 24
Water needs: moderate to high
Soil preferences: slow draining

CALIFORNIA MELICGRASS
Melica californica

Sunset zones 2, 3, 5, 7–9, 14–24
Water needs: seasonal to low once established
Soil preferences: adaptable

ALASKA ONION GRASS
Melica subulata

Sunset zones 1–24
Water needs: seasonal to low once established
Soil preferences: adaptable

Xerophyllum tenax

BULL GRASS
Muhlenbergia emersleyi

Sunset zones 6–24
Water needs: none to seasonal once established
Soil preferences: loamy or clay

LINDHEIMER'S MUHLY GRASS
Muhlenbergia lindheimeri

Sunset zones 6–24
Water needs: none to seasonal once established
Soil preferences: loamy or clay

DEER GRASS
Muhlenbergia rigens

Sunset zones 1–3, 7–11, 14–24
Water needs: seasonal once established
Soil preferences: adaptable

BIGELOW'S BEARGRASS
Nolina bigelovii

Sunset zones 2, 3, 7–16, 18–24
Water needs: low
Soil preferences: adaptable

WILLOW
Salix species native to your area

Sunset zones 1–24

Water needs: moderate water or shallow groundwater
Soil preferences: riparian habitats

CALIFORNIA BULRUSH
Schoenoplectus californicus

Sunset zones 9–24
Water needs: regular to flooded, freshwater to brackish marshes
Soil preferences: slow draining to standing

ALKALI SACATON
Sporobolus airoides

Sunset zones 1–24
Water needs: none to seasonal once established
Soil preferences: loam or clay

PURPLE NEEDLEGRASS
Stipa pulchra

Sunset zones 5–9, 11, 14–24
Water needs: none to seasonal once established
Soil preferences: loam or clay

BEAR GRASS, INDIAN BASKET GRASS
Xerophyllum tenax

Sunset zones 1–7, 14–17
Water needs: none to seasonal once established
Soil preferences: adaptable

Low Perennial Grasses, Sedges, and Rushes

These plants stay under 3 feet tall and prefer sun or part shade. Maintenance is the same for all: remove dead leaves and cut stalks after seed shed in the summer, or simply mow once after seed shed. Many more native species can be used in addition to those listed.

BAD OR NOXIOUS PLANTS	PLANT INSTEAD
Agrostis avenacea (PACIFIC /NEW ZEALAND BENT GRASS) *Anthoxanthum odoratum* (SWEET VERNAL GRASS) *Eragrostis curvula* (WEEPING LOVEGRASS)	*Eragrostis hypnoides* (TEAL LOVEGRASS) *Eragrostis mexicana* (MEXICAN LOVEGRASS) *Hierochloe occidentalis,* syn. *Anthoxanthum occidentale* (WESTERN SWEETGRASS)
Festuca arundinacea (TALL FESCUE)	*Carex barbarae* (SANTA BARBARA SEDGE) *Festuca californica* (CALIFORNIA FESCUE) *Festuca idahoensis* (IDAHO FESCUE)
Stipa tenuissima, syn. *Nassella tenuissima* (MEXICAN FEATHERGRASS) *Stipa brachychaeta* (PUNAGRASS)	*Festuca californica* (CALIFORNIA FESCUE) *Festuca idahoensis* (IDAHO FESCUE) *Juncus balticus* (BALTIC RUSH) *Juncus effusus* (SOFT RUSH) *Juncus patens* (COMMON RUSH) *Sporobolus aroides* (ALKALAI SACATON) *Stipa cernua* (NODDING NEEDLEGRASS) *Stipa lepida* (FOOTHILL NEEDLEGRASS) *Stipa pulchra* (PURPLE NEEDLEGRASS)
Turfgrasses: *Cynodon dactylon* and hybrids (BERMUDA GRASS) *Lolium* species (PERENNIAL RYEGRASS) *Pennisetum clandestinum* (KIKUYU GRASS)	*Carex barbarae* (SANTA BARBARA SEDGE) *Carex filifolia* (THREADLEAF SEDGE) *Carex globosa* (ROUND FRUIT SEDGE) *Carex pansa* (SAND DUNE SEDGE, CALIFORNIA MEADOW SEDGE) *Carex praegacilis* (CLUSTERED FIELD SEDGE) *Carex subfusca* (RUSTY/MOUNTAIN SEDGE) *Carex tumulicola* (FOOTHILL SEDGE) and many others

Carex pansa

SANTA BARBARA SEDGE
Carex barbarae

Sunset zones 4–9, 14–24
Water needs: seasonal once established
Soil preferences: adaptable

THREADLEAF SEDGE
Carex filifolia

Sunset zones 4–9, 14–17, 24
Water needs: seasonal once established
Soil preferences: adaptable

ROUND FRUIT SEDGE
Carex globosa

Sunset zones 4–6, 14–17
Water needs: seasonal once established
Soil preferences: adaptable

SAND DUNE SEDGE, CALIFORNIA MEADOW SEDGE
Carex pansa

Sunset zones 7–9, 11–24
Water needs: seasonal once established
Soil preferences: adaptable

CLUSTERED FIELD SEDGE
Carex praegacilis

Sunset zones 5–9, 14–24
Water needs: seasonal once established
Soil preferences: adaptable

RUSTY/MOUNTAIN SEDGE
Carex subfusca

Sunset zones 7–9, 11–24
Water needs: seasonal once established
Soil preferences: adaptable

FOOTHILL SEDGE
Carex tumulicola

Sunset zones 5–9, 14–24
Water needs: seasonal once established
Soil preferences: adaptable

TEAL LOVEGRASS
Eragrostis hypnoides

Sunset zones 4–6, 14–24
Water needs: seasonal once established
Soil preferences: adaptable

Juncus balticus

WESTERN SWEETGRASS
Hierochloe occidentalis, syn. *Anthoxanthum occidentale*

Sunset zones 4–6, 14–24
Water needs: seasonal once established
Soil preferences: adaptable

BALTIC RUSH
Juncus balticus

Sunset zones 4–9, 14–24
Water needs: seasonal moisture to wet habitats once established
Soil preferences: adaptable, tolerates saline soils

SOFT RUSH
Juncus effusus

Sunset zones 4–9, 14–24
Water needs: seasonal moisture to wet habitats once established
Soil preferences: adaptable, tolerates saline soils

COMMON RUSH
Juncus patens

Sunset zones 4–9, 14–24
Water needs: seasonal moisture to wet habitats once established
Soil preferences: adaptable, tolerates saline soils

ALKALAI SACATON
Sporobolus aroides

See entry under High Perennial Grasses and Sedges.

MEXICAN LOVEGRASS
Eragrostis mexicana

Sunset zones 4–6, 14–24
Water needs: seasonal once established
Soil preferences: adaptable

CALIFORNIA FESCUE
Festuca californica

See entry under High Perennial Grasses and Sedges.

IDAHO FESCUE
Festuca idahoensis

Sunset zones 1–10, 14–24
Water needs: very low
Soil preferences: adaptable

NODDING NEEDLEGRASS
Stipa cernua

Sunset zones 7–9, 11, 14–24
Water needs: low
Soil preferences: adaptable, tolerates saline soils

FOOTHILL NEEDLEGRASS
Stipa lepida

Sunset zones 7–9, 11, 14–24
Water needs: low
Soil preferences: adaptable, tolerates saline soils

PURPLE NEEDLEGRASS
Stipa pulchra

See entry under High Perennial Grasses and Sedges.

Vines and Ground Covers, Evergreen to Semi-Evergreen

These plants prefer sun or part shade. *Sedum laxum* and *Sedum niveum* appreciate afternoon shade. Maintenance is the same for all: remove dead leaves and fruiting heads and shear occasionally. Cut back honeysuckle to control size.

BAD OR NOXIOUS PLANTS	PLANT INSTEAD
Aptenia cordifolia (RED APPLE, HEARTLEAF ICEPLANT)	*Sedum divergens* (CASCADE STONECROP) *Sedum laxum* (ROSEFLOWER STONECROP) *Sedum niveum* (DAVIDSON'S STONECROP) *Sedum spathulifolium* (YELLOW STONECROP) and others
Duchesnea indica (INDIAN MOCK STRAWBERRY) *Dichondra micrantha* (DICHONDRA)	*Fragaria californica* (WOOD STRAWBERRY) *Fragaria chiloensis* (BEACH STRAWBERRY)
Glechoma hederacea (CREEPING CHARLEY, GROUND IVY) *Vinca major* (PERIWINKLE) *Vincetoxicum nigrum,* syn. *Cynanchum louiseae* (BLACK SWALLOW-WORT)	*Arctostaphylos uva-ursi* (KINNIKINNICK) *Asarum caudatum* (WILD GINGER) *Ceanothus hearstiorum* (HEARST'S CEANOTHUS) *Ceanothus prostratus* (MAHALA MAT)
Helichrysum petiolare (LICORICE PLANT)	*Antennaria rosea* (ROSY PUSSYTOES) *Salvia sonomensis* (SONOMA SAGE)
Iceplants: *Carpobrotus edulis* (HIGHWAY ICEPLANT) *Carpobrotus chilensis* (SEA FIG) *Mesembryanthemum crystallinum* (COMMON ICEPLANT), accumulates salt that is released into soil when it dies back	*Abronia maritima* (RED SAND VERBENA) *Abronia umbellata* (PINK SAND VERBENA) *Erigeron glaucus* (SEASIDE FLEABANE) *Extriplex californica* (CALIFORNIA SALTBUSH) *Iva hayesiana* (SAN DIEGO MARSH ELDER, POVERTY WEED) *Jaumea carnosa* (JAUMEA) *Salicornia pacifica* (PICKLEWEED)
Ivy: *Delairea odorata,* syn. *Senecio mikanioides* (CAPE IVY) *Hedera helix* (ENGLISH IVY), *Hedera canariensis* (CANARIAN IVY), and all other ivy relatives *(H. algeriensis, H. azorica, H. colchica, H. cypria, H. hibernica, H. iberica, H. maderensis, H. maroccana, H. nepalensis, H. pastuchovii, H. rhombea)* and hybrids	*Arctostaphylos nevadensis* (PINEMAT MANZANITA) *Arctostaphylos uva-ursi* (KINNIKINNICK) *Baccharis pilularis* var. *pilularis* (DWARF COYOTE BRUSH) *Gaultheria ovatifolia* (OREGON SPICY WINTERGREEN, SLENDER WINTERGREEN, WESTERN TEABERRY) *Vancouveria chrysantha* (GOLDEN INSIDE-OUT FLOWER) *Vancouveria planipetala* (SMALL INSIDE-OUT FLOWER)
Lonicera japonica (JAPANESE HONEYSUCKLE)	*Lonicera interrupta, L. subspicata* (CHAPARRAL HONEYSUCKLE)
Trifolium repens (WHITE CLOVER)	*Lewisia* species *Micromeria douglasii,* syn. *Clinopodium douglasii* (YERBA BUENA) *Oxalis oregana* (REDWOOD SORREL) *Salvia sonomensis* (SONOMA SAGE)

Antennaria rosea

Baccharis pilularis var. *pilularis*

RED SAND VERBENA
Abronia maritima
PINK SAND VERBENA
Abronia umbellata

Sunset zones 17, 24
Water needs: moderate to regular
Soil preferences: well drained

ROSY PUSSYTOES
Antennaria rosea

Sunset zones 1, 2, 7–9, 14–24
Water needs: moderate to regular
Soil preferences: well drained

PINEMAT MANZANITA
Arctostaphylos nevadensis

Sunset zones 1–7, 14–18
Water needs: moderate to regular
Soil preferences: well drained

KINNIKINNICK
Arctostaphylos uva-ursi

Sunset zones 1–9, 14–24
Water needs: moderate to regular
Soil preferences: well drained

WILD GINGER
Asarum caudatum

Sunset zones 1–9, 14–17
Water needs: moderate
Soil preferences: loamy

DWARF COYOTE BRUSH
Baccharis pilularis var. *pilularis*

Sunset zones 5–11, 14–24
Water needs: low once established
Soil preferences: adaptable, well drained

HEARST'S CEANOTHUS
Ceanothus hearstiorum

Sunset zones 5–9, 14–24
Water needs: low
Soil preferences: well drained

MAHALA MAT
Ceanothus prostratus

Sunset zones 1–6, 14–16, 18
Water needs: low
Soil preferences: well drained, volcanic and serpentine

SEASIDE FLEABANE
Erigeron glaucus

Sunset zones 5, 9, 14–24
Water needs: moderate to regular
Soil preferences: well drained

CALIFORNIA SALTBUSH
Extriplex californica

Sunset zone 24
Water needs: moderate to regular
Soil preferences: well drained

Sedum divergens

WOOD STRAWBERRY
Fragaria californica
BEACH STRAWBERRY
Fragaria chiloensis

Sunset zones 4–24
Water needs: moderate
Soil preferences: well drained

**OREGON SPICY WINTERGREEN,
SLENDER WINTERGREEN,
WESTERN TEABERRY**
Gaultheria ovatifolia

Sunset zones 1, 2, 4–6, 14–17
Water needs: moderate to regular
Soil preferences: cool, moist, acid

**SAN DIEGO MARSH ELDER,
POVERTY WEED**
Iva hayesiana

See entry under Perennial Forbs.

JAUMEA
Jaumea carnosa

Sunset zones 4, 5, 8, 9, 14–17, 20–24
Water needs: moderate to regular
Soil preferences: wetlands; tolerates saline conditions

COLUMBIA LEWISIA
Lewisia columbiana
CLIFF MAIDS
Lewisia cotyledon
BITTERROOT
Lewisia rediviva
TWEEDY'S LEWISIA
Lewisia tweedyi

Sunset zones 1–7, 14–17
Water needs: low to moderate
Soil preferences: well drained

CHAPARRAL HONEYSUCKLE
Lonicera interrupta, L. subspicata

Sunset zones 1–24
Water needs: moderate to regular
Soil preferences: adaptable

YERBA BUENA
Micromeria douglasii, syn. *Clinopodium douglasii*

Sunset zones 4–9, 14–24
Water needs: low once established
Soil preferences: adaptable, well drained

187

REDWOOD SORREL
Oxalis oregana

Sunset zones 4–9, 14–24
Water needs: moderate
Soil preferences: loamy

PICKLEWEED
Salicornia pacifica

Sunset zones 17, 24
Water needs: moderate
Soil preferences: well drained, sandy; tolerates saline and alkaline soils

SONOMA SAGE
Salvia sonomensis

Sunset zones 7, 9, 14–24
Water needs: low
Soil preferences: adaptable, well drained

CASCADE STONECROP
Sedum divergens

Sunset zones 1a, 7, 12–24
Water needs: moderate
Soil preferences: rocky, well drained

Vancouveria planipetala

ROSEFLOWER STONECROP
Sedum laxum

Sunset zones 4–7, 15–17
Water needs: low to moderate
Soil preferences: rocky, well drained

DAVIDSON'S STONCROP
Sedum niveum

Sunset zones 7–11, 18–22
Water needs: low to moderate
Soil preferences: rocky, well drained

YELLOW STONECROP
Sedum spathulifolium

Sunset zones 1, 2, 4–9, 14–24
Water needs: moderate to regular
Soil preferences: loamy

GOLDEN INSIDE-OUT FLOWER
Vancouveria chrysantha

Sunset zones 5, 6, 14–17
Water needs: moderate
Soil preferences: cool, moist, acid

SMALL INSIDE-OUT FLOWER
Vancouveria planipetala

Sunset zones 4, 7, 14–17
Water needs: moderate
Soil preferences: cool, moist, acid

Vines and Ground Covers, Deciduous

These plants prefer sun or part shade. Some can be semi-evergreen, depending on the habitat. All of these can be cut down to the ground periodically to remove old or dead tissues and refresh.

BAD OR NOXIOUS PLANTS	PLANT INSTEAD
Asparagus asparagoides (BRIDAL CREEPER)	*Smilax californica* (CALIFORNIA GREENBRIER) *Smilax jamesii* (ENGLISH PEAK GREENBRIER)
Campsis radicans (TRUMPET VINE) *Fallopia baldschuanica*, syn. *Polygonum aubertii* (JAPANESE KNOTWEED, SILVER LACE VINE)	*Aristolochia californica* (PIPEVINE) *Lonicera ciliosa* (WESTERN TRUMPET HONEYSUCKLE) *Lonicera hispidula* (HAIRY HONEYSUCKLE)
Clematis vitalba, syn. *Anemone vitalba* (OLD MAN'S BEARD, TRAVELER'S JOY) *Convolvulus arvensis* (FIELD BINDWEED) *Ipomoea cairica, I. indica* (MORNING GLORIES)	*Calystegia collina* (COAST RANGE FALSE BINDWEED) *Calystegia macrostegia* (ISLAND MORNING GLORY) *Calystegia malacophylla* (SIERRA FALSE BINDWEED) *Calystegia occidentalis* (CHAPARRAL FALSE BINDWEED) *Calystegia peirsonii* (PEIRSON'S MORNING GLORY) *Calystegia purpurata* (PACIFIC FALSE BINDWEED) *Calystegia sepium* (BUGLE VINE) *Calystegia stebbinsii* (STEBBINS' MORNING GLORY) *Clematis lasiantha* (CHAPARRAL CLEMATIS) *Clematis ligusticifolia* (WESTERN WHITE CLEMATIS)
Lamium galeobdolon, syn. *Lamiastrum galeobdolon* (YELLOW ARCHANGEL, GOLDEN DEAD-NETTLE)	*Anemopsis californica* (YERBA MANSA) *Maianthemum dilatatum* (FALSE LILY-OF-THE-VALLEY) *Maianthemum racemosa* (FALSE SOLOMON'S SEAL) *Symphoricarpos mollis* (CREEPING SNOWBERRY) *Vancouveria hexandra* (NORTHERN INSIDE-OUT FLOWER)
Lathyrus latifolius (SWEET PEA)	*Lathyrus vestitus* (PACIFIC PEA)
Wisteria brachybotrys (SILKY WISTERIA) *Wisteria floribunda* (JAPANESE WISTERIA) *Wisteria sinensis* (CHINESE WISTERIA)	*Vitis californica* (CALIFORNIA WILD GRAPE) *Vitis girdiana* (DESERT WILD GRAPE)

189

Aristolochia californica

Calystegia stebbinsii

190

YERBA MANSA
Anemopsis californica

Sunset zones 3, 6–12, 14–24
Water needs: moderate
Soil preferences: riparian

CALIFORNIA PIPEVINE
Aristolochia californica

Sunset zones 5–10, 14–24
Water needs: low to moderate once established
Soil preferences: loamy

COAST RANGE FALSE BINDWEED
Calystegia collina

Sunset zones 7, 8, 14–24
Water needs: low to moderate
Soil preferences: adaptable

ISLAND MORNING GLORY
Calystegia macrostegia

Sunset zones 14–24
Water needs: low to moderate
Soil preferences: adaptable

SIERRA FALSE BINDWEED
Calystegia malacophylla

Sunset zones 1–7, 14–24
Water needs: low to moderate
Soil preferences: adaptable

CHAPARRAL FALSE BINDWEED
Calystegia occidentalis

Sunset zones 1–24
Water needs: low to moderate
Soil preferences: adaptable

PEIRSON'S MORNING GLORY
Calystegia peirsonii

Sunset zones 20–21
Water needs: low to moderate
Soil preferences: adaptable

PACIFIC FALSE BINDWEED
Calystegia purpurata

Sunset zones 2–4, 7–24
Water needs: low to moderate
Soil preferences: adaptable

BUGLE VINE
Calystegia sepium
STEBBINS' MORNING GLORY
Calystegia stebbinsii

Sunset zones 7, 9, 14–24
Water needs: low to moderate
Soil preferences: adaptable

CHAPARRAL CLEMATIS
Clematis lasiantha

Sunset zones 7–9, 14–24
Water needs: moderate
Soil preferences: loam, clay

WESTERN WHITE CLEMATIS
Clematis ligusticifolia

Sunset zones 1–9, 14–24
Water needs: moderate
Soil preferences: loam, clay

Lonicera ciliosa

Vitis girdiana

PACIFIC PEA
Lathyrus vestitus

Sunset zones 21–24
Water needs: moderate
Soil preferences: adaptable

WESTERN TRUMPET HONEYSUCKLE
Lonicera ciliosa

Sunset zones 1, 4–5, 15–17
Water needs: moderate
Soil preferences: adaptable

HAIRY HONEYSUCKLE
Lonicera hispidula

Sunset zones 7–9, 14–24
Water needs: moderate
Soil preferences: adaptable

FALSE LILY-OF-THE-VALLEY
Maianthemum dilatatum
FALSE SOLOMON'S SEAL
Maianthemum racemosa

See entries under Perennial Forbs.

CALIFORNIA GREENBRIER
Smilax californica

Sunset zone 1a
Water needs: low to moderate once established
Soil preferences: loamy

ENGLISH PEAK GREENBRIER
Smilax jamesii

Sunset zones 1a
Water needs: low to moderate once established
Soil preferences: loamy

CREEPING SNOWBERRY
Symphoricarpos mollis

See entry under Low Shrubs.

NORTHERN INSIDE-OUT FLOWER
Vancouveria hexandra

Sunset zones 4–7, 14–17
Water needs: moderate
Soil preferences: cool, moist, acid

CALIFORNIA WILD GRAPE
Vitis californica

Sunset zones 4–24
Water needs: moderate
Soil preferences: loam, clay

DESERT WILD GRAPE
Vitis girdiana

Sunset zones 4–24
Water needs: moderate
Soil preferences: loam, clay

Bulbs, Corms, and Tubers

Bulbs, corms, and tubers prefer sun or part shade. The maintenance requirements are the same for all: remove dead tissues as needed.

BAD OR NOXIOUS PLANTS	PLANT INSTEAD
Allium neapolitanum (ORNAMENTAL WHITE GARLIC) *Arum italicum* (ITALIAN ARUM) *Convallaria majalis* (LILY-OF-THE-VALLEY) *Zantedeschia aethiopica* (CALLA LILY)	*Camassia leichtlinii* (GREAT CAMAS) *Camassia quamash* (SMALL CAMAS) *Trillium ovatum* (WESTERN TRILLIUM, WESTERN WAKEROBIN)
Crocosmia ×*crocosmiiflora* (CROCOSMIA) *Freesia leichtlinii* and hybrids (FREESIA)	*Calochortus* species (CALOCHORTUS) *Erythronium californicum* (CALIFORNIA FAWN LILY) *Erythronium revolutum* (COAST FAWN LILY) *Erythronium tuolumnense* (TUOLUMNE FAWN LILY) *Fritillaria affinis* (CHECKER LILY) *Fritillaria atropurpurea* (SPOTTED FRITILLARY) *Fritillaria biflora* (MISSION BELLS) *Fritillaria camschatcensis* (CHOCOLATE LILY) *Fritillaria liliacea* (FRAGRANT FRITILLARY) *Fritillaria pudica* (GOLD BELL) *Fritillaria recurva* (SCARLET FRITILLARY) *Fritillaria striata* (STRIPED ADOBE LILY)
Watsonia meriana (BULBIL BUGLE LILY)	*Lilium humboldtii* (HUMBOLDT LILY) *Lilium pardalinum* (LEOPARD LILY)

CALOCHORTUS
Calochortus species

Sunset zones: various
Water needs: seasonal, but low to none during summer/fall dormancy
Soil preferences: loamy, porous to heavy clays

GREAT CAMAS
Camassia leichtlinii

Sunset zones 1–9 or 10, 14–17
Water needs: seasonal, but low to none during summer/fall dormancy
Soil preferences: clay

Camassia leichtlinii

Erythronium revolutum

Lilium humboldtii

SMALL CAMAS
Camassia quamash

Sunset zones 1–9 or 10, 14–17
Water needs: seasonal, but low to none during summer/fall dormancy
Soil preferences: clay

CALIFORNIA FAWN LILY
Erythronium californicum

Sunset zones 4–7, 14–17
Water needs: seasonal, but low to none during summer/fall dormancy
Soil preferences: loamy, porous to heavy clays

COAST FAWN LILY
Erythronium revolutum

Sunset zones 1–7, 14–17
Water needs: seasonal, but low to none during summer/fall dormancy
Soil preferences: loamy, porous to heavy clays

TUOLUMNE FAWN LILY
Erythronium tuolumnense

Sunset zones 2–7, 14–17
Water needs: seasonal, but low to none during summer/fall dormancy
Soil preferences: loamy, porous to heavy clays

FRITILLARIA
Fritillaria species

Sunset zones: various
Water needs: seasonal, but low to none during summer/fall dormancy
Soil preferences: loamy, porous to heavy clays

HUMBOLDT LILY
Lilium humboldtii

Sunset zones 1, 2, 7, 14–24
Water needs: seasonal, but low to none during summer/fall dormancy
Soil preferences: loamy to clay

LEOPARD LILY
Lilium pardalinum

Sunset zones 1–7, 14–24
Water needs: seasonal, but low to none during summer/fall dormancy
Soil preferences: loamy to clay

WESTERN TRILLIUM, WESTERN WAKEROBIN
Trillium ovatum

Sunset zones 2–7, 14–17
Water needs: seasonal, but low to none during summer/fall dormancy
Soil preferences: loamy

Maintaining Plants for Fire Resilience

Removing dead or diseased branches and leaves is an essential part of the regular landscape maintenance necessary in wildfire country.

AFTER YOU HAVE STRATEGICALLY SELECTED and placed plants in your defensible space, the most important thing you can do to create a fire-resistant and resilient landscape is to manage the distribution and condition of plant fuels. This means doing maintenance as needed on a regular schedule, even if you have to pay someone else to do it. You cannot live in a wildfire-prone landscape without regular plant maintenance. Nearly all plants and trees used to reduce fire risk require periodic care, such as removing loose bark, dead or diseased branches, and dry leaf litter.

Maintenance has been touched on in the chapter on creating defensible space and in the plant directory. Here we go into greater detail about essential elements of keeping plants healthy such as watering and pruning. We also discuss what to do with the landscape debris you remove.

Handling Pests and Disease

Pests and pathogens wax and wane through the seasons and across years. If you're willing to be patient and accept a little plant damage over time, most pests and some diseases can be controlled simply by promoting biodiversity, providing adequate moisture, and ensuring adequate air flow.

Diverse plants host diverse organisms, and diversity tends to dampen large outbreaks of any one pest species. For pests with no natural enemies, it can help to spray plants with water and a few drops of mild dish soap, sprinkle diatomaceous earth around plants, put out bug traps, and pursue other such remedies. Minimize—or better yet, completely avoid—the use of commercial chemical pesticides, since it is impossible to target a single insect species without also harming other organisms. If serious pest or disease outbreaks persist over several years on particular plants, it is probably time to consider replacing the troubled plant with something else, especially if the sickly plant creates a lot of dead fuel.

Generally speaking, less frequent, deeper watering can promote more drought tolerant plants. Severe drought stress can reduce the ability of plants to produce defensive chemicals or outgrow a disease. Some drought issues can be addressed by pruning (reducing the aboveground biomass) and mulching. Pruning can improve air flow while reducing fuel loads.

Good air flow and sufficient sunshine sometimes are all you need to manage a disease. Creating an air flow map through the seasons can inform you of places where air may stagnate. Areas with little air flow are problematic for species that are susceptible to mildew or other fungal diseases. For example, several native dogwood (*Cornus*) species are susceptible to dogwood anthracnose disease (and nonnative Kousa dogwoods are immune carriers). Shade increases the risk of infection and mortality. Simply planting these dogwoods in areas isolated for fire safety, with good air flow and high light for at least eight hours a day, will allow you to enjoy your dogwoods for years to come.

What about deer and other garden visitors? When shoots are pruned or browsed by, for example, deer or rabbits, some roots die back (and build soil) to compensate. The converse is also true. Browsing of roots by tunneling

RIGHT Deer fencing can keep unwanted visitors out of your garden.

OPPOSITE Micro-spray irrigation can provide fairly even distribution of water without wasting as much as large sprinklers.

animals such as gophers and moles can cause some die-back in the shoots that you may need to prune out, if the plant isn't killed entirely. If you live in an area where shoot- or root-browsing animals become problematic, you can use deer/rabbit fencing and underground caging in focused areas to minimize the problem. This is a great way to avoid using toxic chemicals that might otherwise accumulate in the food chain around you.

Seasonally Appropriate Watering

Water conservation in garden design should be instinctive in the West. The alternative is water extravagance that we can no longer afford. Embracing drought-resistant plants does not conflict with landscaping for fire safety: drought-tolerant gardens can be planted according to fire safety principles. Seasonally appropriate watering keeps plants healthy and maintains higher tissue water content and humidity around the plants (decreasing their chance of combustion). Las Pilitas Nursery gives this advice about chaparral and desert species: "Plants need to have moisture in them when the firestorm comes. Watering dry plants as the fire approaches does not work. Since a wildfire can happen at any time, and weeds have changed the 'normal' fire season, you'll need to water lightly every two weeks if it doesn't rain. Wash the foliage off, but don't get the ground wet."

Many types of irrigation have replaced wasteful overhead sprinklers in the water-hungry West. Drip irrigation has become quite common to improve water use efficiency, but it can actually kill some plants by creating pockets of excessively moist soil surrounded by bone dry soil. Those wet pockets can encourage fungal diseases, while the dry pockets deprive plants of any moisture. The key is to get a fairly even distribution of soil moisture

How to
Tell When Your Plants Need Water

The best way to determine whether your plants need water is to stick your finger into the soil in several places under each plant to check for moisture. Many gardeners can just look at their plants and tell from the orientation and hue of the leaves when plants need more water. You can also test how hydrated plant tissues are by picking a green leaf off a plant and folding it in half. If the leaf is so wilted that it behaves like damp paper and sticks together, expect some leaf die-off when you rehydrate it. If the leaf crunches and breaks apart, that's also a very thirsty plant. If it's pliable and green at the fold, the plant is well hydrated.

Another way to test hydration and ignitability takes a cue from managers of prescribed burns who need to determine if a site is either too wet to burn effectively or too dry to burn safely. Pick off a typical leaf and hold it over a sink or basin with ample water (do this inside where there is no wind to blow any embers or flames anywhere). Touch a lighter flame to the leaf tip for about three seconds. If the leaf ignites and continues to burn after the lighter flame is removed, drop it into the sink and go water your plants, as long as it isn't too hot outside. If the leaf only smolders or goes out completely when the lighter flame is removed, the plant is probably still well enough hydrated.

Rachel likes to do the flame test over her kitchen sink and when finished testing (and making sure the leaf is extinguished), she throws the leaf into her kitchen compost container. She tends to perform this test for any plant of concern in zones 1 and 2. If a leaf indicates that a plant is too dry—that is, if it continues to burn after a lighter is removed—she will increase watering frequency for a couple weeks, then test again.

without overwatering. Micro-spray irrigation does a better job of this without wasting as much water as large overhead sprinklers. Your individual irrigation needs will vary with soil type as well. Deep riparian and heavy clay soils retain more water than fast-draining sandy soils, and water can spread farther horizontally for more even wetting compared to sandy soils.

Beyond irrigation type, the location and timing of irrigation are key for healthy plant growth. If a plant is native to an area that receives regular rainfall, you should supply water year-round. Mediterranean plants should receive more moisture during the growing season, which is late winter through spring. A year or two after planting, those plants should receive little, if any, added water. During extreme drought, occasional watering or spraying down foliage

198

in the early morning or evening can be just enough to prevent die-off without killing the plants with water. Conversely, if you water a chaparral plant (like western redbud, ceanothus, manzanita, or buckeye) during the hottest part of a summer day, you can watch it die before your eyes.

For the most efficient use of irrigation water, apply it directly to the soil during the night or early morning hours. This timing minimizes major sources of evaporative water loss: evaporation of droplets in plant canopies, evaporation from soil surfaces, and evaporation of the irrigation spray before it hits the plants. Watering by sprinkler in mid-to-late afternoon on a hot, dry day can result in up to 45 percent of the water you pay for evaporating before it can be taken up by plants.

Pruning for Fire-Resistant Plants

Pruning is the act of creating spaces in plants, like creating negative spaces in a work of art. From a fire perspective, spaces are the absence of fuel. Proper pruning keeps plants healthy, and healthy plants are more fire resistant and resilient. Ideally, each plant around your home is healthy and has sufficient space to grow, and therefore will require minimal pruning. Some species, such as *Ceanothus*, are susceptible to stem borers and sunburn, which pruning can exacerbate. It's especially important, then, to give these species sufficient space so that the need for pruning is minimized.

During extreme drought, monitoring for and pruning dead and dying plant parts is a key strategy for reducing fire risk. As mentioned earlier, when plants are pruned or grazed, they counterbalance those losses by allowing some fine roots to die off. This is a major mechanism of soil building, which means you can build a little soil while reducing fire risk at the same time. You could also consider pruning up to one-third of the aboveground biomass to reduce water demand, but keep in mind that newly exposed leaves may scald a bit in full sun. This will not harm the plant. For woody species with thin bark, you may need to paint newly exposed trunks with a thin whitewash, one part white latex paint to one part water, to prevent sunscald.

Before you prune, make sure you are ready to do the job properly and safely. Be sure your tools are sharp to avoid shredding branches, and in areas with pathogens of concern (such as those that cause sudden oak death or fire blight), it is important to clean your tools with 70 percent isopropyl (rubbing) alcohol or hydrogen peroxide between individual plants or even cuts. Take precautions not to disturb nesting birds. Check branches for nests, especially during prime nesting season, generally winter through spring.

Pruning strategies

You can use one of several pruning strategies, depending on the growth form of the plant, its size, past pruning, how much dead material is present, and the overall structure you desire. For example, fruit trees are often pruned in an open-centered vase shape to optimize light within the plant. A systematic way to approach pruning is to first eliminate all dead branches or limbs, then cut out branches with narrow (weak) angles or that are competing to be the central leader (main trunk), then eliminate crossing or rubbing branches, then thin any areas that just appear overly dense. Unless you are coppicing, a good guideline is to prune no more than 30 percent of a plant in a given year, so corrective pruning of some plants may take several years to achieve.

Following are descriptions and illustrations of the main pruning strategies for fuel reduction based on growth form. A combination of these strategies may be needed for particular plants over time.

Prune out dead branches or limbs first, then cut out branches with narrow angles, eliminate crossing or rubbing branches, and trim back water sprouts and suckers.

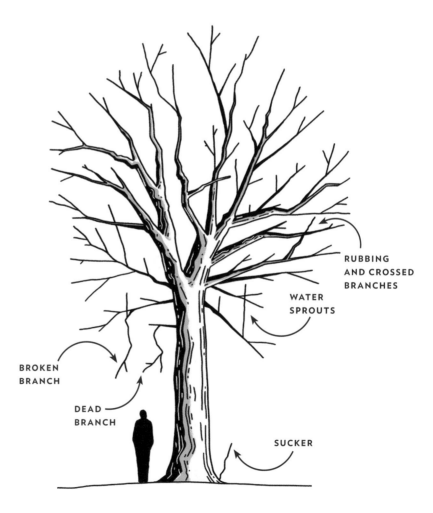

RUBBING AND CROSSED BRANCHES

WATER SPROUTS

BROKEN BRANCH

DEAD BRANCH

SUCKER

Pinching the tips of
new shoots encourages
fuller growth.

PINCHING

Removing the tender tips of shoots on young plants, usually shrubs and
shrublike plants, redirects the plant's energy from growing in a vertical direction into growing horizontally and thus reduces the need for more substantial
pruning later. It stimulates the stem below the pinch to send out new growth.
This is a good strategy for shrubby species such as snowberry (*Symphoricarpos* species).

201

DEADWOODING AND DISEASE REMOVAL

All dead and diseased tissue should be removed from woody plants within
a minimum of 30 feet from structures. Farther from structures, wildlife
habitat such as nesting cavities and acorn woodpecker graneries should be
left intact. Insect galls are unlikely to have a significant impact as long as
plants are sufficiently pruned for their location. Some diseases are indicators that plants should be removed, so you might want to do some research
on particular species. Examples of species that benefit from deadwooding
include cottonwoods and aspens (*Populus* species), willows (*Salix* species),
sycamores (*Platanus* species), elderberries (*Sambucus* species), manzanitas
(*Arctostaphylos* species), Oregon grape (*Berberis aquifolium*), ceanothus
(*Ceanothus* species), and coffeeberries (*Frangula* species).

RENEWAL/STRUCTURAL PRUNING

Renewal pruning focuses on removal of the oldest branches, as well as
crossed branches and branches originating from unhealthy (narrow and
weak) branch crotches. This may also include training a specimen to a
central leader or multileader system up to some desired height. Plants such
as maples (*Acer* species), large manzanitas and ceanothus, Pacific ninebark
(*Physocarpus capitatus*), western redbud (*Cercis occidentalis*), and blue elder-
berry (*Sambucus mexicana*) can benefit.

LIMBING UP OR CROWN LIFTING

Limbing up involves removal of the oldest and lowest branches to allow more light into a tree or shrub and reduce ladder fuels. Large shrubs can be limbed up to appear more like trees and to clear open space around them. Limbing up depends on the size of the plant, and it is generally a good idea to leave at least half to two-thirds of the plant in canopy as opposed to trunk. Limbing up too much of a plant can result in weak trunks that are vulnerable to breaking. Maples (*Acer* species), oaks (*Quercus* species), and hollyleaf cherry (*Prunus ilicifolia*) are just a few of the plants that can benefit.

CANOPY THINNING

Canopy thinning involves removal of individual branches, at the branch collar of a tree or at the ground for shrubs. Proper thinning reduces the density of the canopy but not the size of the tree or shrub. Canopy thinning preserves secondary branches and twigs along the main branches. It allows more light and air through the tree or shrub and displays the bark of its trunk. Candidates include maples (*Acer* species), some oaks (*Quercus* species), red osier dogwood (*Cornus sericea*), ocean spray (*Holodiscus discolor*), Indian plum (*Oemleria cerasiformis*), and mock orange (*Philadelphus lewisii*).

SIZE REDUCTION

There is a right way and a wrong way to reduce the size of a tree that has grown too large for its placement. Topping is the wrong way, as it results in dense canopy fuels and branches vulnerable to breaking later. Reduction cuts, by contrast, selectively remove larger limbs to where they join major

202

Limbing up reduces ladder fuels, canopy thinning allows more light and air through the tree, and size reduction selectively removes larger limbs to bring down height.

LIMBING UP

CANOPY THINNING

SIZE REDUCTION

branches while maintaining good tree form. Trees that might benefit from this treatment include sycamore, oak, maple, or any other tree that had the misfortune to be planted under a power line or other obstruction.

SHEARING OR HEDGING

Shearing or hedging removes all the tips of shrubs without regard to buds or lateral branches and results in topiary shapes such as balls and cubes. This very common technique is a fast way to prune shrubs but not a good idea in fire country. It creates dense growth on the outer edges of a plant, which shades the center and causes the inner leaves and branches to die off. Plants that have been treated this way require corrective thinning before growing season every three years or so to remove dead twigs in the shear zone. Although we recommend against it, if you insist on shearing your hedges in fire country, be sure to keep these plants healthy and free of dead debris! Sheared hedges of plants such as hollyleaf cherry (*Prunus ilicifolia*) and California bay (*Umbellularia californica*) benefit from corrective thinning every few years.

Shearing creates a dense crown, while thinning leaves spaces for air and light to enter.

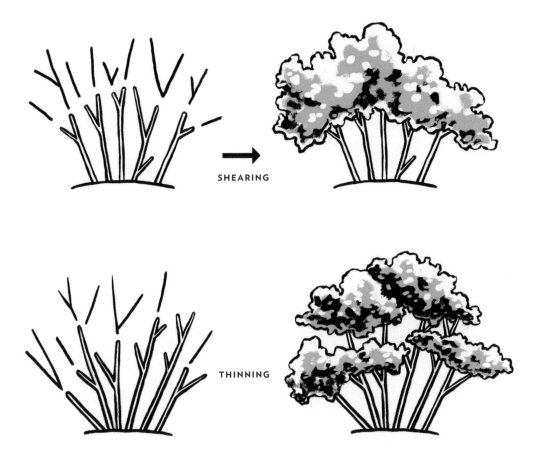

SHEARING

THINNING

COPPICING AND POLLARDING

Coppicing is cutting down shrubs and trees (such as western redbud and oak species) to ground level and allowing shoots to regenerate from the root crown. Coppicing is used to generate tender new growth, particularly important for producing good quality materials for making baskets and tools (such as tongs for handling hot coals). Coppicing can also be used to refresh resprouting chaparral shrubs in zones 2 and 3.

Pollarding is cutting all branches down to main trunks, a technique that can be used to generate branches for fuel, garden stakes, crafts, and other uses. Pollarding is frequently used on nonnative mulberry (*Morus* species) and sycamore trees. Even if the multiple branches that result from each cut are later thinned, this technique is not recommended, as it creates large wounds that often end up rotting (thus becoming a fire hazard) before they can heal.

Basic pruning techniques

There are four basic techniques for correctly pruning woody plants to ensure healthy shoot growth after pruning.

First, branches should be cut at a slight angle, approximately ¼ inch above a bud. An angle that is too steep may result in the bud dying. A cut that is too straight or extends too far above the buds may cause the stub to rot.

Cut branches at a slight angle, ¼ inch above a bud (left). Avoid an angle that is too steep (center) or a cut that is too straight (right).

CORRECT ANGLE

TOO STEEP

TOO STRAIGHT

Second, unless you are simply shearing a shrub (not recommended in fire country), you should always cut branches back to the collar (swollen base) or crotch of a branch, to allow proper healing of the cut. If you cut a branch too long it can sprout a bunch of tiny branches or leave a dead stub that prevents the cut from healing. If you shave a branch beyond the collar, too much into the trunk, you risk causing the trunk to rot and form a cavity before the wound can heal. A healthy cut allows the bark to grow over and seal the wound.

BRANCH COLLAR

CORRECT CUT

TOO FLUSH

STUB TOO LONG

Cut just outside the branch collar (left), not flush with the trunk (center), and don't leave long stubs (right). Flush cuts leave trees open for decay, and long stubs don't heal over, leaving dead fuel.

Third, you should always use a three-step cut to prune any limbs large enough that they might tear the bark where they attach to the tree: (1) under-cut the branch to break the bark connection, (2) cut all the way through a foot or so away from the trunk to reduce branch weight, and (3) do a final clean cut just outside the branch collar, taking care not to rip bark as well.

Cut a branch in three steps to avoid ripping the bark from the trunk beneath an incomplete cut.

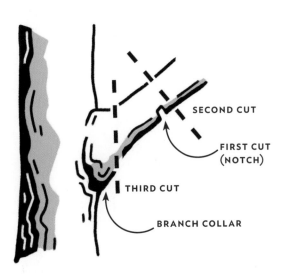

SECOND CUT

FIRST CUT (NOTCH)

THIRD CUT

BRANCH COLLAR

Fourth, if you are establishing new trees, do not remove lower branches until a healthy trunk taper is achieved to support the weight of the tree canopy. Trunk taper develops in trees as lower branches grow, and as trees move with wind. Both of these factors strengthen the trunk. Temporary branches in developing saplings can be shortened and later limbed up once the trunk has become sturdy.

BELOW RIGHT Establishing strong tree trunk taper requires leaving lower branches on the tree until the lower trunk is significantly larger in diameter than the upper trunk or any of the branches.

BOTTOM RIGHT A tree with good trunk taper (left) stands on its own. One with poor trunk taper (center and right) must be staked or is easily blown over by the wind.

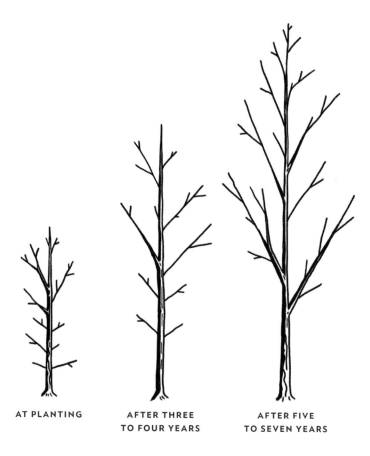

AT PLANTING

AFTER THREE
TO FOUR YEARS

AFTER FIVE
TO SEVEN YEARS

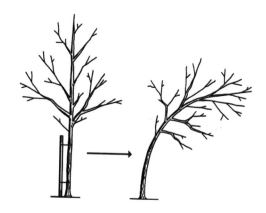

Key Terms

Water sprouts are vigorous upright shoots that grow from latent buds on the trunk or branches of trees. **Suckers** are like water sprouts that grow from the base of a tree trunk.

The **branch collar** is the ridge of woody tissue that forms where a branch attaches to its parent branch or trunk.

Limbing up, also called crown lifting, is the practice of removing the lowest branches on a tree or shrub to eliminate ladder fuels. Lower branches should be left on saplings while trunk taper is being developed, but established trees and large shrubs should be limbed up at least 6 feet from the ground. **Trunk taper** is present when the lower part of a trunk has a greater diameter than the upper part and the branches.

Shearing or hedging, also called heading back, removes the terminal bud on a branch and encourages new shoots to fan out around the cut. The result is growth on the perimeter of a plant and not in the interior.

Thinning removes a branch or limb all the way back to its point of attachment, the branch collar on a larger limb or trunk. It opens up the structure and allows more air and light in.

Pollarding or topping is shearing off the top of a tree at a uniform height, reducing its leader and top branches to stumps that are then open to disease or decay.

Phenology refers to regularly repeated phases in the life cycles of plants and animals and how they are influenced by variations in climate and by habitat factors. Examples include the date of emergence of leaves and flowers and the date of emergence of caterpillar larvae.

When to prune

The ideal time to prune depends on climate, plant phenology, and weather. Major pruning is best done when plants are semi-dormant or dormant, after flowering or fruiting, and when the weather is not too hot or wet. Dormancy occurs during the dry part of the year before winter rains begin (late fall) in our Mediterranean and desert climates, and during winter at higher elevations. Minor pruning can be done most times of the year, as long as the weather is taken into account.

Pruning really shouldn't be done when temperatures are above about 90°F, especially if the plant is in full sun. Wet, high-humidity conditions are

How to
Dispose of Your Unwanted Fuel

After the effort to keep up with pruning and debris pickup, what do you do with all that fuel? If you do not have a regular landscape / bio bin pickup service or can't easily have it hauled away, you have several options for disposal. Not all methods are created equal; some reduce fuels more than others, and some offer more habitat support and reduce carbon emissions more than others. Controlled burning and burning piled woody debris release nutrients to the environment, while composting can create great bird and lizard habitat.

Method	Amount of Fuel Reduction	Degree of Habitat Support	Net Carbon Emissions
Place debris in landscape / yard waste / bio bins, or haul to a waste facility for processing.	high	none	high
Use branches and logs as firewood for burning in a fireplace, wood stove, or fire pit.	moderate	low	high
Do broadcast, prescribed, or controlled burning. (These methods are not appropriate for chaparral habitats, high-elevation bogs, and some other habitats. Consult qualified experts such as prescribed fire associations / burn associations or appropriate agencies in your area.)	high	high, depending on the biotic community	high
Burn piled woody debris (slash).	high	moderate	high
Compost piled debris in a safe, contained area (for example, surrounded by rocks or walls) and/or buried under the soil and allowed to decompose. Also called hügelkultur.	moderate	high	net carbon storage
Chip untreated timber, removed trees, branches, and stumps to create chipper mulch. The type of woodchips produced depends on the type of chipper machine used and the source materials.	moderate	high	net carbon storage

Note: Broadcast, prescribed, and controlled burning are controlled applications of fire under specified environmental conditions with the right timing and permissions; they allow fire to be confined to a predetermined area and produce the fire behavior characteristics required to attain planned resource management objectives. A broadcast burn is a prescribed fire ignited in areas with little or no forest canopy present; broadcast burning is used in grasslands, shrublands, and oak woodlands to restore habitat and reduce fuels. A pile burn is a prescribed fire used to ignite hand- or machine-cut piles of vegetation resulting from pruning or fuel management. Piles are generally burned during the wet season to reduce damage to the residual trees and to confine the fire to the footprint of the pile. Prescribed fire associations / burn associations are communities with trained individuals who can safely execute properly timed prescribed burns.

the worst for spreading fungal and bacterial pathogens, so it is best to avoid pruning within about twenty-four hours of a rain. You can consult various resources online (California Native Plant Society, Oregon State Extension, Trees for Seattle, and even commercial nurseries and garden centers) to determine the ideal time to prune common types of plants based on phenology.

Here is a generalized schedule for pruning in different ecoregions:

- **Coastal ecoregions:** late summer / early fall, late fall / early winter, late spring / early summer
- **Mediterranean and chaparral ecoregions:** late summer / early fall, late spring / early summer
- **Desert ecoregions:** late summer / early fall, late winter / early spring
- **High-elevation ecoregions:** late winter / early spring
- **Great Basin ecoregions:** late spring / early summer.

Biomass Reduction

Beyond pruning, biomass reduction includes removing weeds and reducing fuels in the ground layer as well. Hand pulling, hoeing, spraying hot vinegar, and weed whacking are all safe and effective, along with cleaning up the resulting debris. Using a propane torch to scorch leaves is not advised, not just because you could ignite a fire in the wrong conditions but also because it releases pollutants and greenhouse gases when other effective options are available.

If you must use herbicides, use them judiciously and with sufficient precautions to protect yourself and others. One of our "safest" herbicides, glyphosate (first developed under the trade name Roundup) can kill beneficial gut microbes, even in honeybees, and negatively affect bee behavior and reproduction. Glyphosate has also been linked to non-Hodgkin's lymphoma in at least one meta-analysis and is classified as a carcinogen by the International Agency for Research on Cancer, a division of the World Health Organization. Besides, you still have to clean up the dead plants.

Speaking of cleaning up clippings and weeds, before fire season all landscape debris should be raked out of branches and from underneath plants, just as you would rake combustible debris accumulated against your house. Regular debris cleanup should be done throughout the year to reduce ground-layer fuels. Annual dried plants should be raked up after putting on their floral show and setting seeds. Perennials should be cut back after flowering or fruiting as well. Perennial seed heads can be bundled or scattered around the outer edges of zone 2 for wildlife. Invasive species should be removed or vigorously kept in check.

209

Recovery

Helping Land Heal After Fire

Burned land can often recover without intervention, but in many cases homeowners can help by controlling erosion, taking down trees that pose a hazard, and controlling invasive species.

WE HOPE YOU WILL NEVER HAVE TO DEAL with losing your home or neighborhood to wildfire. However, if you do, excellent resources are available to help you navigate the recovery process and the decisions associated with whether to leave or to stay and rebuild. If you decide to stay, finding your way through the maze of emergency federal, state, local, and nonprofit agencies, insurance companies, and the like can be daunting, to say the least. Search for reputable resources to help in the recovery process, online and in print.

This chapter is not about how to mitigate smoke damage or rebuild your home after a fire. Here we will focus on helping you monitor and support your landscape. Ideally, if you have a large property that isn't close to neighbors, you will let natural ecological succession take place (leaving the land to recover without intervention). However, a purely hands-off approach isn't always an option (in the case of small lots, close neighbors, steep slopes, and safety concerns, for example). Two immediate concerns after fires are erosion and dead standing fuels that pose a threat (such as dead tree snags that might fall). Over the longer term, nurturing healthy regrowth, controlling invasive species, and managing fuel loads should be the top priorities.

Rachel took a mixed approach on her 2-acre property that burned in the 2018 Camp Fire. Areas that were adjacent to wilderness, and not near any neighbors, she mostly left alone, with the exception of a few erosion control measures. In areas closer to her home and neighbors, she removed hazardous trees in addition to erosion control efforts.

Resources for Recovery

Among the resources available to help navigate postfire recovery are these:

- **We wholeheartedly recommend** the *California Native Plant Society Fire Recovery Guide*, available online (www.cnps.org/give/priority-initiatives/fire-recovery), which will undoubtedly be updated periodically.

- **The USDA Natural Resources Conservation Service web page** After the Fire: Resources for Recovery gathers information about how to assess your property in the aftermath of fire and where to find recovery assistance.

- **After the Flames (aftertheflames. com),** a website provided by Coalitions and Collaboratives, Inc., is a collection of actionable best practices for communities impacted by wildfire.

Priorities for the Immediate Aftermath

The immediate aftermath of fire presents many dangers and challenges from burned structures and the environment. If you decide to visit a recently burned area in the built environment, search for valuables, and/or help with cleanup, wearing proper personal protective equipment (PPE) is essential. At a minimum, you should wear an N95 mask, protective clothing covering all your skin, and close-toed shoes with protective booties. Wood ash is not toxic, although it is highly basic and corrosive when mixed with water, but thousands of substances associated with the built environment can leave behind heavy metals and toxic residues.

Materials may still be smoldering as well. Logs, tree snags, buried tree trunks, and peat may smolder for weeks or months. Building materials such as insulation and polyurethane foam in structures can also smolder for prolonged periods before transitioning to open flames. This phenomenon is one of the reasons fire evacuations can be prolonged, as this hazard must be checked.

Once you've been permitted safe access to your home, your first safety priority after ensuring that toxins are secured and smoldering fires are out is to bring down dangerous vegetation in your landscape. Prune or cut down fire-damaged trees that present a serious hazard of falling onto buildings or roads and endangering people or livestock. Keep the debris on site to control erosion while vegetation regenerates. On the other hand, if fire-damaged trees present no falling hazard and if you have room, leave them standing through at least the first postfire growing season. The roots will help hold soil, the standing wood provides incredible wildlife habitat, and time will tell you if a particular tree will outgrow its fire scars.

Then you should clear debris away from any water infrastructure around your home or along roads to ensure water drainage. Culverts, diversion ditches, and constructed swales all should be cleared. Clogged drainage systems are a major cause of erosion, even in the absence of fire. Blocked culverts under roads can hinder safe passage out of your community, particularly since runoff can be many times higher in burned areas.

After you have made sure that drainage infrastructure is working, your focus should be on protecting the soil. This may require diverting water from usual drainage patterns, using sandbags or other materials, to protect vulnerable structures or slopes. It is a good idea to coordinate with neighbors and your community, and experts in stormwater mitigation, to appropriately check and add water diversions.

Any plants that survive a fire, or a lot of blowing ash, would appreciate a bath, even if all you have is nonpotable water. The high pH of ash can damage leaves that are still green, so ash should be rinsed off if possible to minimize tissue burns. If you do not have water to spare, let the leaves burn and the plants recover on their own. Do not use a leaf blower to clear plants or other surfaces of ash. Leaf blowers only resuspend ash particles that are unhealthy to breathe.

Large hardwood trees such as oaks have evolved to withstand fire and if given time are likely to recover fully.

Is Garden Produce Safe to Eat After a Fire?

One of the most common questions immediately after wildfires is whether produce from food production areas impacted by fire is safe to eat. A few plants can accumulate heavy metals from soil—in fact, some are used in phytoremediation, to clean up toxic sites—but most plants do not accumulate significant amounts of heavy metals or other toxins, especially from a short-term event like a wildfire. After the 2018 Camp Fire, which burned almost nineteen thousand structures, fruits and vegetables grown in the area were found to be safe to eat as long as ash was rinsed off.

Adding back organic compost and mulches to food production areas increases soil microbial activity, which can break down chemicals more quickly and bind to some heavy metals, rendering them effectively inert. Lead is harmful at any dose if inhaled or ingested, but plants do not take up lead. Again, as long as you wash off your plants and do not disturb soil where suspected lead contamination may be, your garden produce should be safe to eat.

Protecting the Soil

Soil changes after wildfire, and those changes increase runoff and erosion. Soils can change biologically, nutritionally, and physically. There are things you can do to support soils by replenishing organic matter, avoiding compaction, and controlling erosion.

Replenishing organic matter

Soil is composed of minerals, water, air, and organic matter. Depending on fire intensity, soil organic matter in the top few inches or so can be partially or completely vaporized. More than half of soil organic matter is carbon that can burn like wood, depending on fire intensity and duration. A fast-moving, very hot fire may not burn into soils as dramatically as a low-intensity, slow fire, especially if there is moisture in the soil. Soil types and amount of organic matter present also dictate how much soil changes after fire.

After a burn, soil respiration (an indicator of biological activity) is reduced for a time. Some portion of soil surface microbes, invertebrates, and other shallow soil dwellers die when fire passes through. Toxic compounds from constructed materials—like PCBs (polychlorinated biphenyls), PAHs (polycyclic aromatic hydrocarbons), and heavy metals—can impact soil microbes for a short time as well. Microbial communities are the quickest to recover, however, especially after low-intensity fires. Larger soil organisms repopulate from "cool" patches or deeper soils. A few organisms, like land snails, may take years to migrate back into large burn areas.

Species composition and dominances may shift with changes in soil organic matter and temporarily increased pH on the soil surface from ash. Wood ash ranges in pH between 9 (baking soda) and 11 (ammonia), which is why you should sprinkle it only in small amounts in your compost or garden as a source of nutrients like potassium, phosphorus, and magnesium. Soils high in clay are more able to buffer pH changes caused by ash deposition than soils with a high percentage of sand. Ash from wildfires adds nutrients that will slowly be incorporated into soil by microbes and biogeochemical processes.

A lot of the nutrients in soil that are available to plants—like nitrogen, phosphorus, and potassium (the N-P-K on fertilizer bags)—are contained in soil organic matter. Fire severity in any particular spot determines how much of the soil nutrients are lost from the upper few inches of soil. In low-severity fires, you can actually see an increase in soil organic matter and available nutrients that are released to the soil by the combustion of aboveground plant material. Phosphorus and potassium are depleted from soil above 1200°F, whereas magnesium is depleted above about 1830°F and calcium

Planting lupines, which fix nitrogen from the atmosphere, is one way to build back nitrogen in burned soil.

above 2700°F. Nitrogen and sulfur are lost at temperatures of only a few hundred degrees, so you would expect those nutrients to need replenishing in, say, a vegetable garden that burned. Generally speaking, though, there is no reason to add fertilizers to soil after a burn, especially when they might just run off with the first rains.

Replacing organic matter by applying compost or mulch is a good first step for rebuilding soil health and reducing erosion due to rain splash, wind, and surface flow. But keep in mind that soils build both from above and from below. Plants that have lost aboveground tissues to fire will counterbalance those losses by reducing their root biomass. Those dead roots quickly build organic matter underground.

One way to build back nitrogen in burned soil is to cultivate plants that fix nitrogen from the atmosphere, such as lupines, wild lilac (*Ceanothus* species), and alders (*Alnus* species). Cover crops including annual legumes can be especially effective, but avoid nonnative weedy nitrogen fixers such as rose clover (*Trifolium hirtum*) as they tend to escape into wildlands.

Respecting soil structure

Physical changes also impact soil health. Loss of soil organic matter (including litter and duff on the surface) is associated with losses in soil structure, and loss of structure reduces the ability of water to infiltrate into soil. Poor soil structure can reduce water-holding capacity, much like clay soils that are compressed if you work them when they are too wet. Given the fragility of soils after fire, foot and vehicle traffic should be minimized to avoid further compaction. Around structures, you can cover soil with boards temporarily to reduce soil compaction.

216

This soil in an area burned by the Rim Fire in California has become hydrophobic. Hydrophobic soils repel water and add to water runoff problems after wildfire.

One problem to look out for is the development of a hydrophobic, waxlike layer at or near the soil surface. Plant resins and other compounds produced by some plants and accumulated over time in leaf litter can vaporize and resolidify on soil, making it impervious to water. Sandy soils, which have larger soil pores, are more susceptible to the development of hydrophobic layers because glass (sand) transmits heat more easily than clay, and those larger pores provide bigger spaces for the hydrophobic molecules to accumulate. Interestingly, in areas where combustion temperatures exceed about 572°F at the soil surface, these hydrophobic compounds are consumed and do not precipitate into the soil. Every time it rains, the hydrophobic layer will break down a bit. If little or no rain falls, soils may retain a hydrophobic layer for much longer.

Controlling erosion

The combined loss of soil organic matter and soil structure, and in some cases the development of a hydrophobic layer, can result in extreme surface runoff with the first rains after wildfires, driving erosion. Landslides occur when there are insufficient deep roots and organic matter to hold slopes in place. Wind can also cause erosion as soil particles become airborne. Both wind and water erosion can be blunted using some of the same techniques, by applying materials that reduce the ability of wind and water to carry away soil.

If you live in a burned area near a major watershed creek or river, you want to prevent sediment from flowing into these bodies of water. High sediment/nutrient loads and the high pH of ash can literally suffocate aquatic life in a stream, at least temporarily. Erosion control measures aim to slow down and spread out water so it carries less sediment.

It was long thought that the best prescription for bare, exposed soil was to broadcast annual grasses, throw down straw mulch and wattles, and spray hydromulch everywhere. These tactics have, unfortunately, led to the introduction of some nonnative annual grasses and forbs into burn scars that can make these areas more vulnerable to future ignition and in some situations cause conversion of biotic communities to less desirable, more fire-prone types. Annual grasses do not have very deep root systems, so

---

How to Check for Hydrophobic Soil

How do you know if your soils have become hydrophobic? You can test your soil in several places by scraping away the ash to expose the mineral soil, then placing a few drops of water on the soil and waiting to see if it beads up or percolates into the soil. You should also scrape into the soil a bit, because the hydrophobic layer can sometimes end up a few inches down. If you find you have a hydrophobic layer, get a sense of its thickness by scraping down little by little and testing until you no longer see the water beading up.

217

they do little to anchor soil. Nonetheless, annual grasses are among the first to germinate with early rains, and they easily crowd out native perennial and woody seedlings.

Furthermore, mass aerial seeding appears to be ineffective (and expensive) as a treatment to decrease erosion, may have no effect on depressing invasive species, and can impede the recovery of native species. Application of straw mulches and wattles may reduce erosion if the mulch stays in place, but seeds in straw can contribute to invasions. If you must use straw mulch or bales, use rice, barley, or sterile wheat. Composted wood wattles have been proposed as an alternative to avoid the introduction of foreign seeds, but any organic materials imported to a burn area have the potential to spread pathogens, like the fungal disease that causes sudden oak death. On the other hand, if you have access to a chipper and a lot of burned dead wood on your property, chipping some of it to cover the soil is a good strategy.

The fact that past erosion control measures have in some cases caused lasting ecological damage with little control benefit suggests the need for a more nuanced approach to fire recovery. What else can you use for erosion control? To our knowledge, rocks have never been implicated in spreading plant diseases. Rocks, charred wood, and remnant plant materials on site can be applied strategically as erosion control structures, and to nurse seedlings along in a protected microclimate. Regardless of slope, logs, log debris (branches), or man-made erosion barriers have been shown to significantly reduce erosion and sediment flow into streams after wildfire and improve postfire soil quality. Sandbags, boards, straw bales, drift fencing, and even chain-link fencing can be placed strategically to slow down and spread out water.

To the extent feasible, applying woodchips or debris from the site in mounds perpendicular to flow patterns will help slow water down, causing it to drop sediments and reduce scouring of the soil. If you can divert some water into storm drains, that may help protect sensitive slopes from failing during heavy rains. Strategically placed debris can also rough up surfaces to reduce wind scour. Wherever you imagine water can flow or strong air currents can funnel, that is where you should place obstructions.

All of these applications have the added benefit of creating habitat for critters. Creating different microhabitats through erosion control measures such as rocks and branches fosters the establishment of diverse species. The soil ecosystem, microbes, invertebrates, burrowing animals, plants— all respond to the changed environment, and nutrient cycling continues.

In the WUI, erosion mitigation should be prioritized in developed areas, in drainage areas, and in landslide hazard areas. Developed areas are most likely to see damaging traffic, and drainage areas need attention to reduce sediment release into streams. Consult with your local Natural Resources

Key Terms

Hydrophobic soils are soils found at or just below the soil surface that repel water as a result of intense heat vaporizing plant resins and depositing them as a waxy coating around soil particles.

Wattles are rolls of netting stuffed with straw, composted wood, coconut fibers, or other organic material, designed and installed to slow down stormwater runoff and prevent sediment from washing into bodies of water.

Hydromulch is a mixture of organic matter, fertilizer, seed, and water blown through a sprayer to cover large areas of bare soil quickly.

Serotinous cones are cones that remain attached to a tree and closed until heat stimulates the cone scales to open and release seeds.

Fire followers are plant species that respond positively to environmental cues like charred soil, smoke, and increased sunlight and nutrients after wildfires, especially after some rain.

Fire intensity refers to the amount of radiant energy (heat) released by a fire at a given point in time. **Fire severity** refers to the impact of a fire on an ecosystem such as loss of trees or reduction of biodiversity.

A **snag** is a standing dead or dying tree, often missing a top or most of the smaller branches. A **snag forest** is a patch of snags caused by high-intensity fires, widespread insect outbreaks, or other major disturbances. Such a forest provides rich, productive habitat for diverse species

219

Conservation Service (NRCS) representative, cooperative extension and/or master gardener program, and fire safe council to determine the best ways to control erosion on your land. Funding likely will be available to defray costs associated with erosion control measures. Mitigation for landslide hazards should be left up to professionals, but you should certainly let county or state officials know if you are concerned about a particular landslide threat.

Life returns in abundance after fire scours the forest floor.

Life Returns: Natural Regeneration

Magical things happen after wildfires. Bright green slips of new growth emerge like sparkling emeralds against a charcoal backdrop. Patches that burned hotter leave cream-colored ash, etched shadows of fallen trees that were completely consumed. Plants that resprout from roots and charred stems emerge first. Seedlings begin to emerge after significant rains. Some species explode with exuberant growth in the absence of a competing canopy, putting on amazing floral shows. Some conifers have serotinous cones that open only when heated, and some chaparral species require smoke for germination. Fire followers such as bush mallows (*Malacothamnus* species) emerge almost exclusively within the first couple of years after a fire and may not be seen again until after the next fire, decades or a century later.

Fires are generally good for most plants, provided they (1) occur within the range of fire frequencies and timing that are appropriate for the particular wildland biotic community, and (2) those wildland communities are not further disturbed to the point that nonnative species invade and the community is converted to something else. Fires result in more light reaching soil surfaces, some increase in available nutrients, and often higher overall productivity and diversity as communities regenerate.

The pattern and rhythm of regeneration depends on the biotic community, the timing and severity of the fire, the fire size, the interval of time since the last disturbance or wildfire, soils, topography, and the weather patterns that follow. In Mediterranean and desert climates especially, the active growing season for most organisms is late winter and spring. As a consequence, spring fires tend not to burn as hot but can be far more destructive for plants, wildlife, and insects. Regardless, life always returns after wildfire. Fire can be a regenerative force. It is our job to steward that regeneration so burned areas continue to support native plants and animals sustainably.

Wildfire severity and plant regeneration

Wildfires are by nature patchy, with areas of low-intensity burns mixed with hot crown fires, depending on the biotic community, the condition and distribution of fuels, and the wind. Wildfires leave a mix of low- to high-severity impacts. Fire severity is a measure of the amount of ecological change caused by a burn, and it can range from simple combustion of fine detritus on the ground to incineration of entire tree or shrub canopies. If you live in a mixed-conifer WUI, you are more likely to see patchy fire severity after a burn than if you live in a chaparral WUI.

Low-intensity fires burn the ground layer in forests, woodlands, deserts, and grasslands, resulting in low-severity disturbance. In high-elevation peat bogs, however, low-intensity fires can smolder into organic peat that may be yards thick and cause ecosystem state change, from peatland to open water—a high fire severity impact.

Moderate-severity fire in forests and woodlands results in occasional canopy burns and some death of saplings and trees. High-severity fire results in complete or almost complete aboveground mortality. Mature chaparral tends to burn into the canopy—that is, with high severity. High-severity fires create snags, or standing dead wood, in forests and chaparral, resulting in extremely rich feeding areas for insects, birds, reptiles, amphibians, and mammals as these patches regenerate after fire.

Different biotic communities recover at different rates, just as different conifer species disperse at different rates across landscapes. Many researchers have reported the same overall recovery of vegetation regardless of fire severity, although large-scale, high-severity burns may require longer to regenerate naturally. Scientists have also found that most wildfires occurring today are of low and moderate intensity, and the less widespread

221

Snags from high-severity fires offer critical habitat for a variety of native species of plants and animals.

high-intensity burns often end up supporting the highest levels of native plant and wildlife species as they regenerate, without our intervention.

As far as fire extent goes, larger fires are not necessarily bad. They can create vast areas where wildlife and plants are slow to recolonize. Unburned and lower-severity patches are important nurseries for that process.

Monitoring regrowth to support native species

When it comes to wildfire recovery, there are two kinds of plants: those that resprout and those that reseed. Some plants can do both. Most conifers do not survive canopy fires (redwoods and giant sequoias are exceptions); thus, you would expect them to regenerate from seeds after severe fires. Most oaks and riparian species can resprout, but depending on the amount of damage to the cambium beneath the bark, they may resprout only to die a year or three later. For resprouters, resist the impulse to cut out and remove dead wood until you see new growth and know where to cut. An exception might be when all the bark is gone, the wood is completely charred, and you need extra woody material to create erosion-control structures.

Herbaceous perennial plants will either regenerate from underground storage structures (roots, bulbs, corms, tubers, and rhizomes) or from seeds in soil (seed bank). Fleshy perennials like daffodils, with underground storage structures, do very well after fires because their storage organs are protected and their competitors aboveground have been removed. Annuals depend solely on seed. In high-severity fire, some of the seed bank gets destroyed, but buried seeds and seeds that disperse in wind can help recover ground layer vegetation within a few years, depending on the moisture available.

Plants that resprout from underground roots and shoots are likely to recolonize much faster than plants from seeds, especially if wildfire is followed by a drought year. Resprouters can grow back quite thickly and can increase to high fuel loads within a few years, even before dead trees (snags) fall down. You will need to monitor regrowth, and thin to maintain your defensible zones as you did before the fire.

Among the greatest challenges after fire is invasion by noxious species that capitalize on abundant, freshly cleared space and reduced competition. Invasive species can be kept in check if you can recognize the plants and remove them regularly, once the soil has received some rain. Since the 2018 Camp Fire, for example, many vacant lots have become

222

Resprouters can grow back thickly and add to fuel loads within a few years

Fire Severity *and* Biodiversity

The patchiness of fire in wildlands can actually foster greater biodiversity across landscapes. High-severity patches can teem with diverse life for years after the fire. Researchers and experience tell us that a wealth of flowering shrubs and plants can spring up in the wake of a high-intensity fire, attracting countless species of flying insects—bees, dragonflies, butterflies, and flying beetles. Birds such as the mountain bluebird feed on the flying insects there and nest in snag forest habitat. Shrub-nesting birds raise their young in the native mountain chaparral that regrows after fire.

Three and four years after the 2013 Douglas Complex Fire in southern Oregon, researchers counted twenty times more individuals and eleven times more species in areas that experienced high fire severity relative to areas with the lowest fire severity. Even species that require old-growth habitat—such as spotted owls, Mexican spotted owls, fishers, and martins—prefer to hunt in unlogged snag forests due to the high density of prey. This points to the importance of allowing high-severity burn areas to recover without removal of burned snags. Thoughtful responses like this can foster the dynamic health of all our wildlands and wildlife.

overrun with massive populations of Scotch broom (*Cytisus scoparius*). This shrub puts on a beautiful display of yellow flowers in spring, but it crowds out native plant communities, is toxic to most livestock, and creates a seed bank that can persist for at least eighty years.

Depending on the severity of the burn and the habitat you live in, the succession of the plants in your landscape will have different time frames to "go back to normal." Most people want to go back to normal as soon as possible, but it's important to let your plants have time to regenerate/sprout on their own first. Observing what grows back can give you ideas for how to best move forward. As plants regenerate/sprout, get rid of any invasive species you see. Don't wait until they get too big!

If you are unsure about some of the plants germinating or resprouting after a fire, especially grasses, seek advice from your county cooperative extension office or master gardeners, or post photos on the free iNaturalist app for identification (iNaturalist.org).

Our Fire Future

Deer have adapted
to live with wildfire,
and so can we.

FIRE IS BOTH A POWERFULLY DESTRUCTIVE and a powerfully creative force. Many species have evolved adaptations so heavily reliant on fire that they cannot reproduce without it. Pyrophytes and fire followers often depend on heat or smoke for seed release or germination. Species adapted to sunny environments require fire to periodically reduce competition from their shade-tolerant neighbors. Snag forests of dead trees, charred chaparral skeletons, and blackened grasslands support rich food webs, including decomposers, insects, birds, and mammals. As recovery from fire proceeds, nutrient-enriched flowers, fruits, and cones abound.

Fire can be an almost magical disturbance that resets the clock in a place. Forest Service researcher and later professor in the School of Forestry at UC Berkeley Harold Biswell, an early advocate of prescribed burning, wrote in 1980, "Keep in mind that fire is a natural part of the environment, about as important as rain and sunshine. . . . Fire has always been here and everything good evolved with it . . . we must work more in harmony with nature, not so much against it." We need to learn to build homesteads that are as fire resilient as the wildlands and wildlife that surround us.

Preparing for a healthy and sustainable fire future will require us to focus on adequately preparing for fire in our built communities, supporting fire in modern landscapes, and protecting the integrity of wildlands as the WUI expands.

Community Preparedness

The safety of your home depends on every link—every structure, every defensible space, every wildfire action plan—in your community. Community preparedness begins with getting to know your neighbors, at whatever scales necessary for the safety of your fireshed. If you are in a cul-de-sac, you and your neighbors should have a plan to ensure everyone's relative safety and ability to evacuate, especially for individuals with mobility issues or pets with special needs. Regular communication and planning should occur at each level in the hierarchy of your community: your neighborhood, your subdivision, your district, your town or city. This has several aspects.

Communication. Everyone must feel that they have permission and allowance for candid communication when someone spots a hazard in their own or a neighbor's yard. You and your neighbor(s) might not agree on some aspect or timing of creating defensible space. It is essential to develop channels to mitigate any disagreements for the good of the community.

Fire ecology education. Communities should regularly engage in educational outreach and updates for fire safety, tailored to the community. For example, there are many interpretations of what constitutes defensible space, and abundant misinformation. Your understanding of basic fire ecology and the ecology of the wildlands near you should be based on the latest recommendations from reliable sources.

Policy alignment. Community policies should coincide with fire readiness recommendations. Any policies that impede fire readiness—for example, homeowners' association or county policies—should be reviewed and reconciled with fire readiness recommendations in your state.

Wildfire action plans. Every individual household should have a current wildfire action plan (WAP), and every community should also have a Community Wildfire Protection Plan to prepare for vegetation management and evacuation. In California, there are state-, county-, and sometimes town-focused fire safe councils to help with this type of planning.

Since having to evacuate during the 2018 Camp Fire, Rachel has become acutely aware of the need to plan for conditions when it is too difficult or unsafe to evacuate. Her family didn't find out about the fire until fairly late because of the location of her home. By the time they evacuated, most routes were impassable. For some folks there were no routes out. Some individuals had to abandon trapped or burning vehicles and try to escape on foot or by hitching a ride with someone else. In other cases, fire personnel had to divert people to large parking lots or defend building perimeters to protect people who could not evacuate before the flames moved through. All communities in fire risk areas should create designated safe places that are sufficiently marked and regularly advertised, much like tsunami zones on parts of our coasts.

Fuel reduction programs. To combine what they need in order to be fire ready with practices that support ecological health, communities can apply through local fire safe councils for grants for fuel reduction programs. These monies can be used to decrease fuel densities and reduce plant competition

How to

Prepare a Personal Wildfire Action Plan

Wildfire action plans (WAPs) empower families to prepare for wildfire events. These plans are proactive and thus can provide a sense of control by formalizing what to do in the event of a wildfire emergency. Each family's WAP will be different, depending on where you live and your family characteristics and requirements. Ideally, you should have a WAP for every family member, pet, and farm animal so important individual details are not missed. You should have hard copies of your WAP in a binder, as digital copies may not be accessible during an emergency.

A WAP includes an evacuation plan for your household that designates several emergency meeting locations outside the hazard area, as well as several different escape routes from your home and community. It also includes a family communication plan that names an out-of-area friend or relative as a single point of contact for communication among family members in case of separation. The planning process also includes gathering/preparing emergency supplies, creating an action plan checklist, and encouraging mental and physical readiness for a wildfire event through conversations and drills.

There are a number of online resources to help you and your family create your WAP. Here are a few:

- **The Ready, Set, Go! program** of the International Association of Fire Chiefs offers a twelve-page booklet where you can record your personal wildfire action plan. Go to www.wildlandfirersg.org and click on "Are YOU Wildfire Ready?" in the menu bar.

- **The California Department of Forestry and Fire Protection (CAL FIRE) Prepare for Wildfire web page** offers the Ready for Wildfire app, which helps you build your personalized wildfire preparedness plan and sends you text messages on active CAL FIRE incidents. You can also download brochures and watch a video on its Ready, Set, Go! program. Go to www. readyforwildfire.org/prepare-for-wildfire/ ready-set-go/.

- **Ready,** an official website of the US Government, offers suggestions for wildfire preparedness (www.ready.gov/wildfires) and how to make an emergency plan (www.ready.gov/plan).

227

so the remaining plants are less vulnerable to drought stress. Grants are available for brush and tree reduction and thinning, chipping (one of Rachel's favorite local programs to manage fuels on her property when pile burning is not an option), pile burning allowances, goat and sheep grazing, invasive species removal, prescribed fire, and even for native plant revegetation. Funding sources include government agencies such as CAL FIRE (www.fire.ca.gov/grants/), the Oregon Department of Forestry (www.oregon.gov/odf/), and the Washington State Department of Natural Resources (www.dnr.wa.gov/FireDistrictAssistance), as well as nonprofit organizations like the Washington State Fire Adapted Communities Learning Network (www.fireadapted-washington.org/roles/).

Volunteer programs. Communities can also tap into the power of volunteerism. Many hands make light work. Explore partnerships with local civic organizations, nonprofit organizations, businesses, government agencies,

Community Preparedness Resources

Your community may have a Community Wildfire Protection Plan (CWPP), generally available through your county fire safe organization. CWPPs are an excellent added layer of insurance that you are living in a cooperative community where fire safety guidelines are observed. Fire safe organizations provide additional helpful information, such as generalized evacuation maps that you can download for your wildfire action plan, as well as tips for fire safety and "fire smart" contractor contacts. See the Fire Safe Marin website (firesafemarin.org) as an example.

Here are some other good community preparedness resources:

• **The Fire-Adapted Communities program of the US Fire Administration** (part of the Federal Emergency Management Agency, FEMA) offers bulletins on how to create a fire-adapted community and how to prepare a Community Wildfire Protection Plan (www.usfa.fema.gov/wui/communities/).

• **The Firewise USA program of the National Fire Protection Association** provides a collaborative framework to help neighbors in a geographic area get organized, find direction, and take action to increase the ignition resistance of their homes and community and to reduce wildfire risks at

and your neighbors. Nothing brings people together like working toward common goals. In Lake County, Oregon, community members take a survey to identify areas of concern and mitigate problems on private property. In Australia and New Zealand, community fire brigades are common, groups of specially trained volunteers who stay behind for a certain window of time to assist stranded people and extinguish ember-ignited spot fires (in addition to community preparations before fires occur).

Smarter Building and Zoning in the WUI

WUI communities are attractive areas for growth not only because of the allure of living nearer to nature but also because housing tends to be cheaper than in cities. We need to agree on building and zoning policies to make the WUI safer. Our current practices are not working, as evidenced by the

the local level (www.nfpa.org/Public-Education/Fire-causes-and-risks/Wildfire/Firewise-USA).

- **The Wildfire Risk to Communities website** (wildfirerisk.org) created by the US Forest Service offers interactive maps, charts, and resources to help communities understand, explore, and reduce wildfire risk.

- **The California Fire Safe Council (CFSC, cafiresafecouncil.org)** provides education to the residents of California on the dangers of wildfires and how they can be prevented. The CFSC funnels grants to local community groups working on wildfire prevention activities such as defensible space, community fire planning, and education.

- **The Oregon Wildfire Response and Recovery web page** of the State of Oregon (wildfire.oregon.gov) gathers tools and resources for monitoring evacuation levels and the current wildfire situation, preparing for wildfire, and recovering from wildfire. Oregonians can sign up for local emergency alerts at ORAlert.gov.

- **The Fire Program of OSU Extension Service** (extension.oregonstate.edu/fire-program) gathers information on fire awareness and fire preparedness. OSU Extension Service Forestry and Natural Resources offers a collection of YouTube videos on various forestry topics, including wildfire (www.youtube.com/channel/UCeBjJplE8rAroG3bI0WZNFQ/videos).

- **The Washington State Fire Adapted Communities Learning Network** (www.fire-adaptedwashington.org) gathers people to have frank, open conversations about learning to live with wildfire in Washington and to take action to protect local communities.

number of structures burning every year. More funding needs to be used for fire readiness that reduces fire risks to the built environment, as opposed to simply fighting wildfires. We must focus on why and how our communities burn, using history, fire science, and research as a guide.

There are many regulations that codify ways to reduce the chances of losing structures in West Coast states. California has an extensive set of fire codes and regulations, which is regularly updated. Oregon and Washington defer to the latest International Fire Code, which is also updated every few years. The International Code Council works with governments to advocate for fire-resistant construction in communities at risk from wildfire. Its International Wildland-Urban Interface Code (www.iccsafe.org/products-and-services/wildland-urban-interface/) establishes regulations to safeguard life and property in the built environment.

Demand for new housing will continue to escalate, but laws, codes, and regulations should incentivize building up, not out into higher-fire-risk areas. This will allow us to keep wildlands for wildlife, put fewer people in harm's way, and create more sustainable solutions for communities moving into the future.

Some wildland areas are restricted from building due to landslide hazards or rare species or habitats. Given the number of buildings that have been lost in wildfires during the past few decades, a new layer of building restriction should include consideration of fire risk—with respect to canyons and topographic saddles that regularly funnel prevailing fire season winds, with respect to ability to evacuate, and with respect to defensibility. Essentially, building should be restricted in areas where wildfire season winds create topographic "chimneys" that draw fire through them.

Buildings should also have adequate setbacks from ridges. Homes positioned too close to ridges are more vulnerable to ignition not just from firebrands but also from radiant heat. Certain building densities and construction materials should be banned from high-fire-risk areas as well. Wood fences, for example, are notorious for spraying embers and fostering house ignitions.

WUI communities that have burned have a golden opportunity to build more fire-resilient neighborhoods. These communities need to revisit fire codes and policies for structures, roads and traffic, and public infrastructure, and they need to designate safe gathering areas in the event of an uncontrolled wildfire. We should be thinking of our communities (especially those in higher risk locations) like fire marshals do buildings, with maximum allowable capacities based on the number of exit routes, which should be proportional to population. Residents of Paradise and Magalia discovered after the 2018 Camp Fire that zoning laws in the past didn't consider evacuations for wildfire, despite the existence of town evacuation plans (that turned out to be inadequate). Paradise had six evacuation routes, but the fast-moving fire closed

some, and traffic jams made others impassable, leaving just one main way to get out that was inadequate for the number of people living there.

These ridge communities are not unique in the WUI. If communities are in areas that are difficult to evacuate, evacuation planning should include designated safe havens. Across the central and southeastern United States in Tornado Alley, most communities design and build community tornado shelters. Why can't we design and build community fire shelters, rather than creating them ad hoc in the middle of a WUI firestorm? Planning must include worst-case scenarios and the safest possible options not just for residents but also for the fire professionals putting their lives at risk.

WUI communities that have not burned must learn from the communities that have burned. Beyond reviewing and updating fire codes and policies, these communities should consult with fire experts to discuss any mitigation needed to improve fire resilience with respect to development (avoiding extreme fire-prone areas), evacuation capacities, and community wildfire protection/action plans. In San Diego, California, one neighborhood was intentionally designed and maintained to survive wildfire because of what had been learned from previous fires in the area, and it worked! Houses were constructed to comply with fire-focused building codes, yards are under

Homes positioned too close to ridges, like this one that burned in Laguna Niguel, California, in May 2022, are more vulnerable to ignition from firebrands and radiant heat, particularly when fire season winds are funneled toward them.

strict regulations for defensible space (year-round), and full-time inspectors monitor yards and hazards in the community. When the 2007 Witch Creek Fire burned through the adjacent chaparral habitat, this interface community lost only a few yard plants and garbage cans; no homes or lives were lost. This should be a model for all WUI communities in the future.

A proposal that has been gaining attention in many areas of the country where disasters affecting communities are expected to recur is managed retreat. This is simply the purposeful relocation of people, buildings, and other infrastructure away from highly hazardous places. Managed retreat has been planned, for instance, in low-lying flood-prone areas along the Mississippi

Key Terms

A **pyrophyte**, literally "fire lover," is a species that depends on fire to survive and regenerate.

A **fireshed** is a distinct area where social and ecological concerns about wildfire combine and intertwine. Wildfires operate at large scales that require us to think and act with the good of the whole fireshed in mind.

Fire safe councils are community-based organizations that work to make communities less vulnerable to wildfire through educational programs and projects such as creating firebreaks and assisting homeowners with special needs in creating defensible space.

Firebreaks are obstacles to the spread of fire, such as open space or areas where trees are thinned and pruned to reduce the potential of catching fire but retain enough crown to shade the ground.

A **wildfire action plan (WAP)** is a plan developed by individual families to give forethought to evacuation, communication, and supplies to have on hand for a wildfire emergency.

A **Community Wildfire Protection Plan (CWPP)** is a plan developed at the community level to identify and plan needed fuel reduction treatments and to recommend measures for homeowners to take to reduce ignitability of structures in the WUI.

Fire brigades are community emergency response teams.

Managed retreat is the purposeful movement of people, buildings, and other infrastructure away from highly hazardous places.

232

River. Managed, wholesale retreat from existing high-risk wildfire areas likely isn't realistic for WUI communities, but banning development in extremely high-risk fire areas in those communities may well be. It makes sense to engineer and design our communities to live with fire, just as we need to design our buildings to be more fire resistant.

Returning Fire to Landscapes

Fire must be recognized as an integral part of our landscapes. But many of our biotic communities and landscapes have changed and are changing in ways that will require managing fire differently. Historic fire suppression, the loss of traditional ecological knowledge (TEK) about burning practices and effects, the introduction of invasive species that change fire dynamics, plus the shadow of climate change—all pose challenges to returning fire to landscapes.

Fire frequency decreased on most western forested landscapes coincident with the spread of Old World infectious diseases among, and genocide of, Native Americans (First Peoples) in the mid-to-late 1800s. Ethnoecologist Kat Anderson tells us that fire was "the most significant, effective, efficient, and widely employed vegetation management tool of California Indian tribes." Native Americans used fire to manage rich natural resources for foods, basketry, cooking, hunting, and protection, as well as dyes, musical instruments, clothing, and games. They used prescribed fire in their "wildland-urban interface" areas to protect villages. As tribes lost significant population, and as most of their ancestral lands were taken away, fewer fires occurred.

After the creation of the US Forest Service in 1905 and the Great Fire of 1910 (which burned 3 million acres in Idaho, Montana, Washington, and British Columbia), policies promoting fire suppression over prescribed fire were codified. These policies were developed not just because fire was demonized but also to support the logging industry's assets. (Note that the roughly hundred years of fire suppression did not apply to all biotic communities—not, for example, to most chaparral and to very high elevation forests—and does not describe many areas on our public lands today.)

Before European settlement, virgin timberlands generally had much taller, larger trees than the second- and third-growth forests we know today. These larger trees tended to be more fire resistant if for no other reason than that their bark was thicker and their branches were so much higher above the ground. A combination of fire suppression and logging led to higher fuel densities, so that wildfires caused more damage to built environments, along with higher levels of soil disturbance and landslide events. In timberlands in particular, clear-cutting and lingering slash piles can make a site more vulnerable to intense fires just a few years after clearing, significantly retarding recovery.

Smokey Bear first appeared in a 1944 poster and since then has become a highly recognizable symbol of the US Forest Service campaign to vanquish wildfire.

Fires in these new forests have become more expensive to suppress, and expanding WUI communities have become more difficult to defend, leaving little budget for fire management programs.

Changes in fuel characteristics are intimately connected to invasive species now resident in our region. Out of roughly 6,500 plant species in California, 1,100 species, subspecies, and varieties of nonnative plants have become naturalized, 183 of which are considered noxious pests by the California Department of Fish and Wildlife. Almost all of these noxious pests are problematic in Oregon and Washington as well. Managing invasive species requires learning specific methods to control them, including when to employ or avoid fire. Even some nonnative animal species—such as feral pigs, goats, and horses; nutria; and perhaps even roof rats and eastern squirrel species—are changing fire conditions.

In the shadow of climate change, we will see more extreme weather events, including extreme droughts and flood events, a reduction in glaciers and annual snowpack, earlier spring runoff, rising sea levels, and a longer fire season with more forest and desert area burned each year. Climate change will bring warmer daytime and nighttime temperatures, which will increase drought stress and fuel temperatures, making ignition easier and fire management trickier. Some woody species under these conditions will experience greater die-off, generating more dead fuels. Increased soil exposure will exacerbate drying.

All of these factors make the reintroduction of fire as a tool to improve ecosystem health a tricky proposition. It requires careful planning, skillful execution, and the support of regulatory agencies. An idea gaining traction in fire landscapes around the world is that communities should have trained individuals who can safely execute properly timed prescribed burns. These might include landowners, volunteer fire departments, nongovernmental organizations such as the Washington Prescribed Fire Council (waprescribedfire.org), Native Americans using traditional ecological knowledge, and other community members who receive fire training and work together to implement prescribed burns on private lands. Humboldt and Butte Counties in California, for example, have such associations. These associations can provide a place where experience is gained and shared.

Changing Our View of Fire

We need to acknowledge that a lot of habitats in the West require fire to maintain healthy and resilient ecosystems, and that fire suppression will only continue our path to fires that are deadly and destructive for humans. We must recognize that protecting homes and families is not about controlling wildfire but rather reducing the flammability of our homes, landscapes, and communities. Overall, we need to change how society views fire. Fire is not something to be prevented; fire is something we can coexist and evolve with, moving into the future.

Fire is an inevitable ecological process that varies in ignition source, severity, size, behavior, and frequency in every biotic community of our beautiful West Coast states. Returning prescribed fire and letting some wildfires burn in unpopulated areas is the best approach we can take to reduce fire hazards, and it is a matter of cultural justice for Native communities. We need to look to Native American tribes for perspective, advice, and assistance. In addition, we can insist on changes in policies to restore (and increase) cultural burning. Fire has been a natural phenomenon in our western landscapes for millennia, and most wildlife and habitats have evolved adaptations to fire. We can all adapt better to fire as well.

Resources and Further Reading

There are many, many online resources for wildfire updates, fire safety planning, and wildfire recovery. Here is a partial list for your convenience. Inclusion here does not represent an endorsement, nor does the absence of other reliable resources indicate our lack of support. While you explore and learn more, you will gain increased knowledge about how to promote wildfire safety, planning, evacuation, and recovery.

Current Wildfire Information

The InciWeb Incident Information System (inciweb.nwcg.gov/) provides a map of major wildfires burning, updated daily, along with links for national wildland fire agencies and organizations, and coordination centers for regional information.

The National Interagency Fire Center (www.nifc.gov/fire-information/nfn) provides news and updates on current fires, and coordinates various fire agencies and resources around the country, including the National Interagency Coordination Center with weather and fire prediction services by region. Northwest, for Washington and Oregon, gacc.nifc.gov/nwcc/; Northern California, gacc.nifc.gov/oncc/index.php; Southern California, gacc.nifc.gov/oscc/index.php.

The US Forest Service gathers various wildfire information resources on its Public Fire Information Websites page (www.fs.usda.gov/science-technology/fire/information).

The California Department of Forestry and Fire Protection (CAL FIRE) Incidents web page (www.fire.ca.gov/incidents/) maps active fires.

The Oregon Department of Forestry Fire Information and Statistics web page (www.oregon.gov/odf/fire/pages/firestats.aspx) maps active large wildfires.

The Washington Department of Natural Resources Information on Wildfires web page (www.dnr.wa.gov/Wildfires) gathers many sources of information on active wildfires.

Wildfire Preparedness and Prevention

The CAL FIRE web page at www.fire.ca.gov/ is a source for fire preparedness, guidelines, and grants. CAL FIRE has a web page on defensible space at www.readyforwildfire.org/prepare-for-wildfire/get-ready/defensible-space/.

The University of California, Division of Agriculture and Natural Resources (UCANR) supports a website with prefire mitigation and postfire recovery suggestions, ucanr.edu/sites/postfire/Homeowners_Guide_to_Recovering_from_Wildfire/.

The Oregon Department of Forestry curates numerous links related to wildfire preparedness, conditions, and restrictions at www.oregon.gov/odf/Fire/Pages/default.aspx.

The Washington State Department of Natural Resources offers resources on preparedness and prevention on its Prepare for Wildfire web page (www.dnr.wa.gov/programs-and-services/wildfire/ wildfire-preparedness) and Wildfire Prevention web page (www.dnr.wa.gov/WildfirePrevention).

California Chaparral Institute. 2020. *From the House Outward: Protecting Your Home from Wildfire*, booklet available at californiachaparral.org/fire/ protecting-your-home/.

California Native Plant Society (CNPS). 2019. Defensible space and landscaping, *Fire Recovery Guide*, booklet available at www.cnps.org/give/priority-initiatives/ fire-recovery.

Federal Emergency Management Agency (FEMA). September 2008. *Home Builder's Guide to Construction in Wildfire Zones*, technical fact sheet available at www.fema.gov/sites/default/files/2020-08/ fema_p_737_0.pdf.

Fire Safe Marin. 2020. Video: "What is defensible space? Get to know your zero zone," www.youtube.com/ watch?v=bPlLXb_MHuo.

——. 2020. Harden Your Home: How to Protect Your Home from Wildfires (web page), www.firesafemarin. org/home-hardening.

——. 2021. Video: "Creating defensible space and fire resistant landscapes," www.youtube.com/ watch?v=5YTqPfAQkis&t=1889s.

——. 2022. Defensible Space (web page), www.firesafe- marin.org/fire-smart-yard/defensible-space.

Hanson, Nikki. 2020. How to collaborate with your landscape: Creating fire-resistant habitat (web page), Grassroots Ecology, www.grassrootsecology.org/ from-the-field/creating-fire-resistant-habitat.

Jennings, Trip, dir. 2022. *Elemental*. Portland, OR: Balance Media.

Las Pilitas Nursery. Landscaping your home in a fire area (web page), www.laspilitas.com/fire.htm.

Masterson, Linda. 2012. *Surviving Wildfire: Get Prepared, Stay Alive, Rebuild Your Life. A Handbook for Home- owners*. Masonville, CO: PixieJack Press.

National Fire Prevention Association. 2019. Public Educa- tion: Preparing homes for wildfire (web page), www. nfpa.org/Public-Education/Fire-causes-and-risks/ Wildfire/Preparing-homes-for-wildfire.

National Fire Protection Association. 2015. Video: "Your Home Can Survive a Wildfire," www.youtube.com/ watch?v=vL_syp1ZScM.

University of Nevada, Reno Extension. 2020. *Wild- fire Home Retrofit Guide*, available at www. readyforwildfire.org/wp-content/uploads/ Wildfire_Home_Retrfit_Guide-1.26.21.pdf.

Native Plants and Fire

Bornstein, Carol, David Fross, and Bart O'Brien. 2005. *California Native Plants for the Garden*. Los Olivos, CA: Cachuma Press.

Brenzel, Kathleen Norris, ed. 2012. *The New Sunset West- ern Garden Book*, 9th edition. New York: Time Home Entertainment.

Ferguson, Gary. 2017. *Land on Fire: The New Reality of Wildfire in the West*. Portland, OR: Timber Press.

Fross, David, and Dieter Wilken. 2006. *Ceanothus*. Port- land, OR: Timber Press.

Hanson, Chad T. 2021. *Smokescreen: Debunking Wildfire Myths to Save Our Forests and Our Climate*. Lexington: University Press of Kentucky.

Kauffmann, Michael, Tom Parker, and Michael Vasey. 2021. *Field Guide to Manzanitas: California, North America, and Mexico*, 2nd edition. Humboldt County, CA: Backcountry Press.

Keator, Glenn. 1998. *The Life of an Oak: An Intimate Portrait*. Heyday Books and the California Oak Foundation.

Kimmerer, Robin Wall. 2013. *Braiding Sweetgrass: Indigenous Wisdom, Scientific Knowledge, and the Teachings of Plants*. Minneapolis, MN: Milkweed Editions.

Logan, William Bryant. 2006. *Oak: The Frame of Civilization*. New York: Norton.

Pavlik, Bruce M., Pamela C. Muick, Sharon G. Johnson, and Marjorie Popper. 1993. *Oaks of California*. Cachuma Press and the California Oak Foundation.

Tallamy, Douglas W. 2021. *The Nature of Oaks: The Rich Ecology of Our Most Essential Native Trees*. Portland, OR: Timber Press.

Wagtendonk, Jan W. van, Neil G. Sugihara, Scott L. Stephens, Andrea E. Thode, Kevin E. Shaffer, and Jo Ann Fites-Kaufman (eds.), James K. Agee (foreword). 2018. *Fire in California's Ecosystems*, 2nd edition, revised. Berkeley: University of California Press.

238

Source Notes

Introduction

Chiodi, Andrew M., Brian E. Potter, and Narasimhan K. Larkin. 2021. Multi-decadal change in western US nighttime vapor pressure deficit. *Geophysical Research Letters* 48 (15): e2021GL092830. doi. org/10.1029/2021GL092830

Congressional Research Service. 2021. In Focus: Wildfire Statistics. IF10244 Version 56. Updated October 4, 2021. crsreports.congress.gov

Crockett, Joseph L., and A. Leroy Westerling. 2018. Greater temperature and precipitation extremes intensify western U.S. droughts, wildfire severity, and Sierra Nevada tree mortality. *Journal of Climate* 31: 341–354. doi.org/10.1175/JCLI-D-17-0254.1

Forister, Mathew L., C. A. Halsch, C. C. Nice, J. A. Fordyce, T. E. Dilts, J. C. Oliver, K. L. Prudic, A. M. Shapiro, J. K. Wilson, and J. Glassberg. 2021. Fewer butterflies seen by community scientists across the warming and drying landscapes of the American West. *Science* 371: 1042–1045. doi.org/10.1126/science.abe5585

Forister, Matthew L., Emma M. Pelton, and Scott H. Black. 2019. Declines in insect abundance and diversity: We know enough to act now. *Conservation Science and Practice* 1: 1–8. doi.org/10.1111/esp2.80

Gershunov, Alexander, Tamara Shulgina, Rachel E. S. Clemesha, Kristen Guirguis, David W. Pierce, Michael D. Dettinger, David A. Lavers, Daniel R. Cayan, Suraj D. Polade, Julie Kalansky, and F. Martin Ralph. 2019. Precipitation regime change in Western North America: The role of Atmospheric Rivers. *Scientific Reports* 9: 9944. doi.org/10.1038/s41598-019-46169-w

Goss, Michael, Daniel L. Swain, John T. Abatzoglou, Ali Sarhadi, Crystal A. Kolden, A. Park Williams, and Noah S. Diffenbaugh. 2020. Climate change is increasing the likelihood of extreme autumn wildfire conditions across California. *Environmental Research Letters* 15: 1–14. doi.org/10.1088/1748-9326/ab83a7

Hanson, Chad T. 2021. *Smokescreen: Debunking Wildfire Myths to Save Our Forests and Our Climate*. Lexington: University of Kentucky Press.

Iglesias, Virginia, Anna E. Braswell, Matthew W. Rossi, Maxwell B. Joseph, Caitlin McShane, Megan Cattau, Michael J. Koontz, Joe McGlinchy, R. Chelsea Nagy, Jennifer Balch, Stefan Leyk, and William R. Travis. 2021. Risky development: Increasing exposure to natural hazards in the United States. *Earth's Future* 9 (7): e2020EF001795. doi.org/10.1029/2020ef001795

Ikeda, Kyoko, Roy Rasmussen, Changhai Liu, Andrew Newman, Fei Chen, Mike Barlage, Ethan Gutmann, Jimmy Duhia, Aiguo Dai, Charles Luce, and Keith Musselman. 2021. Snowfall and snowpack in the Western US as captured by convection permitting climate simulations: Current climate and pseudo global warming future climate. *Climate Dynamics* 57: 2191–2215. doi.org/10.1007/s00382-021-05805-w

Jolly, Matt W., Mark A. Cochrane, Patrick H. Freeborn, Zachary A. Holden, Timothy J. Brown, Grant J. Williamson, and David M.J.S. Bowman. 2015. Climate-induced variations in global wildfire danger from 1979 to 2013. *Nature Communications* 6: 7537. doi.org/10.1038/ncomms8537

Kawahara, Akito Y., Lawrence E. Reeves, Jesse R. Barber, and Scott H. Black. 2021. Opinion: Eight simple actions that individuals can take to save insects from global declines. *Proceedings of the National Academy of Sciences* 118: e2002547117. doi.org/10.1073/pnas.e2002547117

Kimmerer, Robin Wall. 2013. *Braiding Sweetgrass: Indigenous Wisdom, Scientific Knowledge, and the Teachings of Plants.* Minneapolis, MN: Milkweed Editions.

Kramer, Heather A., Miranda H. Mockrin, Patricia M. Alexandre, Susan I. Stewart, and Volker C. Radeloff. 2018. Where wildfires destroy buildings in the US relative to the wildland–urban interface and national fire outreach programs. *International Journal of Wildland Fire* 27: 329–341. doi.org/10.1071/WF17135

Kramer, Heather. A., Miranda H. Mockrin, Patricia M. Alexandre, and Volker C. Radeloff. 2019. High wildfire damage in interface communities in California. *International Journal of Wildland Fire* 28: 641–650. doi.org/10.1071/WF18108

Lopez, Hosmay, Robert West, Shenfu Dong, Gustavo Goni, Ben Kirtman, Sang-Ki Lee, and Robert Atlas. 2018. Early emergence of anthropogenically forced heat waves in the western United States and Great Lakes. *Nature Climate Change* 8: 414–420. doi.org/10.1038/s41558-018-0116-y

Moritz, Max A., Enric Batllori, Ross A. Bradstock, A. Malcolm Gill, John Handmer, Paul F. Hessburg, Justin Leonard, Sarah McCaffrey, Dennis C. Odion, Tania Schoennagel, and Alexandra Syphard. 2014. Review: Learning to coexist with fire. *Nature* 515: 58–66. doi.org/10.1038/nature13946

Radeloff, Volker C., David P. Helmers, H. Anu Kramer, Miranda H. Mockrin, Patricia M. Alexandre, Avi Bar-Massada, Van Bustic, Todd J. Hawbaker, Sebastián Martinuzzi, Alexandra D. Syphard, and Susan I. Stewart. 2018. Rapid growth of the US wildland-urban interface raises wildfire risk. *Proceedings of the National Academy of Sciences* 115: 3314–3319. doi.org/10.1073/pnas.1718850115

Rosenberg, Kenneth V., Adriaan M. Dokter, Peter J. Blancher, John R. Sauer, Adam C. Smith, Paul A. Smith, Jessica C. Stanton, Arvind Panjabi, Laura

Helft, Michael Parr, and Peter P. Marra. 2019. Decline in North American avifauna. *Science* 366: 120–124. doi.org/10.1126/science.aaw1313

Short, Karen C. 2021. Spatial wildfire occurrence data for the United States, 1992–2018 (FPA_FOD_20210617), 5th edition. Fort Collins, CO: Forest Service Research Data Archive. doi.org/10.2737/RDS-2013-0009.5

van Klink, Roel, Diana E. Bowler, Konstantin B. Gongalsky, Ann B. Swengel, Alessandro Gentile, and Jonathan M. Chase. 2020. Meta-analysis reveals declines in terrestrial but increases in freshwater insect abundances. *Science* 368 (6489): 417–420. Erratum corrected 26 June 2021. doi.org/10.1126/science.aax9931

Wagner, David L., Eliza M. Grames, Matthew L. Forister, May R. Berenbaum, and David Stopak. 2021. Insect decline in the Anthropocene: Death by a thousand cuts. *Proceedings of the National Academy of Sciences* 118 (2): 1–10. doi.org/10.1073/pnas.2023989118

Wright, Jonathon S., Rong Fu, John R. Worden, Sudip Chakraborty, Nicholas E. Clinton, Camille Risi, Ying Sun, and Lei Yin. 2017. Rainforest-initiated wet season onset over the southern Amazon. *Proceedings of the National Academy of Sciences* 114: 8481–8486. doi.org/10.1073/pnas.1621516114

Habitat: Your Biotic Community and Ecoregion

Bond, Monica L., Derek E. Lee, Rodney B. Siegel, and James P. Ward, Jr. 2009. Habitat use and selection by California spotted owls in a postfire landscape. *Journal of Wildlife Management* 73: 1116–1124. doi.org/10.2193/2008-248

Chase, Jonathan M., Shane A. Blowes, Tiffany M. Knight, Katharina Gerstner, and Felix May. 2020. Ecosystem decay exacerbates biodiversity loss with habitat loss. *Nature* 584: 238–243. doi.org/10.1038/s41586-020-2531-2

Fusco, Emily J., John T. Finn, Jennifer K. Balch, R. Chelsea Nagy, and Bethany A. Bradley. 2019. Invasive grasses

240

increase fire occurrence and frequency across US ecoregions. *Proceedings of the National Academy of Sciences* 116: 23594–23599. doi.org/10.1073/pnas.1908253116

Galbraith, Sarah M., James H. Cane, Andrew R. Moldenke, and James W. Rivers. 2019. Wild bee diversity increases with local fire severity in a fire-prone landscape. *Ecosphere* 10(4): e02668. doi.org/10.1002/ecs2.2668

Griffith, Glenn E., James M. Omernik, David W. Smith, Terry D. Cook, Ed Tallyn, Kendra Moseley, and Colleen B. Johnson. 2016. Ecoregions of California (poster): Open-File Report 2016–1021. doi.org/10.3133/ofr20161021

Haddad, Nick M., Lars A. Brudvig, Jean Clobert, Kendi F. Davies, Andrew Gonzales, Robert D. Holt, Thomas E. Lovejoy, Joseph O. Sexton, Mike P. Austin, Cathy D. Collins, William M. Cook, Ellen I. Damschen, Robert M. Ewers, Bryan L. Foster, Clinton N. Jenkins, Andrew J. King, William F. Laurance, Douglas J. Levey, Chris R. Margules, Brett A. Melbourne, A. O. Nicholls, John L. Orrock, Dan-Xia Song, and John R. Townshend. 2015. Habitat fragmentation and its lasting impact on Earth's ecosystems. *Scientific Advances* 1:e1500052. doi.org/10.1126/sciadv.1500052

Hanson, Chad T. 2015. Use of higher-severity fire areas by female Pacific fishers on the Kern Plateau, Sierra Nevada, California, USA. *Wildlife Society Bulletin* 39: 497–502.

———. 2021. *Smokescreen: Debunking Wildfire Myths to Save Our Forests and Our Climate.* Lexington, KY: University of Kentucky Press.

Hanski, Ilkka. 2011. Habitat loss, the dynamics of biodiversity, and a perspective on conservation. *Ambio* 40: 248–255. doi.org/10.1007/s13280-011-0147-3

Kagan, James S., Rachel L. Brunner, and John A. Christy. 2019. *Classification of the Native Vegetation of Oregon.* Portland, OR: Oregon Biodiversity Information Center. inr.oregonstate.edu/sites/inr.oregonstate.edu/files/2019-classification-native-vegetation-oregon.pdf

Myers, Norman, Russell A. Mittermeier, Cristina G. Mittermeier, Gustavo A. B. da Fonseca, and Jennifer Kent. 2000. Biodiversity hotspots for conservation priorities. *Nature* 403 (6772): 853–858. doi.org/10.1038/35002501

Radeloff, Volker C., David P. Helmers, H. Anu Kramer, Miranda H. Mockrin, Patricia M. Alexandre, Avi Bar-Massada, Van Bustic, Todd J. Hawbaker, Sebastián Martinuzzi, Alexandra D. Syphard, and Susan I. Stewart. 2018. Rapid growth of the US wildland-urban interface raises wildfire risk. *Proceedings of the National Academy of Sciences* 115: 3314–3319. doi.org/10.1073/pnas.1718850115

Rocchio, F. Joseph, and Rex. C. Crawford. 2015. *Ecological Systems of Washington State: A Guide to Identification.* Natural Heritage Report 2015-04. Washington State Department of Natural Resources. www.dnr.wa.gov/publications/amp_nh_ecosystems_guide.pdf

Sawyer, John, Todd Keeler-Wolf, and Julie M. Evens. 2009. *A Manual of California Vegetation*, 2nd edition. Sacramento, CA: California Native Plant Society Press.

Spyreas, Greg. 2019. Floristic quality assessment: A critique, a defense, and a primer. *Ecosphere* 10(8): e02825. doi.org/10.1002/ecs2.2825

The Nature and Behavior of Fire

Babrauskas, Vytenis. 2002. Ignition of wood: a review of the state of the art. *Journal of Fire Protection Engineering* 12: 163–189. doi.org/10.1106/104239102028711

Brooks, Matthew L., Richard A. Minnich, and John R. Matchett. 2018. Southeastern Deserts bioregion. In Jan W. Wagtendonk, Neil G. Sugihara, Scott L. Stephens, Andrea E. Thode, Kevin E. Shaffer, and Jo Ann Fites-Kaufman (eds.), *Fire in California's Ecosystems*, 2nd edition. Berkeley, CA: University of California Press.

Finney, Mark A., Jack D. Cohen, Jason M. Forthofer, Sara S. McAllister, Michael J. Gollner, Daniel J. Gorham, Kozo Saito, Nelson K. Akafuah, Brittany A. Adam, and Justin D. English. 2015. Role of buoyant flame dynamics in

241

wildfire spread. *Proceedings of the National Academy of Sciences* 112: 9833–9838. doi.org/10.1073/pnas.1504498112

Gabbert, Bill. 2021. PBS explains how fire whirls and fire tornados form. Wildfire Today. wildfiretoday.com/2021/09/02/pbs-explains-how-fire-whirls-and-fire-tornados-form/

Gershunov, Alexander, Janin Guzman Morales, Benjamin Hatchett, Kristen Guirguis, Rosana Aguilera, Tamara Shulgina, John T. Abatzoglou, Daniel Cayan, David Pierce, Park Williams, Ivory Small, Rachel Clemesha, Lara Schwarz, Tarik Benmarhnia, and Alex Tardy. 2021. Hot and cold flavors of southern California's Santa Ana winds: Their causes, trends, and links with wildfire. *Climate Dynamics* 559: 1–14. doi.org/10.1007/s00382-021-05802-z

Ghaderi, M., Maryam Ghodrat, and Jason J. Sharples. 2021. LES simulation of wind-driven wildfire interaction with idealized structures in the Wildland-Urban Interface. *Atmosphere* 12: 1–17. doi.org/10.3390/atmos12010021

Halofsky, Jessica E., David L. Peterson, and Brian J. Harvey. 2020. Changing wildfire, changing forests: The effects of climate change on fire regimes and vegetation in the Pacific Northwest, USA. *Fire Ecology* 16: 24. doi.org/10.1186/s42408-019-0062-8

Keeley, Jon E., and Alexandra D. Syphard. 2019. Twenty-first century California, USA, wildfires: Fuel-dominated vs. wind-dominated fires. *Fire Ecology* 15: 24. doi.org/10.1186/s42408-019-0041-0

Lunder, Zeke. September 13, 2021. Lassen Park and Caribou Wilderness fire severity—9/11/2021. The Lookout. the-lookout.org/2021/09/13/lassen-park-and-caribou-wilderness-fire-severity-9-11-2021/

Lynn, Christopher Dana. 2014. Hearth and campfire influences on arterial blood pressure: Defraying the costs of the social brain through fireside relaxation. *Evolutionary Psychology* 12: 983–1003. doi.org/10.1177/147470491401200509

Ottmar, Roger D., and David V. Sandberg. 1985. Calculating moisture content of 1000-hour timelag fuels in western Washington and western Oregon. Research Paper PNW-336. Portland, OR: US Department of Agriculture, Forest Service, Pacific Northwest Forest and Range Experiment Station.

Pyne, Stephen J., Patricia L. Andrews, and Richard D. Laven. 1996. Wildland fire fundamentals, in *Introduction to Wildland Fire*. New York: John Wiley and Sons.

Reigel, Gregg M., Richard R. Miller, Carl N. Skinner, Sydney E. Smith, Calvin A. Farris, and Kyle E. Merriam. Northeastern Plateau bioregion. In Jan W. Wagtendonk, Neil G. Sugihara, Scott L. Stephens, Andrea E. Thode, Kevin E. Shaffer, and Jo Ann Fites-Kaufman (eds.), *Fire in California's Ecosystems*, 2nd edition. Berkeley, CA: University of California Press.

Short, Karen C. 2021. Spatial wildfire occurrence data for the United States, 1992–2018 (FPA_FOD_20210617), 5th edition. Fort Collins, CO: Forest Service Research Data Archive. doi.org/10.2737/RDS-2013-0009.5

Sikkink, Pamela G., Duncan C. Lutes, and Robert Keane. 2009. Field guide for identifying fuel loading models. General Technical Report RMRS-GTR-225. Fort Collins, CO: US Department of Agriculture, Forest Service, Rocky Mountain Research Station.

Sinha, S., A. Jhalani, and A. Ray. 2004. Modelling of pyrolysis in wood: A review. *Journal of Solar Energy Society of India* 10: 41–62.

Srock, Alan, Joseph Charney, Brian Potter, and Scott Goodrick. 2018. The hot-dry-windy index: A new fire weather index. *Atmosphere* 9: 279–289. doi.org/10.3390/atmos9070279

Storey, Michael Anthony, Owen F. Price, Miguel Almeida, Carlos Riveiro, Ross A. Bradstock, and Jason J. Sharples. 2021. Experiments on the influence of spot fire and topography interaction on fire rate of spread. *PLOS One* 16: e0245132. doi.org/10.1371/journal.pone.0245132

242

Hardening Your Home Against Fire

Federal Emergency Management Agency (FEMA). September 2008. *Home Builder's Guide to Construction in Wildfire Zones*. Technical Fact Sheet Series, FEMA P-737. www.fema.gov/sites/default/files/2020-08/fema_p_737_0.pdf

Fire Safe Marin. 2020. Harden Your Home: How to Protect Your Home from Wildfires. www.firesafemarin.org/home-hardening

Restaino, Christina, Susan Kocher, Nicole Shaw, Steven Hawks, Carlie Murphy, and Stephen L. Quarles. 2020. *Wildfire Home Retrofit Guide*. University of Nevada, Reno, Extension. www.readyforwildfire.org/wp-content/uploads/Wildfire_Home_Retrfit_Guide-1.26.21.pdf

Takahashi, Fumiaki. 2019. Frontiers in Mechanical Engineering. Whole-House Fire Blanket Protection From Wildland-Urban Interface Fires. Department of Mechanical and Aerospace Engineering, Case Western Reserve University, Cleveland, OH, United States. www.frontiersin.org/articles/10.3389/fmech.2019.00060/full

Creating Defensible Space

Brandle, James R., Laurie Hodges, John Tyndall, and Robert A. Sudmeyer. 2009. Windbreak practices. In H. E. Garrett (ed.), *North American Agroforestry: An Integrated Science and Practice*, 2nd edition. Madison, WI: American Society of Astronomy. www.kansasforests.org/rural_forestry/rural_docs/NAAgroforestry%20Chapter%205%20WB%20Yield%20Brandle.pdf

Stephens, S. L., Jens T. Stevens, Brandon M. Collins, Robert A. York, and Jamie M. Lydersen. 2018. Historical and modern landscape forest structure in fir (*Abies*)-dominated mixed conifer forests in the northern Sierra Nevada, USA. *Fire Ecology* 14: 7. doi.org/10.1186/s42408-018-0008-6

What to Plant, Where, and When

Archibald, S., Gareth P. Hempson, and Caroline Lehmann. 2019. A unified framework for plant life-history strategies shaped by fire and herbivory. *New Phytologist* 224: 1490–1503. doi.org/10.1111/nph.15986

Berkeley Urban Bee Lab. n.d. Seasonal bee gardening. www.helpabee.org/seasonal-bee-gardening.html

Brunet, Johanne, Magaret W. Thairu, Jillian M. Henss, Rosabeth I. Link, and Joshua A. Kluever. Pamela K. Diggle, ed. 2015. The effects of flower, floral display, and reward sizes on bumblebee foraging behavior when pollen is the reward and plants are dichogamous. *International Journal of Plant Sciences* 176: 811–819. doi.org/10.1086/683339

Cui, Xinglei, Adrian M. Paterson, Sarah V. Wyse, Md Azharul Alam, Kevin J. L. Maurin, Robon Pieper, Josep Padulles Cubino, Dean M. O'Connell, Djessie Donkers, Julien Breda, Hannah L. Buckley, George L. W. Perry, and Timothy J. Curran. 2020. Shoot flammability of vascular plants is phylogenetically conserved and related to habitat fire-proneness and growth form. *Nature Plants* 6: 355–359. doi.org/10.1038/s41477-020-0635-1

Faita, M. R., E.D.M. Oliveira, V. V. Alves, A. I. Orth, and R. O. Nodari. 2018. Changes in hypopharyngeal glands of nurse bees (*Apis mellifera*) induced by pollen-containing sublethal doses of the herbicide Roundup. *Chemosphere* 211: 566–572.

Fragoso, Fabiana P., Qi Jiang, Murray K. Clayton, and Johanne Brunet. 2021. Patch selection by bumble bees navigating discontinuous landscapes. *Scientific Reports* 11: 8986. doi.org/10.1038/s41598-021-88394-2

Fusco, Emily J., John T. Finn, Jennifer K. Balch, R. Chelsea Nagy, and Bethany A. Bradley. 2019. Invasive grasses increase fire occurrence and frequency across US ecoregions. *Proceedings of the National Academy of Sciences* 116: 23594–23599. doi.org/10.1073/pnas.1908253116

Garbolotto, Matteo M., Susan J. Frankel, and Bruno Scanu. 2018. Soil- and waterborne *Phytophthora* species linked to recent outbreaks in Northern California restoration sites. *California Agriculture* 72: 208–216. doi.org/10.3733/ca.2018a0033

Grissell, Eric. 2001. *Insects and Gardens: In Pursuit of a Garden Ecology.* Portland, OR: Timber Press.

Keator, Glenn. 1998. *The Life of an Oak: An Intimate Portrait.* Berkeley, CA: Heyday Books and the California Oak Foundation.

Logan, William Bryant. 2006. *Oak: The Frame of Civilization.* New York: Norton.

Luo, Qi-Hua, Jing Gao, Chang Liu, Yu-Zhen Ma, Zhi-Yong Zhou, Ping-Li Dai, Chun-Sheng Hou, Yan-Yan Wu, and Qing-Yun Diao. 2021. Effects of a commercially formulated glyphosate solutions at recommended concentrations on honeybee (*Apis mellifera* L.) behaviors. *Nature Scientific Reports* 11: 2115. doi.org/10.1038/s41598-020-80445-4

Mader, Eric, Matthew Shepherd, Mace Vaughan, Scott Hoffman Black, and Gretchen LeBuhn. 2011. *The Xerces Society Guide Attracting Native Pollinators: Protecting North America's Bees and Butterflies.* North Adams, MA: Storey Publishing.

Motta, Erick V. S., Kasie Raymann, and Nancy A. Moran. 2018. Glyphosate perturbs the gut microbiota of honey bees. *Proceedings of the National Academy of Sciences* 115: 10305–10310. doi.org/10.1073/pnas.1803880115

Nathan, Emery, Keely Roth, and Alexandria Lynn Pivovaroff. 2020. Flowering phenology indicates plant flammability in a dominant shrub species. *Ecological Indicators* 109: 105745. doi.org/10.1016/j.ecolind.2019.105745

Quarles, Stephen, and Ed Smith. 2011. The combustibility of landscape mulches. University of Nevada Cooperative Extension. SP-11-04. naes.agnt.unr.edu/PMS/Pubs/1510_2011_95.pdf

Schierenbeck, Kristina. 2021. The genetic consequences of hybridization between California native plant species with closely related taxa. *Artemisia* 48: 25–29.

Seide, Vanessa Eler, Rodrigo Cupertino Bernardes, Eliseu José Guedes Pereira, and Maria Augusta Pereira Lima. 2018. Glyphosate is lethal and Cry toxins alter the development of the stingless bee *Melipona quadrifasciata.* *Environmental Pollution* 243: 1854–1860. doi.org/10.1016/j.envpol.2018.10.020

Simpson, Kimberley J., Brad S. Ripley, Pascal-Antoine Christin, Claire M. Belcher, Caroline E. R. Lehmann, Gavin H. Thomas, and Colin P. Osborne. 2016. Determinants of flammability in savanna grass species. *Journal of Ecology* 104: 138–148. doi.org/10.1111/1365-2745.12503

Syphard, Alexandra D., Teresa J. Brennan, and Jon E. Keeley. 2014. The role of defensible space for residential structure protection during wildfires. *International Journal of Wildland Fire.* doi.org/10.1071/WF13158

Tallamy, Douglas W. 2019. *Nature's Best Hope: A New Approach to Conservation That Starts in Your Yard.* Portland, OR: Timber Press.

———. 2021. *The Nature of Oaks: The Rich Ecology of Our Most Essential Native Trees.* Portland, OR: Timber Press.

Maintaining Plants for Fire Resilience

California Chaparral Institute. 2020. From the house outward: Protecting your home from wildfire. california-chaparral.org/fire/protecting-your-home/

Zhang, Luoping, Iemaan Rana, Rachel M. Shaffer, Emanuela Taioli, and Lianne Sheppard. 2019. Exposure to glyphosate-based herbicides and risk for non-Hodgkin lymphoma: A meta-analysis and supporting evidence. *Mutation Research* 781: 186–206. doi.org/10.1016/j.mrrev.2019.02.001

Recovery: Helping Land
Heal After a Fire

Abatzoglou, John T., David E. Rupp, Larry W. O'Neill, and Mojtaba Sadegh. 2021. Compound extremes drive the western Oregon fires of September 2020. *Geophysical Research Letters* 48: 8. doi.org/10.1029/2021GL092520

Bright, Benjamin C., Andrew T. Hudak, Robert E. Kennedy, Justin D. Braaten, and Azad Henareh Khalyani. 2019. Examining post-fire vegetation recovery with Landsat time series analysis in three western North American forest types. *Fire Ecology* 15: 8. doi.org/10.1186/s42408-018-0021-9

Brooks, Randy. University of Idaho Extension. Forestry Information Series. Fire No. 5.

California Native Plant Society. 2019. *Fire Recovery Guide*. www.cnps.org/wp-content/uploads/2019/08/cnps-fire-recovery-guide-2019.pdf

Certini, Giacomo. 2005. Effects of fire on properties of forest soils. *Oecologia* 143: 1–10. doi.org/10.1007/s00442-0041788-8

Certini, Giacomo, Daniel Moya, Manuel Esteban Lucas-Borja, and Giovanni Mastrolonardo. 2021. The impact of fire on soil-dwelling biota: A review. *Forest Ecology and Management* 488: 118989. doi.org/10.1016/j.foreco.2021.118989

Copeland, Stella M., Seth M. Munson, John B. Bradford, Bradley J. Butterfield, and Kevin L. Gunnell. 2019. Long-term plant community trajectories suggest divergent responses of native and nonnative perennials and annuals to vegetation removal and seeding treatments. *Restoration Ecology* 27: 821–831. doi.org/10.1111/rec.12928

Downing, William M., Meg A. Krawchuk, Garrett W. Meigs, Sandra L. Haire, Jonathan D. Coop, Ryan B. Walker, Ellen Whitman, Geneva Chong, and Carol Miller. 2019. Influence of fire refugia spatial pattern on post-fire forest recovery in Oregon's Blue Mountains. *Landscape Ecology* 34: 771–792. doi.org/10.1007/s10980-019-00802-1

Falk, Donald A., Adam C. Watts, and Andrea E. Thode. 2019. Scaling ecological resilience. *Frontiers in Ecology and Evolution* 7: 1–16. doi.org/10.3389/fevo.2019.00275

Fernández, Cristina, and José A. Vega. 2021. Is wood strand mulching a good alternative to helmulching to mitigate the risk of soil erosion and favour the recovery of vegetation in NW Spain? *Landscape and Ecological Engineering* 17: 233–242. doi.org/10.1007/s11355-020-00439-2

Halofsky, Jessica E., David L. Peterson, and Brian J. Harvey. 2020. Changing wildfire, changing forests: The effects of climate change on fire regimes and vegetation in the Pacific Northwest, USA. *Fire Ecology* 16: 4. doi.org/10.1186/s42408-019-0062-8

Hanson, Chad T. 2021. *Smokescreen: Debunking Wildfire Myths to Save Our Forests and Our Climate*. Lexington, KY: University of Kentucky Press.

Hrelja, Iva, Ivana Šestak, and Igor Bogunović. 2020. Wildfire impacts on soil physical and chemical properties—A short review of recent studies. *Agric. Conspec. Sci.* 85(4): 293–301.

Hubbert, Ken R., Pete M. Wohlgemuth, and Jan L. Beyers. 2012. Effects of hydromulch on post-fire erosion and plant recovery in chaparral shrublands of southern California. *International Journal of Wildland Fire* 21: 155–167. doi.org/10.1071/WF10050

Isaacson, Kristofer P., Caitlin R. Proctor, Q. Erica Wang, Ethan Y. Edwards, Yoorae Noh, Amisha D. Shah, and Andrew J. Whelton. 2021. Drinking water contamination from the thermal degradation of plastics: Implications for wildfire and structure fire response. *Environmental Science Water Research and Technology* 7: 274. doi.org/10.1039/d0ew00836b

Keeley, Jon E., and Alexandra D. Syphard. 2017. Different historical fire-climate patterns in California. *International Journal of Wildland Fire* 26: 253–268. doi.org/10.1071/WF16102

245

Keeley, Jon E., and Juli G. Pausas. 2018. Evolution of 'smoke' induced seed germination in pyroendemic plants. *South African Journal of Botany* 115: 251–255. doi.org/10.1016/j.sajb.2016.07.012

Keeley, Jon E., and Alexandra D. Syphard. 2019. Twenty-first century California, USA, wildfires: Fuel-dominated vs. wind-dominated fires. *Fire Ecology* 15: 24. doi.org/10.1186/s42408-019-0041-0

Kim Eun-Jung, Jeong-Eun Oh, and Yoon-Seok Chang. 2003. Effects of forest fire on the level and distribution of PCDD/Fs and PAHs in soil. *Science of the Total Environment* 311:177–189. doi.org/10.1016/S0048-9697(03)00095-0

López-Vincente, Manuel, Henk Kramer, and Saskia Keesstra. 2021. Effectiveness of soil erosion barriers to reduce sediment connectivity at small basin scale in a fire-affected forest. *Journal of Environmental Management* 278: 111510. doi.org/10.1016/j.jenvman.2020.111510

Martin, Drew, Mai Tomida, and Brian Meacham. 2016. Environmental impact of fire. *Fire Science Reviews* 5:5. doi.org/10.1186/s40038-016-0014-1

Masterson, Linda. 2012. *Surviving Wildfire: Get Prepared, Stay Alive, Rebuild Your Life. A Handbook for Homeowners.* Masonville, CO: PixieJack Press.

Peppin, Donna, Peter Z. Fule, Carolyn Hull Sieg, Jan L. Byers, and Molly E. Hunter. 2010. Post-wildfire seeding in forests of the western United States: An evidence-based review. *Forest Ecology and Management* 260: 573–586.

Rhoades, Charles C., Alex T. Chow, Timothy P. Covino, Timothy S. Fegel, Derek N. Pierson, and Allison E. Rhea. 2019. The legacy of a severe wildfire on stream nitrogen and carbon in headwater catchments. *Ecosystems* 22: 643–657. doi.org/10.1007/s10021-018-0293-6

Santoso, Muhammad A., Eirik G. Christensen, Jiuling Yang, and Guillermo Rein. 2019. Review of the transition from smouldering to flaming combustion in wildfires. *Frontiers in Mechanical Engineering* 5: 1–20. doi.org/10.3389/fmech.2019.00049

Simard, Martin, William H. Romme, Jacob M. Griffin, and Monica G. Turner. 2011. Do mountain pine beetle outbreaks change the probability of active crown fire in lodgepole pine forests? *Ecological Monographs* 81: 3–24. doi.org/10.1890/10-1176.1

Stevens-Rumann, Camille, and Penelope Morgan. 2019. Tree regeneration following wildfires in the western US: A review. *Fire Ecology* 15: 15. doi.org/10.1186/s42408-019-0032-1

UC Cooperative Extension of Sonoma County. 2020. Produce Safety After Wildfire. ucanr.edu/sites/SoCo/files/315093.pdf

USDA Natural Resources Conservation Service (NRCS). 2000. Soil Quality Resource Concerns: Hydrophobicity. Soil Quality Information Sheet. USDA NRCS Soil Quality Institute. www.nrcs.usda.gov/Internet/FSE_DOCUMENTS/nrcs142p2_051899.pdf

Williams, A. Park, John T. Abatzoglou, Alexander Gershunov, Janin Guzman-Morales, Daniel A. Bishop, Jennifer K. Balch, and Dennis P. Lettenmaier. 2019. Observed impacts of anthropogenic climate change on wildfire in California. *Earth's Future* 7: 892–910. doi.org/10.1029/2019EF001210

Woolley, Travis, David C. Shaw, LaWen T. Hollingsworth, Michelle C. Agne, Stephen Fitzgerald, Andris Eglitis, and Laurie Kurth. 2019. Beyond red crowns: Complex changes in surface and crown fuels and their interactions 32 years following mountain pine beetle epidemics in south-central Oregon, USA. *Fire Ecology* 15: 4. doi.org/10.1186/s42408-018-0010-z

246

Our Fire Future

Anderson, M. Kat. Berkeley. 2005. *Tending the Wild: Native American Knowledge and the Management of California's Natural Resources*. Berkeley, CA: University of California Press.

Arax, Mark. August 2019. Gone—Decades of greed, neglect, corruption, and bad politics led to last year's Paradise fire, the worst in California history. It should never have happened. It will happen again. *California Sunday Magazine*. story.californiasunday.com/gone-paradise-fire

Biswell, Harold. 1980. Fire ecology: Past, present, and future. Keynote talk presented at the American Association for the Advancement of Science, Ecology Section, Davis, California, June 23, 1980.

Collins, Brandon M., Jay D. Miller, Jeffrey M. Kane, Danny L. Fry, and Andrea E. Thode. 2018. Characterizing fire regimes. In Jan W. Wagtendonk, Neil G. Sugihara, Scott L. Stephens, Andrea E. Thode, Kevin E. Shaffer and Jo Ann Fites-Kaufman (eds.), *Fire in California's Ecosystems*, 2nd edition. Berkeley, CA: University of California Press.

Daniels, Mark L., Scott Anderson, and Cathy Whitlock. 2005. Vegetation and fire history since the Late Pleistocene from the Trinity Mountains, northwestern California, USA. *The Holocene*, 15(7): 1062–1071. doi.org/10.1191/0959683605hl878ra

Dennison, Phillip E., Simon C. Brewer, James D. Arnold, and Max A. Moritz. 2014. Large wildfire trends in the western United States, 1984–2011. *Geophysical Research Letters* 41: 2928–2933. doi.org/10.1002/2014GL059576

Editorial: California leaders downplay the dangerous effects of sprawl during wildfires. August 7, 2019. *Los Angeles Times*. www.latimes.com/opinion/story/2019-08-06/wildfire-sprawl-development

Peterson, Molly. June 12, 2019. One potential solution to deadly fires in the wilderness: Don't build there. KQED. www.kqed.org/science/1943266/one-potential-solution-to-fires-in-the-wilderness-dont-build-there

Sommer, Lauren. June 3, 2019. This California neighborhood was built to survive a wildfire. And it worked. KQED. www.kqed.org/science/1941685/this-california-neighborhood-was-built-to-survive-a-wildfire-and-it-worked?fbclid=IwAR1x-Lo5Chz3DGHzsKdkzHq4Vgdue7TzUdTkjqeXYd-swCn2eQqxKNd_IEDRM

Sugihara, Neil G., Jan W. Van Wagtendonk, and Jo Ann Fites-Kaufman. 2018. Fire as an ecological process. In Jan W. Wagtendonk, Neil G. Sugihara, Scott L. Stephens, Andrea E. Thode, Kevin E. Shaffer and Jo Ann Fites-Kaufman (eds.), *Fire in California's Ecosystems*, 2nd edition. Berkeley, CA: University of California Press.

247

Acknowledgments

I WISH TO THANK JOYCE WINKLER for retrieving me from a house fire to experience more of life. We are here but for fortune.

I have been blessed with family and friends who inspire lifelong learning through example. I am especially indebted to my father, Ben E. Edwards III, who engenders good in everyone, along with the notions that we should love what we do, figure things out, and work hard. I am grateful to Jennifer Jewell for introducing us to Stacee at Timber Press, and to our local "literary society" of strong women who motivate each other to pursue whatever strikes. My partner, Chris, and my children, Adeline, Nathaniel, and Gwendolyn, are a beloved and forgiving source of strength. I would also like to thank all of the folks who have made available their knowledge and advocacy for native plants and environments.

Rachel and I thank Timber Press, and Lorraine Anderson for her careful editing, which turned our ideas into an accessible guide. Most of all, I thank Rachel for coming up with this idea and being such a great writing partner. This book could not have come to fruition without what we each brought to the project.

—Adrienne

I WANT TO THANK MY HUSBAND for his support of my efforts to put this book together, and the inspiration he gave me to research fire in the first place. I also want to thank Adrienne for having the confidence that I lacked to get the idea for this book into production.

—Rachel

Photography and Illustration Credits

Courtesy of Firezat, page 76

Kari Greer, page 87

Google Earth, page 69 top

Saxon Holt, pages 98, 103

Landfire.gov (CONUS 2012 Summarized Map Complete Collection JPG) Fire Regime Group Map, page 36

Robbi Pengelly / *Sonoma Index-Tribune*, page 93

George Rose / Getty Images, page 69 bottom

Staehle, Albert. 1945. "Smokey says - Care will prevent 9 out of 10 forest fires!." Special Collections, USDA National Agricultural Library. https://www.nal.usda.gov/exhibits/speccoll/items/show/453, page 234

Courtesy of the University of Nevada, Reno Extension, Living With Fire Program, page 66

Courtesy of Washington State Department of Natural Resources, page 88

ALAMY

Danita Delimont, page 224

Nature Picture Library, page 220

ZUMA Press, Inc, page 231

DREAMSTIME

Alinka2408, page 197

Andreistanescu, page 10

Bozhdb, page 213

Salvador Ceja, page 19

Linda Cook, page 59

Steven Cukrov, page 120

Erin Donalson, pages 20, 38

Bonandbon Dw, page 13 top

Steve Estvanik, page 221

Larry Gevert, page 78

Jamie Hooper, page 107

Scott Jones, page 215

Amelia Martin, page 24 left

Chokchai Poomichaiya, page 210

John Rehg, page 15

Daniel Ripplinger, page 106 left

Emma Ross, page 106 right

Stevehymon, page 12 top

Tab 1962, page 74

Andreas Tychon, page 118

FLICKR

Patrick Alexander, pages 148, 156 right

BVC Members, page 196

National Interagency Fire Center / Idaho Department of Lands, page 51

National Interagency Fire Center / Kari Greer, pages 12 bottom, 49, 81, 83, 97

Used under a CC BY 2.0 license

Bureau of Land Management / Jennifer McNew, page 192

Tom Brandt, page 126 top

Tom Hilton, pages 172, 176 bottom left

John Rusk, pages 140 right, 141, 147 left, 176 top right, 183, 188, 190 top, 190 bottom

249

Index

A

accelerants, on decks, 74
Acer species, 202
Acer circinatum, 131
Actostaphylos species, 112
aerial / canopy fuels, 50
aerial / crown / canopy fire, defined, 48
After the Fire web page (USDA Natural Resources Conservation Service), 212
After the Flames website (aftertheflames.com), 212
Agrostis pallens, 111
Ailanthus altissimus, 107
air flow, promotion of, 196
alders, 216
Alnus species, 216
Anderson, Kat, 233
animal species, 234. *See also* wildlife
annuals, 84, 209, 217–218, 222. *See also* grasses: annuals
annuals and biennials, 173–178
architecture, and plant flammability, 110
art, 82, 85, 87
Arundo donax, 24
aspect / exposure, 58, 59, 61. *See also specific entries in plant directory*
    defined, 60
Atriplex species, 110
Australia, volunteers in, 229

B

bad plants, 106, 107, 121, 122. *See also specific plant categories*
barbecue appliances, 67, 74
bare root plants, 114–115
barriers, 60, 61
beach species, 179
bee mimics, 107. *See also* pollinators

bees, 107, 119, 152, 209. *See also* pollinators
Bermuda grass, 107
biennials and annuals, 173–178
biochar, 41
    defined, 43
biodiversity
    defined, 16
    and fire severity, 223
    increasing, 84, 119
    and native plants, 102, 219
    and pest and disease control, 195–196
    and plant selection, 104
    reduction of, 23, 28
biodiversity hot spots, 21, 34, 121
biomass reduction, 23, 209
biome types, 29
biotic communities, 30–34
    defined, 33
birds, 14, 199, 223
Biswell, Harold, 225
botanists / naturalists, 122
bottlebrush, 113
boxwood, 102
Braiding Sweetgrass (Kimmerer), 18
branch collar, defined, 207
broadcast burn, defined, 208
Bromus tectorum, 24, 113
broom shrubs, 24
Buddleja davidii, 122
budget considerations, 63, 69, 70, 77, 219, 228, 230
building ignitions, 53
built environment, defined, 16
bulbs, 112, 222
bulbs, corms, and tubers, 192–193
bumblebees, 104. *See also* pollinators
burning of pruning and debris residue, 208
bush mallows, 220

Butte County, California, 234
butterflies, 14, 107. *See also* pollinators
butterfly bush, 122

C

cafiresafecouncil.org, 229
calcium, 215–216
CAL FIRE (California Department of Forestry and Fire
    Protection), 13, 52, 227, 228
Calflora (calflora.org), 105
California
    biome types, 29
    Camp Fire in, 56, 66, 97, 214, 222–223, 226, 230–231
    Carr Fire in, 54
    climate zones in, 52
    community preparedness resources in, 229
    Dixie Fire in, 57
    ecoregions, 30
    El Dorado Fire in, 41
    fire-safe gardens in, 121
    invasive species in, 25
    North Complex Fire in, 57
    Oakland firestorm of 1991 in, 56
    plant communities in, 31
    Santiago Canyon Fire in, 56
    Tubbs Fire in, 69
    wetlands history, 12
    wildfires in, 13, 26
    wind patterns in, 54, 55
    Witch Creek Fire in, 232
California bay (plant), 203
California Department of Fish and Wildlife, 234
California Department of Forestry and Fire Protection
    (CAL FIRE), 13, 52, 227, 228
California fescue, 111
California Fire Safe Council (CFSC), 229
California Invasive Plant Council (Cal-IPC), 25
California Native Plant Society, 31, 105, 212
Callistemon citrinus, 113
Calscape Garden Planner, 105
Calscape online tool (calscape.org), 105
Camp Fire (California), 56, 66, 97, 214, 222–223,
    226, 230–231
camphor tree, 113
canopy / aerial / crown fire, defined, 48
canopy / aerial fuels, 50
canopy thinning (pruning strategy), 202

canyons, and wind patterns, 93
carbon and carbon storage, 23, 40, 41, 47, 117,
    208, 214
carcinogens, 209
Carlton Complex Fire (Washington), 88
Carpobrotus chilensis, 112
Carpobrotus edulis, 112
Carr Fire (Redding, California), 54
Cascades, 27, 56, 105
Ceanothus species, 199, 216
cedar, as organic mulch, 117
Centaurea solstitialis, 24
chaparral habitats and plants
    and 2007 Witch Creek Fire, 232
    and aspect, 59
    coppicing of, 204
    defined, 35
    and fire recovery, 220, 225
    and fire return interval, 37
    and fire severity, 221
    and plant flammability, 113
    pruning schedule, 209
    and removal of native species, 28
    and sudden oak death, 108
    watering, 47, 199
    and zone 4, 88, 90
characteristic species, 34
    defined, 33
charcoal, 41
cheatgrass, 24, 28, 113
Chinook winds, 55, 56
clary sages, 107
Classification of Native Vegetation (Oregon), 31
Cleveland sage, 11
climate, 50–53, 61, 117
climate change
    and fire risk, 12
    impact on ecosystem functions, 23
    impact on fire behavior, 60–61, 233, 234
    and measurement of species types, 24
    regional effects of, 102
    as threat to biodiversity, 17
clinometer or clinometer app, 61
clusters of plants, 84, 86, 87, 89, 92, 108
Coalitions and Collaboratives, Inc., 212
coastal ecoregions, 209
Coast Range (California), 56
color and fire, 40–41

252

combustible materials, 70, 77
    defined, 73
combustion, 40–41
    defined, 43
community fire preparedness, 226–233
Community Wildfire Protection Plans (CWPPs), 226, 228
    defined, 232
compass apps, 61
composting, 208
conduction, defined, 42–43
cones, serotinous, 220
    defined, 219
convection, defined, 43
convective heat, defined, 42
copper chloride, 41
coppicing (pruning strategy), 204
corms, 222
    bulbs, corms, and tubers, 192–193
Cornus species, 196
Cortaderia selloana, 107, 111, 112
cost considerations, 63, 69, 70, 77, 219, 228, 230
county cooperative extension offices, 219, 223
cover crops, 216
cracks in roofing material, 65
crown / canopy / aerial fire, defined, 48
crown lifting / limbing up (pruning strategy). *See* limbing
        up / crown lifting (pruning strategy)
cultivars, 108
    defined, 109
cyanide, 137
Cynodon dactylon, 107
cypress, as organic mulch, 117
Cytisus multiflorus, 24
Cytisus scoparius, 24, 94, 113, 223

D

daffodils, 222
dams or weirs, 27
deadwooding (pruning strategy), 201
debris buildup, and plant flammability, 110
debris cleanup, 209, 213. *See also specific entries in
        plant directory*
deciduous species, 101. *See also specific plant
        categories*
decks, 72, 74–75, 81–82
decomposed granite, as mulch, 118
deep ripping or plowing of land, 27

deer, 196, 225
defensible space
    and community preparedness, 226
    creation of, 18, 79–97
    defined, 16, 96
    on sloping terrain, 59
    and zone system, 80–81, 89, 94
desert plants and ecoregions
    biome types, 29
    and fire, 37, 221
    mulch for, 118, 119
    pruning schedule, 209
    in shelterbelts, 93
    and timing of planting, 117
    watering of, 47
"Diablo wind" (term), 56
direct flame contact, 64, 65, 72, 79
disease control, 195–197, 199, 201, 207–209, 218.
        See also specific entries in plant directory
disease removal (pruning strategy), 201
diversity of species. *See* biodiversity
Dixie Fire (California), 57
dogwood anthracnose disease, 196
dominant species, 34
    defined, 33
door trim, 72
dormancy, 114, 117, 207. *See also specific entries in
        plant directory*
Douglas Complex Fire (Oregon), 223
drainage, 27, 117, 218
drip irrigation, 197
drought
    and fire risk, 48, 199
    and fuels, 45
    method for watering plants during, 47, 197, 198–199
    reducing drought stress, 113, 196, 227–228
    and timing of planting, 117
dry rot or decaying wood, and structure assessment, 65
duff, defined, 48

E

eastern filbert blight, 145
eaves, firescaping of, 70–71
Ecological Systems of Washington State (Washington
        Natural Heritage Program), 31
ecoregions, 30, 209
        defined, 33

edge effects, defined, 28
edge habitats vs. interior habitats, 22–23
edible plants, 104–106
El Cerrito (California area), 13
El Dorado Fire (California), 41
elevation, 58, 60, 61
ember screens, 71
embers / firebrands
 defined, 73
 as ignition source, 64, 65, 69, 70–71
 and outdoor art, 85
 and risk to structures, 13, 15, 66, 77, 79
 and vegetation clearing, 94
 and wind, 53, 94
emergency alerts, 229
emergency vehicles, 96–97
English ivy, 24
EPA (US Environmental Protection Agency), 30
erosion control, 27, 211, 213, 214, 216, 217–219
Eugene, Oregon, 107
European settlement, 26, 30
evacuation, 97, 226, 227, 228, 230–231
evacuation orders, defined, 73
evacuation warnings, defined, 73
evaporative water loss, 199
evergreen conifers, 121
evergreen species. *See specific plant categories*
exposure. *See* aspect / exposure
extension.oregonstate.edu/collection/native-plant-
  gardening, 105
extension.oregonstate.edu/fire-program, 229

F
Federal Emergency Management Agency (FEMA), 34, 228
fencing and fences, 89
 and animal pests, 196, 197
 in interface WUI areas, 97
 regulations against, 230
 in zone 1, 83
 in zone 2, 85–86
fertilizers, 215–216, 219
Festuca californica, 111
fine fuels, defined, 48
Fire-Adapted Communities program, 228
fire behavior, 58–61
 defined, 43
fire behavior and effects software, 48

fire blight, 199
firebrands. *See* embers / firebrands
firebreaks, defined, 232
fire brigades, 229
 defined, 232
fire codes and regulations, 230, 231
fire ecology education, 226
fire enablers, 17, 24, 106, 107, 108, 113
fire followers, 220, 225
 defined, 219
fire hazards, and structures, 63–77
fire intensity, defined, 219
Fire Program of OSU Extension Service, 229
fire recovery, 211–223
Fire Recovery Guide (California Native Plant Society), 212
fire recovery resources, 212
fire regimes, 30, 34, 35–37, 102
 defined, 35
fire-resilient landscapes, building, 11–19
fire-resistant plants, 109–113
 defined, 109
fire-retardant plants, 109, 110
 defined, 109
fire retardants (term), 75, 76–77
 defined, 73
fire return intervals, 35–37
 defined, 35
fire risk
 aids to understanding, 34
 and climate change, 12
 to communities, 229, 230
 and fire behavior, 45
 and habitat quality, 25–28
 and Scotch broom, 113
 weather-related, 52
 and winds, 56
fires. *See also* wildfires
 and habitat fragmentation, 22–28
 nature and behavior of, 39–61
 policy changes, 235
 as tool to improve ecosystem health, 234
fire-safe gardens, 79, 121–193
Fire Safe Marin website (firesafemarin.org), 228
fire safe organizations and councils, 97, 219, 227, 228
 defined, 232
firescaping, 15
 defined, 16
fire season, going away during, 67

254

fire severity, 221–222, 223
    defined, 219
firesheds, defined, 232
fire shelterbelts, 90–94
    defined, 96
fire suppression, 27, 35–37, 89, 233, 235
    defined, 35
fire tornadoes, 54
fire triangle, 53
fire whirls, 54
Firewise USA program, 15, 228–229
Firezat, 76
First Street Foundation, 34
flame lengths, 59–60
    defined, 60
flame or fire buoyancy, 43, 44, 65
    defined, 43
flames, risk from, 64, 65, 72, 79
flame test, 198
flammability, 109–114, 235
defined, 109
flammable materials, defined, 73
flash points / ignition points, 45, 110
    defined, 48
fleshy perennials, 222
foehn (föhn) winds, 54–57, 93
    defined, 58
forbs, 110, 111, 112, 159–172, 217
    defined, 109
forests, 29, 49–50, 221. See also trees
foundation plantings, 116
fuel arrangement, 49–50
fuel breaks, 84
fuel compactness, defined, 48
fuel-dominated fires, 54
    defined, 58
fuel load management and fuel loading / fuel
        volume, 46, 47–48, 94–95, 211, 222
    defined, 48
fuel management, defined, 96
fuel moisture, 45–47
    defined, 48
fuel reduction programs, 227–228
fuel reduction zone (zone 3), 80, 86–88, 89
fuels
    defined, 48
    disposal of, 208
    and fire policy, 233–234

and fire risk, 37
homes as, 63
impact on fire behavior, 43, 44–50, 60–61
management of, 96, 195–209, 211
reduction of, 35, 89–90
role in fire, 40–41, 42–50, 84, 96
in zone 3, 86
fuel volume. See fuel load management and fuel loading /
    fuel volume
funding sources, for community preparedness, 219, 228,
    230. See also cost considerations

G
gaps, nooks, and crannies, and structure assessment, 65
garbage cans, 82
gardenplanner.calscape.org, 105
garden produce safety, 214
gardens, residential, 79, 121–193
giant reed, 24
glass panes, trim, seals, outlets, and weather stripping, 66
glass surfaces, 72–73
Glen Ellen, California, 93
glyphosate, 209
Goodall, Jane, 21
good plants, 106, 107
Google Earth, 61
gophers, 197
granite, decomposed, as mulch, 118
grasses and grasslands
    after wildfires, 223, 225
    annuals, 12, 24, 25, 26, 28, 94, 217–218
    biome type, 29
    flammability of, 110, 111–112, 113
    as fuel, 49
    high perennial grasses and sedges, 179–181
    low perennial grasses, sedges, and rushes, 182–184
    in zone 2, 83
grazing, 26, 111, 112, 199, 228
Great Basin ecoregions, pruning in, 209
Great Fire of 1910, 233
ground covers
    fire-resistant, 109
    vines and ground covers, deciduous, 189–191
    vines and ground covers, evergreen to semi-
        evergreen, 185–188
ground fuels, 49, 50
groundwater depletion, 27

255

growth forms, 111–112, 200–204. *See also* life
 forms, and plant flammability
growth rate, and plant flammability, 110
gutters, 69–70

H

habitat degradation, defined, 28
habitat fragmentation, 16, 18, 21–28, 102, 104
 defined, 28
habitat quality / health, 25–28, 88–90
habitats, and adaptations to fire, 235
habitats, creation and support of, 11–19, 230
habitat zone (zone 4), 80, 88–90
Halsey, Richard, 94
hardening of homes, 63–77
hazards.fema.gov/nri/wildfire, 34
heading back (pruning strategy). *See* shearing
 (pruning strategy)
heat, role in fire, 40
heat transfer, 42–43
hedging (pruning strategy). *See* shearing
 (pruning strategy)
herbaceous plants, 84, 86, 159–172, 222
 defined, 96, 109
herbicides, 209
high-elevation ecoregions, pruning in, 209
high-hazard properties, 81, 82, 83, 86, 88, 89
high perennial grasses and sedges, 179–181
high salt content, and plant flammability, 110
highway iceplant, 112
hollyleaf cherry, 202, 203
home chemicals, 68
homes / houses. *See also* structures
 as fuel, 63
 hardening of, 63–77
 preparation for going away, 67
 in wildland areas, 13–15
honeysuckle, 185
horizontal fuel arrangement, 49
horizontal spacing, for trees and shrubs, 95
horseradish, 106
hoses, 82
Hot-Dry-Windy Index, 52
 defined, 58
hot spots, 90
houses / homes. *See* homes / houses
hügelkultur, 208

Humboldt County, California, 234
hummingbirds, 107. *See also* pollinators
hydromulch, defined, 219
hydrophobic soils, 216–217
 defined, 219
hydrozones, 84
 defined, 96

I

ignition points / flash points. *See* flash points / ignition points
ignition-resistant materials, defined, 73
ignition sources, 41, 55, 58, 64, 65
impounding water, 27
iNaturalist app (iNaturalist.org), 25, 223
inorganic mulches, 119
inr.oregonstate.edu/biblio/classification-native-
 vegetation-oregon-2019, 31
inr.oregonstate.edu/orbic/rare-species/ rare-species-
 oregon-publications, 31
insects, 14, 118
interface WUI areas, 13–15, 97
 defined, 12, 16
interior habitat, defined, 28
interior habitats vs. edge habitats, 22–23
intermix WUI areas, 13–15, 96
 defined, 12, 16
International Association of Fire Chiefs, 227
International Fire Code, 230
invasive species
 as bad plants, 122
 and changes to fire dynamics, 233
 control of, 211, 222–223
 crowding out of, 114
 and debris cleanup, 209
 and erosion control, 218
 as fuels, 94, 234
 and habitat fragmentation, 23–25
 introduction of, 18, 21
 and loss of biodiversity, 28
 and plant selection, 19, 106, 107
 removal of, 88, 89–90, 100
 as threat to native biodiversity, 17
invasivespecies.wa.gov, 25
Inventory of Rare and Endangered Plants of California
 (California Native Plant Society), 31
irrigation, 47, 118, 196, 197–199

J

Jepson Flora Project, 30
Joshua tree, 32, 34

K

key terms
    abour fire behavior, 43
    about community preparedness, 16, 232
    about fire policy, 35
    about fire recovery, 219
    about fuels, 48
    about habitat, 28
    about plant communities, 33
    about plant selection, 109
    about pruning, 207
    about structure fires, 73, 96
    about topography, 60
    about wind, 58
Kimmerer, Robin Wall, 18

L

ladder fuels, 49, 50, 202, 207
    defined, 48
lag time, 46
    defined, 48
Laguna Mountains (California), 13
Laguna Niguel, California, 231
Lake County, Oregon, 229
laminar flow of air and water, 90
LANDFIRE program (landfire.gov/frg.php), 37
landform shapes, 58, 60, 61
landscape fabrics, as mulch, 118–119
landscapes, 11–19, 99–113, 195–209
landscaping plans, 39
landslides, 217, 218, 219, 230
land snails, 215
large broadleaf evergreen trees, 123–124
large deciduous trees, 125–127
laser leveling, 27
Las Pilitas Nursery (laspilitas.com), 105, 197
lawns, 14, 92, 94, 107, 111
lead contamination, 214
lean, clean, and green zone (zone 2), 79–80, 83–86, 89, 118, 144
leaves, tests for ignitability, 198
leeward vs. windward sides of mountains, defined, 58

legumes, 216
life forms, and plant flammability, 110, 111. *See also*
        growth forms
limbing up / crown lifting (pruning strategy), 202, 206
    defined, 207
lint buildup, 65
litter, defined, 48
live oaks, 93
logging industry, 233
The Lookout website, 53
low perennial grasses, sedges, and rushes, 182–184
low shrubs, 151–158
Lunder, Zeke, 53
lupines, 215, 216

M

magnesium, 215
maintenance requirements for plants, 102, 103, 195–209.
        See also specific entries in plant directory
Malacothamnus species, 220
Mammoth Lakes, California, 29
managed retreats, 232–233
    defined, 232
A Manual of California Vegetation (California Native
        Plant Society), 31
manzanitas, 102, 112–113
maple trees, 202
master gardeners, 219, 223
Mediterranean ecoregions, 117, 209, 221
Mediterranean sage, 107
medium deciduous trees, 131–133
medium evergreen to semi-evergreen trees, 128–130
metal flashing, 69, 72, 74–75
Mexican feather grass, 111, 112
micro-spray irrigation, 196, 197–198
mining, 27
mint, 106
Mississippi River, 232–233
mixed-conifer WUIs, 221
Mojave Desert, 32, 34
moles, 197
Mono winds, 56, 57
Morton, Charlie, 41
Morus species, 204
moss removal, 66
moths, 107. *See also* pollinators
mountain bluebird, 223

mountains, and wind-dominated wildfires, 54–57
mulberry species, 204
mulch and mulching, 100, 117–119, 196, 217, 218
    defined, 109

N

N95 masks, 212
Nassella tenuissima, 111, 112
National Fire Danger Rating System, 46–47
National Fire Protection Association, 228–229
National Fuel Moisture Database (NFMD), 46
National Risk Index website (FEMA), 34
National Weather Service, 52, 53
Native Americans, 25–26, 233, 234, 235
native plants
    before European settlement, 30
    with flammable qualities, 103
    online lists, 105
    and plant selection, 18, 19, 102–104, 107, 121–193
    in WUI areas, 100
native plant societies, 104, 105, 122
Native Plant Society of Oregon, 105
native species
vs. nonnative species, 17
promotion of, 109
rate of growth, 116
and recovery after wildfires, 222–223
removal of, 28
naturalists / botanists, 122
natural resource agencies, 104
Natural Resources Conservation Service (NRCS),
    218–219
Nerium oleander, 107, 113
nests, 201
The New Sunset Western Garden Book (2012), 100
New Zealand, 229
nitrogen, 23, 215–216
noncombustible materials, 70, 74–75, 77, 80, 81–83, 89
    defined, 73
noncombustible zone (zone 1), 79, 80, 81–83, 89,
    118, 144
nonnative species
    as fire enablers and fire enhancers, 24, 112
    vs. native species, 17
    and plant flammability, 113
    and plant selection, 104–108, 121, 122
nonorganic mulches, 118–119

North Complex Fire (California), 57
noxious plants, 106, 121, 122. *See also specific
    plant categories*
npsoregon.org, 105
"nurse" boulders, 113
nurseries, 104, 105

O

Oakland firestorm of 1991 (California), 56
oak trees, 104, 202, 204
oak wilt, 125
oils and resins, 113
old-growth habitats, 223
oleander, 107, 113
ORAlert.gov, 229
Oregon
    biome types, 29
    climate zones in, 52
    community preparedness resources, 229
    Douglas Complex Fire in, 223
    ecoregions, 30
    invasive species in, 25
    plant communities in, 31
    wildfires in, 13
    wind patterns in, 54, 55
Oregon Biodiversity Information Center of the Institute
        for Natural Resources at Oregon State University,
        31
Oregon Department of Forestry, 228
Oregon Department of Forestry Fire Information
        and Statistics web page, 52
Oregon Invasive Species Council (OISC), 25
Oregon State University's Extension Service, 105
Oregon Wildfire Response and Recovery web page, 229
organic matter in soil, 214–216
organic mulches, 117–118, 119
oxygen, role in fire, 40, 42, 43, 49, 53

P

Pacific Decadal Oscillation, 12
Pacific Palisades, California, 12
Palm Springs, California, 79, 100
pampas grass, 107, 108, 111, 112
Paradise, California, 97
pathogens, 118
paving stones, 82

peat bogs, 221
perennial forbs, 159–172
perennials, 84, 209. *See also specific plant categories*
personal protective equipment (PPE), 212
pest control, 195–197
pesticides, 14, 17, 196
petunias, 100
phenology, defined, 207
phosphorus, 215
Phytophthora species, 108
Phytophthora ramorum, 108, 118
pile burn, defined, 208
pinching (pruning strategy), 201
Pineapple Express, 55
placement, and planting techniques, 116–117
plant alliances, 34
    defined, 33
plant associations, 34
    defined, 33
plant communities, 31, 34
    defined, 33
plant directory, about, 101
plants
    adaptations to fire, 225
    clusters, in zone 2, 84
    clusters, in zone 3, 86, 87
    densities, 89
    drought-resistant plants, 197
    health of, 114–117
    maintenance requirements, 100–101, 102, 103,
        195–209. *See also specific entries in plant directory*
    planting techniques for, 116–117
    selection of, 100–113, 121–193
    shapes, 101
    size of, 115, 116, 202–203
    washing, after wildfires, 213
plastic films, as mulch, 118, 119
play equipment, 85
plowing or deep ripping of land. *See* deep ripping or
        plowing of land
pollarding (pruning strategy), 204
pollinators, 11, 14, 17, 100, 104, 106, 107. *See also specific
        entries in plant directory*
pollution, 23
Ponderosa pine, 49
poor plants, 106, 107, 121, 122. *See also specific entries
        in plant directory*
potassium, 215

potted plant starts, 114–115
precipitation, 46, 47, 50. *See also* rainfall
prescribed fires / prescribed burns, 46, 198, 208, 225,
        233, 234, 235
    defined, 35
pruning. *See also specific entries in plant directory*
    basic techniques for, 204–206
    for biomass reduction, 196
    for fire-resistant plants, 199–209
    plant acceptance of, 116
    for plant maintenance, 95, 113
    root pruning, 115
    timing of, 207–209
Prunus ilicifolia, 202, 203
purple needlegrass, 111
pyroclouds, 53, 54
    defined, 58
pyrolysis / smoldering combustion, 110. *See also* thermal
        pyrolysis / smoldering combustion
    defined, 43, 109
pyrophytes, 225
    defined, 232

Q
Quercus species, 202

R
rabbits, 196
radiant heat, 55, 64, 65, 71, 72–73, 79
    defined, 42
radiation, defined, 43
rainfall, 198, 217, 218, 219. *See also* precipitation
rain gutters, 69–70
raised bed gardens, 85
raking of debris, 209
rareplants.cnps.org, 31
rare species, 31, 34
Ready, Set, Go! program, 227
Ready for Wildfire app, 227
Ready website, 227
recovery rates, 221
Redding, California, 54
red flag warnings, 52, 53
    defined, 58
regeneration after fires, 220–223
regulations and fire codes, 230, 231

259

relative humidity, defined, 58
renewal/structural pruning, 201
reservoirs, 27
resilience, defined, 16
resins and oils, 113
resprouters, 222
rhizomes, 222
ridges, 230, 231
riparian areas, invasives in. *See specific entries in plant directory*
rips in window or door screens, 66
Risk Factor (First Street Foundation), 34
roaches, 118–119
rocks, as mulch, 118, 119
rocks, for erosion control, 218
roofs, 63, 65, 68–69, 72
root pruning, 115
roots, 114–115, 116, 117, 196–197, 222
rose clover, 216
Roundup, 209
rushes, low perennial grasses, sedges, and rushes, 182–184

S
SAFE (Sustainable and Fire Safe) Landscapes blog, 18
safe places, designated, 226
sage, 107
sagebrush, 29
Salcedo, Tracy, 93
saltbush, 110
Salvia species, 107
Salvia aethiopsis, 107
Salvia clevelandii, 11
Salvia pratensis, 107
Salvia sclarea, 107
San Diego, California, 231–232
Santa Ana winds, 55–56
Santa Margarita, California, 105
Santa Rosa, California, 11, 69
Santa Ynez Mountains, 55
Santiago Canyon Fire (California), 56
savannas, 29
Scotch broom, 24, 94, 113, 223
screens, rips in, 66
sea fig, 112
sedges
    high perennial grasses and sedges, 179–181
    low perennial grasses, sedges, and rushes, 182–184

sediments, 217, 218, 219
Sedum laxum, 185
Sedum niveum, 185
seeds and seed banks, 113, 114, 134, 145, 151, 222, 223
self-sustaining fires, defined, 40
serotinous cones, 220
    defined, 219
shade and sun, 225. *See also specific plant categories*
shearing (pruning strategy), 203
    defined, 207
shelterbelts, 90–94. *See also* fire shelterbelts
shredded rubber, as mulch, 118
shrublands, 29
shrubs
    flammability of, 110, 112–113
    low shrubs, 151–158
    medium evergreen to semi-evergreen trees, 128–130
    mulch for, 119
    planting techniques, 116
    pruning of, 199–209
    in shelterbelts, 91–93
    small trees / large shrubs, deciduous, 145–150
    small trees / large shrubs, evergreen, 134–144
    spacing of, 95
    in zone 2, 83–84
    in zone 3, 86, 87
shutters, 72
siding, assessment of, 71–72
Sierra Nevada, 27, 55, 56, 89
size of plants, 115, 116, 202–203
size reduction (pruning strategy), 202–203
slope, 58, 59, 61, 95
    defined, 60
small trees / large shrubs, deciduous, 145–150
small trees / large shrubs, evergreen, 134–144
Smokey Bear, 234
smoldering combustion / thermal pyrolysis. *See* pyrolysis / smoldering combustion; thermal pyrolysis / smoldering combustion
snag forest habitats, 221, 223, 225
    defined, 219
snails, 215
snow, and timing of planting, 117
snowberry species, 201
soffits, 70–71
soil amendments and nutrients, 116–117, 215–216
soil compaction, 216
soil pH, 215

260

soil preferences. *See specific entries in plant directory*

soil protection, after wildfires, 213, 214–219

soil structure, loss of, 216–217

soil types, 198, 214, 216–217

Sonoma Valley (California), 93

Spanish broom, 94

Spartium junceum, 24, 94

species evenness, defined, 28

species richness, defined, 28

spiders and spiderwebs, 14, 64, 66, 74, 77, 86

spot fires, 53, 229

 defined, 58, 73

sprinklers, overhead, 197, 198

sprinkler systems, 75–76

stand-replacement fires, defined, 35

stem borers, 199

Stipa pulchra, 111

storm drains, 218

stormwater runoff, 219

straw, 217, 218

structure assessment, 64–68

structure fire blankets / structure wraps, 75, 76, 77

structures, 63–77. *See also* homes

succulents, 19, 110–111, 112

suckers, defined, 207

sudden oak death, 108, 118, 199, 218. *See also specific entries in plant directory*

sulfur, 216

sun and shade, 225. *See also specific entries in plant directory*

sunburn, 199

Sundowner winds, 55, 56

Sunset climate zones, 100, 122. *See also specific entries in plant directory*

 defined, 109

sunsetwesterngardencollection.com/climate-zones, 122

sunshades, 74

surface fire, defined, 48

surface fuels, 49, 50

sycamore trees, 204

Symphoricarpos species, 201

synthetic mulches, 118–119

T

tamarisk, 24

Tamarix species, 24

temperature, as factor in climate, 50

terms, key. *See* key terms

thermal pyrolysis / smoldering combustion, 41, 118, 212. *See also* pyrolysis / smoldering combustion

thermal stress, 72

thinning (pruning strategy), 203

 defined, 207

timing of planting, 117

tools, 199

topography, 43, 44–45, 54, 58–61

topping (pruning strategy), defined, 207

toxic species, 107, 137. *See also specific entries in plant directory*

toxins, after wildfires, 212, 214, 215

traditional ecological knowledge (TEK), 233

 defined, 16

tree of heaven, 107–108

trees. *See also* forests

 deciduous. *See specific plant categories*

 densities, 89

 evergreens. *See specific plant categories*

 and fire, 109

 in firebreaks, 232

 and fire severity, 219, 221

 flammability of, 110, 112–113

 hardwood, 213

 large broadleaf evergreen trees, 123–124

 large deciduous trees, 125–127

 medium deciduous trees, 131–133

 medium evergreen to semi-evergreen trees, 128–130

 mulch for, 119

 planting techniques, 116

 pruning of, 199–209, 232

 removal of, 211, 212–213

 in shelterbelts, 91–93

 small, in zone 2, 83–84, 85

 small trees / large shrubs, deciduous, 145–150

 small trees / large shrubs, evergreen, 134–144

 spacing of, 95

 in zone 3, 86–87

Trifolium hirtum, 216

trunk taper, 69, 95, 206

 defined, 207

Tubbs Fire (California), 69

tubers, 222

 bulbs, corms, and tubers, 192–193

turbulence, wind, 54, 55, 90–94

turbulent flow of air and water, 90–94

261

U

ucanr.edu/blogs/Safelandscapes, 18
ucjeps.berkeley.edu/eflora/geography.html, 30
Umbellularia californica, 203
underlayment, 68–69, 72
Understand Risk web page (Wildfire Risk to
    Communities), 34
USDA hardiness zones, 122
USDA Natural Resources Conservation Service, 212
US Department of the Interior, 37
US Environmental Protection Agency (EPA), 30
US Fire Administration, 228
US Forest Service, 37, 46, 52, 229, 233, 234
US National Park Service, 41
US National Vegetation Classification, 34
    defined, 33
utilities, shutting off, 67

V

vegetation, 15, 27, 79–81, 82, 93
vegetation.cnps. org, 31
vents, 70, 71
Venturi effect, 93
    defined, 96
vertical fuel arrangement, 49–50
vertical spacing, for trees and shrubs, 95
vines and ground covers, deciduous, 189–191
vines and ground covers, evergreen to semi-evergreen,
    185–188
volatile compounds, and plant flammability, 110
volunteer programs, 228–229

W

Waldo Canyon, Colorado, 12
walls, 75, 90–91, 93–94
Wasatch winds, 56
Washington
    biome types, 29
    Carlton Complex Fire in, 88
    climate zones in, 52
    community preparedness resources in, 229
    ecoregions, 30
    invasive species in, 25
    plant communities in, 31
    wildfires in, 13
    wind patterns in, 54, 55

Washington Department of Natural Resources
    Information on Wildfires web page, 52
Washington Invasive Species Council (WISC), 25
Washington Native Plant Society, 105
Washington Natural Heritage Program (WNHP), 31
Washington Prescribed Fire Council
    (waprescribedfire.org), 234
Washington State Department of Natural Resources,
    31, 228
Washington State Fire Adapted Communities
    Learning Network, 228, 229
Washington State Noxious Weed Control Board, 25
water conservation, 102, 103, 197–199
water erosion, 217. *See also* erosion control
water infrastructure, and debris cleanup after
    wildfires, 213
watering, 196, 197–199
water needs. *See specific entries in plant directory*
water sources and pumps, 75–76
water sprouts, defined, 207
water tanks, 85
wattles, 217, 218
    defined, 219
weather, and fire behavior, 43, 44–45, 47, 50–58,
    60–61
weather apps, 52
WeatherUnderground.com, 57
weather vanes or wind socks, 57
weed-barrier fabrics, 82, 118–119
weeds, 119
weirs or dams, 27
West Coast bentgrass, 111
West Coast states, 11–19, 230, 235. *See also* California;
    Oregon; Washington
western redbud, 204
wetlands, in California, 12
whitewash, applied after pruning, 199
wildfire action plans (WAPs), 226, 227
    defined, 232
wildfire behavior, 39–61
wildfire fuels. *See* fuels
wildfire.oregon.gov, 229
wildfirerisk.org/understand-risk/, 34
Wildfire Risk to Communities website
    (wildfirerisk.org), 34, 229
wildfires. *See also* fires
    community preparedness for, 226–229
    defined, 16

262

extreme fire events, 11–19
    statistics and history, 12–15, 41
wildfire sprinkler systems, defined, 73
Wildfire web page (FEMA), 34
wildflowers, 114
wildland communities, 11, 220–221
Wildland Fire Assessment System, 46
wildland fuel reduction zone (zone 3), 80, 86–88, 89
wildland-urban interface areas (WUIs), 13–15.
       See also interface WUI areas; intermix WUI areas
    building and zoning in, 229–233
    defined, 16
    and fire support, 225
    and habitats, 17–18, 21–37
    and support for wildness, 99–100
Wildland-Urban Interface Code, 230
wildland vegetation, defined, 109
wildlife
    and adaptations to fire, 235
    diversity of, 84
    habitats for, 15–19, 208, 218
    and native plant inclusion, 102
    value, and plant selection, 104
    in WUI areas, 100
wildlife resources, 104
wild lilac, 216
windbreaks. *See* fire shelterbelts
wind-dominated fires, 54–57, 58, 64, 84, 90
    defined, 58
wind erosion, 217. *See also* erosion control
WindFinder.com, 57
window trim, 72
winds and wind patterns, 48, 52, 53–58, 61, 77, 90–91,
       230, 231
wind scour (erosion type), 218
wind socks or weather vanes, 57
wind turbulence, 54, 55, 90–92
Witch Creek Fire (California), 232
wnps.org, 105
wood ash, 215
wood chips, composted, 118
woodlands, 29. *See also* forests
wood piles, 87–88
woody plants, 89, 90, 115, 116–117
    defined, 109
WUIs. *See* wildland-urban interface areas (WUIs)

Y
yard furniture, 82, 84–85, 87
yellow starthistle, 24
Yucca brevifolia, 34

Z
zone 1, 79, 80, 81–83, 89, 118, 144
zone 2, 79–80, 83–86, 89, 118, 144
zone 3, 80, 86–88, 89
zone 4, 80, 88–90
zone system, 80–81, 89, 94

263

ADRIENNE EDWARDS, PHD, is a botanist, plant ecologist, garden designer, and environmental consultant. She began her botanical odyssey in the Southeast, spent time botanizing in the Midwest, and since 2006 has lived and worked in northern California. After more than thirty years of experience teaching, researching, and consulting, plants continue to be her muse. She is currently a faculty lecturer at California State University, Chico.

RACHEL SCHLEIGER, MS, is a plant ecologist who specializes in restoration ecology. She has lived in the Sierra Nevada foothills most of her life. Her family and property survived the deadliest and most destructive western fire on record, the 2018 Camp Fire. Since then, she has developed a curriculum to teach about wildfire, both in person and online through Butte College. She is currently a faculty lecturer at both Butte College and California State University, Chico.